FAST
FORWARD

Martin Giese
Matthias Hilpert

FAST
FORWARD

ACCELERATING B2B SALES
FOR STARTUPS

This book is dedicated to entrepreneurs worldwide,
the ingenious risk-takers who will drive real change
with abundant energy, courage, and grit.
We are privileged to work with you.

TABLE OF CONTENTS

ABOUT THE AUTHORS
AND CONTRIBUTORS

Matthias Hilpert

Matthias learned his first lesson in sales while working his after-school job: washing cars for company executives. He picked up luxury cars from executives' offices, drove them to the next car wash, and dropped them off again. Of course, it was all about the driving, not the 20 Deutschmarks for the wash. But then again… why not charge a little bit more? Maybe 50 Deutschmarks? Eventually, he ended up charging 150 Deutschmarks, having now enjoyed the money as much as the driving.

Before launching his career in international marketing, sales and board-level management, Matthias studied Business, Philosophy, and Artificial Intelligence at FAU Nuremberg, University of Edinburgh, and LMU Munich. In 1999, fresh out of university, he founded Avalas.com, Germany's first mobile internet portal. He went on to spend more than 20 years in telecommunications, working for Vodafone, Orange, and Salt worldwide. His last role in this field was as the Chief Commercial Officer of Orange Switzerland, running a €1 billion business operation. In this capacity, Matthias contributed to a successful private equity investment cycle for Apax Partners, generating €800 million in enterprise value.

As CEO of MH2 Capital, Matthias has now turned full-time investor, focusing on early-stage technology with a portfolio of 20+ investments, real estate and public assets. Matthias' investments are driven by his passion to push Germany's and Europe's competitiveness forward by fostering innovation both through start-ups and large corporations.

Matthias has sold

- to B2B and B2C segments
- software and hardware
- with deal sizes ranging from €5 to €50 million
- via direct and indirect channels
- at customers' premises, over the phone and email, online and in shops
- via inbound and outbound channels
- taking anywhere from 15 minutes to two years to close a deal
- by himself and by managing sales teams of 500+ people

Martin Giese

Martin's first business sale funded the launch of a student-edited school newspaper when he was 14 years old. With youthful naiveté, Martin simply walked into a local bookstore and convinced the owner to sponsor the back page of the newspaper for 50 Deutschmarks.

Martin studied law and journalism in Hamburg, Geneva, and Singapore, and later earned a Master of Public Administration from Harvard and an MBA from MIT Sloan. While in Boston, Martin landed his first sales job for a local startup (Frictionless Commerce, later acquired by SAP). Here he built an entire merchant network from scratch by intensive cold-calling.

As an entrepreneurial jack-of-all-trades, Martin loves to improve business systems through the use of analytics, negotiations and business model design. He transitioned into operating roles after advising the private equity buyers of Kabel Deutschland on the purchase of the company in 2003. At Kabel Deutschland, he led teams from marketing and sales reporting to business intelligence and controlling, thereby providing the analytic backbone for a combination of B2C and B2B sales and marketing channels that delivered more than €100 million in annual revenue growth. This allowed for Kabel Deutschland's IPO to launch in 2010 and later be acquired by Vodafone in 2013.

As Managing Director for the Kabel call center subsidiary and operations director for the Vodafone Germany call centers, Martin developed a significant B2C sales channel by leveraging the company's 50 million annual service contacts as an upselling opportunity. Martin's sales-through-service approach and some of his innovative supplier contract designs were recognized as a global best practice for Vodafone.

Since 2019, Martin has been the Managing Director of the Munich-based deep tech incubator XPRENEURS by Europe's premier entrepreneurship center UnternehmerTUM. He is an active business angel with a dozen investments and regularly gives lectures in leading programs such as the EMBA at TU Munich, the EMBA at Frankfurt School, the Center for Digital Technology and Management, and the University of Passau. Martin is also the author of "Startup Finanzierung", Germany's most comprehensive guide on startup financing.

Contributors

Tai Alegbe – Co-Founder & CEO, **Contingent**

Bill Aulet – Managing Director, Martin Trust Center for MIT Entrepreneurship, **MIT Sloan School of Management**

Jörg G. Beyer – Co-Founder & former Co-CEO, **LeanIX**

Tiffani Bova – Global Growth Evangelist, **Salesforce** and WSJ Bestselling Author, Growth IQ

Peter Carlsson – Co-Founder & CEO, **Northvolt**

Charles Delingpole – Founder & CEO, **ComplyAdvantage**

Nicolas Dessaigne – Co-Founder & Board Member, **Algolia**

Erez Galonska – Co-Founder & CEO, **Infarm**

Christoph Janz – Co-Founder & Managing Partner, **Point Nine Capital**

Philipp Koch-Büttner – Co-Founder & COO, **Lengoo**

Kai Leppanen – former SVP, Global Accounts, **Opera** & Chief Global Sales Officer, **Liana**

Daniel Metzler – Co-Founder & CEO, **Isar Aerospace**

Alex Meyer – Co-Founder & Partner, **42CAP**

Stephen Millard – Operating Partner & Chief Platform Officer, **Notion**

Bastian Nominacher – Co-Founder & Co-CEO, **Celonis**

Avinoam Nowogrodski – Co-Founder & former CEO, **Clarizen**

Dr. Felix Reinshagen – Co-Founder & CEO, **NavVis**

Veronika Riederle – Co-Founder & CEO, **Demodesk**

Jonas Rieke – COO, **Personio**

Matt Robinson – Co-Founder & Board Member, **GoCardless**

Dr. Stephan Rohr – Co-Founder & CEO, **TWAICE**

Neil Ryland – Chief Revenue Officer, **Peakon**

Paul Salazar – Head of Sales Central Europe, **Couchbase**

Arun Srinivasan – Founder & CEO, **Clarisights**

Ben Stephenson – Co-Founder & CEO, **Impala**

Gregor Stühler – Co-Founder & CEO, **Scoutbee**

Chris Tottman – Co-Founder & General Partner, **Notion**

Dr. Oliver Trinchera – Co-Founder & CEO, **Kinexon**

Ognyan Vasilev – EMEA B2B Industries Advisory and GoToMarket, **Salesforce**

Michael Wax – Co-Founder & CEO, **Forto**

Miki Yokoyama – Managing Director, **TechFounders**

Moritz Zimmermann – Co-Founder & former CTO, **Hybris**

Firmin Zocchetto – Co-Founder & CEO, **Payfit**

For a full description of the contributors' companies, please refer to the List of Contributors' Companies in the Appendix.

FOREWORD

by Bastian Nominacher,
Co-Founder and Co-CEO of Celonis

Fast Forward: Accelerating B2B Sales for Startups is motivated by the desire to help startup founders master the crucial sales side of the entire journey from first sales to €100 million ARR. This book demystifies the sales journey, breaking it down into clear phases, and is packed with hands-on, pragmatic advice.

Martin Giese and Matthias Hilpert, two seasoned operators and business angels, relied not only on their own vast experience, but also secured contributions from a fantastic lineup of successful founders across Europe and beyond. As a result, they put their finger on many of the common mistakes that can create fundamental risk for otherwise promising startups.

There are several common themes in the successful journey of building an outstanding B2B company. Many of these describe the journey that Alexander Rinke, Martin Klenk, and I undertook in building Celonis. Over the past decade, we have focused on enabling companies to unlock their capacity to maximize their business performance. This accelerated our growth from a student consulting project into a world leader for digital intelligent execution systems, powered by our market leading process mining software. Today, Celonis is headquartered in New York and Munich – and we have 15 offices worldwide.

1

Sales is often considered a mythical thing. But founders, especially engineers, need to recognize that selling is a serious profession that should be approached just as systematically as any other area of a startup's business.

One critical success factor for the first two or three years of a company is that sales must be led by one of the founders. This is the phase the authors call "Explore & Learn." Only later does the process become more standardized. At Celonis, we now have hundreds of people dedicated to our go-to-market activities.

A founder can sell on an entirely different level to a sales representative. A founder can change the rules if that helps close the deal, while a rep can only change the product or change the pricing.

After this initial phase, the challenges are standardization, automatization, organization building, and organizational learning. The authors call this "Standardize & Optimize." This is reflective of our experience at Celonis, where at first it was trial and error and not at all standardized.

Then we analyzed what worked and what didn't. We realized we could talk the prospective customer's ear off about our product's advantages, but what excited them most was a live demo. Once we showed them what our software could do, they were hooked.

It was only after a couple of years that we realized customers always ask the same questions. In response, we used our insights to create a sales package answering all those frequently asked questions. That kind of standardization helped us tremendously in scaling the business.

In this book, Martin and Matthias do a great job explaining that while you formally sell to a legal entity, it's the people who matter. For founders, it's crucial to understand their customers' decision-making structures and processes. It's essential to know how to get to the decision-makers. Procurement managers do not make the actual purchasing decision, they merely decide on terms and conditions.

Readers will also find pertinent advice on segmenting their market based on their startup's parameters and criteria. Startups often target customers based on the wrong criteria. It is important to focus on the segments where you see the most significant scope and opportunity to scale – at least to start with. Do not make the mistake of trying to boil the ocean.

There is no general rule as to how big deals should be at a specific stage – it entirely depends on the business model. But founders need to consider that the sales cycle is different for different-sized customers: the process takes longer for a €1 million deal than for a €50,000 deal. Some startups make the mistake of focusing on smaller companies, as they find it easier to get appointments. That might be the case, but it still doesn't help to close deals if your product is, for example, too expensive for your target audience.

If you're looking to understand how to sell, my advice is to shadow someone selling professionally. Visit a call center and listen to the conversations with sales representatives. Accompany a field sales rep for a week and see how they prepare and conduct their meetings. And to save time and avoid mistakes, read this book.

Munich, February 2021   Bastian Nominacher
                                      Co-Founder & Co-CEO, Celonis

1 - INTRODUCTION

Why we wrote this book

As operators-turned-business angels, we invest our own money in startups and hold a combined portfolio of more than 30 companies. To date, we have discussed the "how to" of company building and sales activities with thousands of founders.

In our conversations, we found that selling an innovation to corporate customers (business-to-business, or B2B) is one of the hardest nuts to crack for founders.

Hardly a day goes by where a startup team doesn't approach us with a sales-related problem. This can be anything – from failing to generate excitement with the customers to endlessly long sales cycles and salespeople that don't live up to their promise.

Not surprisingly, when Matthias held a workshop at Martin's deep tech incubator XPRENEURS on "The road to €1 million B2B revenue," the participants were excited about learning more. However, neither of us were aware of a comprehensive and consistent source to guide the founders toward a more structured B2B sales approach.

Following our own advice, we set out to test, sharpen, and validate our ideas on B2B sales with startup founders from our network.

The result of that work is this book – combining our 40 years of experience as operators in B2B sales with the insights of 32 successful founders from all stages of the journey: from €1 million to €100 million revenue.

The 10 most frequent mistakes founders make in B2B sales

The challenges we most frequently encounter in our conversations with startup founders occur all along the B2B sales journey:

Mistake 1: Outsourcing sales to "experts" too early

If you have no IT background, you wouldn't presume to tell your software engineer how to code your product. So why would you try to sell your product yourself if you have no experience in sales?

Early sales is different because it's all about establishing a continuous feedback loop between your business model, your product, and your customer. Like a spider in the web, only you are in the central position necessary to successfully sell in the beginning. Only later on will you need a sales organization to scale what you have begun.

> → In Chapter 2, you'll learn how successful B2B sales starts with *you* as your company's first and only sales person, and then how it evolves together with your growing business.

Mistake 2: Starting with an overly wide market segment

Many founders start their sales endeavors with a vision in mind of a widely used product with many different use cases in mind. While this may be realistic for many startups *eventually*, targeting too many different customers *from the outset* makes it hard to find a good product/ market fit as well as customers.

→ In Chapters 3 and 4, you will learn how to define manageable and meaningful market segments, and how to pinpoint the decision-makers within your target companies.

Mistake 3: Building a product without constant customer feedback

With the widespread application of the Lean Startup methodology, this mistake has become less prevalent – but still too many founders (especially those with a technical background) spend too much time in the lab instead of going out and getting feedback from their customers. So what does this have to do with sales? Everything! Because asking someone to buy your product is guaranteed to give you honest feedback on whether you're solving enough pain for customers to actually give you money for it.

→ In Chapter 5, you'll learn why solving a pain point is key for selling, and how you can prove that your product is the best painkiller on the market.

Mistake 4: Charging too little

Pricing is complex and often underestimated as a concept to create value. That explains why many founders initially charge too *little* money for their product. Underpricing your solution triggers a number of issues. It signals that your product's value is lower, which creates distrust in buyers. And if it doesn't account for the complex purchasing processes within your corporate customers, you risk your own profitability. The good thing is that few B2B customers are put off by pricing that is (too) high. If everything else fits well, you can always negotiate.

→ In Chapter 6, you'll get to know the different types of revenue and pricing models. Beyond the math, you'll also learn about the psychology behind "aiming high."

Mistake 5: Confusing a pilot with a customer

When is a customer a customer? Many founders (often pushed by investor pressure to prove product/market fit) proudly report their first customer signatures when in reality, they have merely signed contracts on free pilot projects. Unfortunately, a "Death by 1,000 Pilots" is often the consequence.

→ In Chapter 7, you'll learn how to frame a deal into contracts and T&Cs that are both good for you and attractive for your customer.

Mistake 6: Sticking with a set sales process for too long

Sales, especially conversations with your customers, can teach you a lot – but you can use those insights only if you have set up your processes for fast iteration and learning. If you try to standardize your sales process too early (perhaps in order to delegate it to a team), you'll miss out on valuable lessons for your product and process.

→ In Chapter 8, we'll share an outline of a sales process that is tailored to enable learning and iterating as much as possible. In Chapters 9 and 10, we follow up with hands-on advice and best practices on how to actually talk to your customers and how to negotiate a deal.

Mistake 7: Not pushing for "No" soon enough

For fear of missing a deal, founders hesitate to push for "No" hard enough. In other words, they don't qualify their prospects rigorously enough in the early stages of the sales process. This way, they'll waste a lot of valuable resources on customers that are unlikely to sign a contract and don't spend enough time on the more accessible candidates.

→ In Chapter 11, you'll learn how to manage the pipeline of all customers you're currently in contact with and how to make sure you only talk to the right ones.

Mistake 8: Flying by the seat of your pants

You can only manage what you measure. But sloppy maintenance of your CRM database and managing sales based on how things *feel* at the moment (or what your sales managers tell you they feel) is all too often representative of the status quo.

Curiously enough, sometimes the problem with SaaS products also lies on the other side of the coin: data overload. When you can literally measure everything, what do you focus on to keep track of your sales process and pipeline?

→ In Chapter 12, you'll find out how to measure the performance of your sales team. Chapter 13 then shows you what metrics to keep an eye on so you can track your business's overall health.

Mistake 9: Neglecting the role of people for growth

Hiring for sales is hard, maybe the hardest challenge of all. How do you know who you want? And will the people you hire today still be the best bet for your startup one or two years from now? Almost all founders struggle with questions on how to build their sales organization. Our advice: ask for help and hire for experience. At a certain level of complexity, "been there, done that" tops everything.

→ In Chapters 14 and 15, you'll master the art and science of building your sales organization and designing a remuneration system that aligns your people's goals with your business's goals.

Mistake 10: Focusing all your sales resources on acquiring new customers

More customers mean more revenue, so you keep adding more customers to your base. But what about your existing customer base? Many founders neglect *selling* more to the one market segment whose doors are already wide open for their proposals.

> → In Chapter 16, you'll get to know the most important levers for keeping and growing the revenue you make from your existing customers.

Why you need a different approach to sell to companies

Typical sales guides are tailored to selling to an individual consumer. They teach you how to become, in essence, a convincing seller in a one-on-one conversation.

They do not, however, teach you anything about the *process* of selling that is required to win a *company* as a customer.

The difference between business-to-consumer (B2C) sales and business-to-business (B2B) sales is a source of confusion for many startup founders we talk to. So what's the difference?

B2C versus B2B sales

B2C sales - Products sold to private consumers often have a comparatively lower value (less than €1,000, often less than €100). The decision to purchase is typically made fast, based on simple criteria – sometimes even emotionally and impulse-driven (think of that Apple Watch you saw in the store and just *had* to have).

Also, the purchase decision is usually made by a single decision-maker who's also in control of their own budget. Once the purchase is made, the transaction is over (although smart companies try to build on and expand their customer base).

B2B sales - The process leading up to a B2B purchase decision in contrast can take anywhere from one to 24 months or more. This is due to the higher transaction value and the more complex decision criteria that need to be fulfilled.

Even more, it is a result of the diverse set of professional decision-makers that are involved. The lengthy process is, however, not necessarily a bad thing, as it implies a commitment to a long-term relationship with the customer.

As a result, if you want to sell something to private consumers, sales do play a role, but only as part of the larger marketing mix.

This makes sense: given the large number of customers and the low transaction value. It is just much more efficient to prepare the customer's mind via advertising to make the purchasing decision on her own instead of convincing every single customer individually.

This is why books on B2C sales usually focus narrowly on the psychology of sales conversations – where the entire sales process from first contact to purchase can be completed within a single or very few interactions.

The purchasing process of companies is often more complex – as are the products for B2B customers. A fully standardized approach would not work all that well here.

The activities of the direct or indirect sales force play a much bigger role – and are much more strategic and diverse – in B2B sales.

B2C sales	B2B sales
<€1K value	€10K - €1M value
Single decision-maker	Team of decision-makers and influencers
Simple decision-making criteria	Complex set of decision-making criteria
Highly standardized	Standardized and customized
No or low lead time	1-12 months lead time
Single transaction	Long-term relationship
→ **Marketing focus**	→ **Sales focus**

Selling different kinds of B2B products

Of course, by juxtaposing B2C and B2B like this, we are drawing images of the extremes that are not always as clear-cut in reality and can transition from one to the other.

A growing number of software companies like Dropbox or Slack initially focus on sales to individuals using a B2C-style toolkit. As long as their products are used by individuals within a company, the purchasing process resembles that of B2C products. Over time, however, the target company might want to purchase a larger number of seats with more professional functionalities and to embed the software deeper into the organization. As the number of licenses or seats increases, the sales process takes on more top-down or B2B characteristics: at this stage, it addresses a buying or decision-making team rather than individual users.

The lessons on B2B sales in this book will be applicable to a wide range of B2B products.

Nevertheless, most of the B2B sales cases in this book will focus on sales with high-value propositions that are addressed to a team of corporate decision-makers. The archetype of this case is a Software-as-a-Service (SaaS) product delivering an annual average customer value (ACV) ranging from €10,000 to €1 million. With this type of product, the startup aims for a customer relationship that lasts over several years.

Why B2B sales is founders' business

If you have founded a startup that offers products or services to corporate customers, chances are high that your academic and professional background has nothing to do with sales. So why should you read a book on sales? That's not your field, right?

The reason is because you're a startup founder now. And what matters is that you must get customers to buy your product.

No sales = no startup

The survival chance of your startup depends on a pass-or-fail question: are there paying customers?

Naturally, if your startup is just launching, you won't have full order books yet. In the early stages, it might also make sense to collaborate with your customers in exchange for their investment in co-development or the data and access they are giving you.

At some point, though, there's no way around it: You need a paying customer. Nothing else – not a great product, not an amazing team, not a pile of awards – is proof that you are on the right track. By definition, having someone who buys your stuff is the one necessary condition required to running a company. And to get companies to buy from you, you need sales.

The secret window into your customers' brains

Without sales, there is no way to know what your customers actually think about your product.

As you are building your product, you want to make it as useful as possible for your future customers. But how do you know what is useful to them?

No matter how much you think you know about your customer (for example, from your own industry experience), you will only know the full picture if you enter into an actual conversation with them. And no conversation is as effective as a sales conversation – talk is cheap, but a sale is proof that you've struck a nerve.

This is an essential part of why sales is so important (and in our view: why it's so much fun!) particularly in the early stages of your startup. The conversations and interactions you will have during the sales process will deliver key information that you can use to develop your product and technology. In the later stages, the information helps you with strategic planning, expanding and diversifying your growing company.

> In B2B, there is no alternative to founder sales. Today, we have hundreds of employees and I'm still in on every OEM sale. Not because I want to micromanage it, but because I need to know what keeps the customer awake at night. Otherwise, I risk losing touch with the market.
>
> **— Gregor Stühler, Co-Founder & CEO, Scoutbee**

Investors love startups who can sell

Without sales, it's hard to gain the traction necessary to convince investors of financing your startup.

Like other investors, we have a long list of criteria such as team quality, market size and type, and product execution when we're evaluating an investment in an early-stage startup. What we are looking for is proof that your startup has the potential for fast growth.

The one criterion that trumps all others is customer traction or – even better – revenue traction. If you can prove that you are successful in selling your product to paying customers, you are well on your way to a "yes" from investors.

Why you can do sales regardless of your background

If you're like most startup founders, you will have no experience in sales from university or your previous career. So you might be wondering, "If sales is so essential, shouldn't it be done by an expert? After all, you wouldn't let just anyone take charge of programming or financial planning."

If you're starting from scratch, you're in good company. Like many founders who end up doing a lot of sales for their startup, we also did not start our careers in sales based on any sales-specific academic background.

We hadn't even been especially eager to get into sales. In Europe, sales doesn't always have the best image. At the very best, some salespeople are admired as "sales wizards" – natural charmers who can mystically woo customers into buying anything. But for the most part, "sales reps" are seen as annoying pests who see sales as a game of grit: if you just knock on enough doors, you can sell sand in a desert.

Only once we got into the field, we changed our view on the profession completely. That's when we found out that reducing sales success to charm or grit, however, disregards one fundamental truth:

Salesmanship can be learned like any other discipline.

Over time and with experience, what appears like intuition reveals itself to be a logical result, based on established principles and truths. Sales is more math than magic.

Learn how to sell from 30 top-tier operators

Throughout this book, we have included advice on B2B sales from those who've actually "been there" – startup founders from all across Europe.

From unicorns to just-launched ventures, all of them share stories about their insights and the pitfalls they faced (or fell in) while building their startups.

In the course of writing the book, we held more than 40 hour-long interviews. To both our excitement and pain, we soon realized that we had generated many more insights than we were able to condense into the limited pages available in this book.

To make the full experience and deep insights of our contributing startup founders accessible to you, we launched our companion website www.fastforwardbook.com.

On the website, you'll find extended versions of the conversations we had with successful founders about all aspects of the B2B sales we touch on in this book. We have also included a number of helpful resources, such as building sales materials, designing sales metrics and checklists, to help you negotiate the best deals.

We hope that through this book and our website, you can benefit not only from the insights from our experience as operators, but from the experience of the entire startup scene.

Do you miss a topic or have comments about our book? Just shoot us a message at hello@fastforwardbook.com or connect with us on LinkedIn. We welcome any feedback on Fast Forward (and anything about sales for startups, really). Please get in touch, we are looking forward to hearing from you!

Now let's get going – let's move your startup *fast forward!*

2 - COMPANY BUILDING PHASES

The roadmap for your startup's sales journey

It's common to speak of different startup stages and your startup's stage depends on the milestones you've achieved so far: a working prototype and team (seed stage), first revenue and traction (early stage), and, finally, growth and profits (late stage).

In B2B sales, startups typically go through two phases. We call them the *Explore & Learn* phase and the *Standardize & Optimize* phase.

The transition from the *Explore & Learn* phase to the *Standardize & Optimize* phase is driven only by one factor: relevant market feedback.

Indicators for this are typically the number of customers served and revenue generated. Because the key indicator is external market feedback, not the internal efforts made or time elapsed, there is no set point in time where the transition automatically happens.

Which sales phase you start from determines your approach and mindset (strategy) as well as your way of working as a team (process).

The following overview gives you a first indication of the topics and challenges that move into focus with each stage. That doesn't mean the others are "finished" with the advancement into the next stage – it just means that you don't iterate on them quite as often anymore.

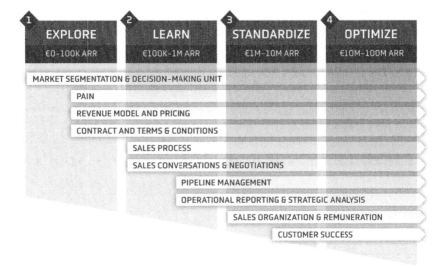

The keywords in this figure are also the topics we're going to address throughout this book. But first, let's look at them from a bird's-eye view, so you know what to expect.

The Explore & Learn phase

What this phase is about

The *Explore & Learn* phase is all about learning as much about the market as possible.

> Sales is such an essential area of your business. You can't just hand it off to someone else. As a founder, you have to go through the process yourself to understand it. In the beginning, sales is a very entrepreneurial activity. How do you find someone with a need? How do you get their contacts?
>
> — **Bastian Nominacher, Co-Founder & Co-CEO, Celonis**

As a founder, your job in the *Explore & Learn* phase is to identify three key pieces of information:

1. The right kind of customer
2. Your product's most important and quantifiable monetary benefits for this customer
3. Your customer's pricing sensitivity

To gather this information, you need to understand your customers' current solutions (if they use any) and your competitors' shortcomings. Against those, you need to pitch the key features that differentiate your product. Finally, you want to trigger buying interest in your customers using the right price. This process is called product discovery.

> One of my biggest lessons was: technology is not a product. A product is something that fulfills a customer need. That's not necessarily the case for a technology out of the university.
>
> Often the general advice to founders is: be laser-focused on a specific niche when you enter the market. That's cool when you start out with a product that addresses a specific problem. But we started out with a technology, not a product with a pre-defined use case. So before we built anything, we went out and pitched our vision to people in different industries. Only after trying to sell to 100 or 200 people, we knew what product we wanted to build, and whom we wanted to build it for.
>
> **— Stephan Rohr, Co-Founder & CEO, TWAICE**

Venture capital investor Alex Meyer points out whose responsibility this task falls on:

> Without founder sales, there's no product discovery. And without product discovery, there's no product/market fit.
>
> **— Alex Meyer, Co-Founder & Partner, 42CAP**

In the *Explore & Learn* phase, it is paramount to keep your learning cycles short.

This sounds deceptively easy, but we have seen many, many founders fail at this part. There's always a *little* more research to be done and a *little* more fine-tuning on the prototype until you're "ready"...

The challenge is to ignore the uncomfortable feeling of being "too early." Stick to our version of the Lean Startup philosophy: If you are not embarrassed when you make the first sales call to your customer, you've started your sales process too late.

In the *Explore & Learn* phase, you need to tune your working mode 100% toward getting information fast. You can best achieve this if you establish an iterative, efficient process of

1. Deciding frequently
2. Implementing your decisions fast
3. Validating the results of your decisions using the feedback of your potential customers

None of these sales tasks involve making actual money. That's because the *Explore & Learn* phase is all about building the basis for making money later – when you know how and from whom.

Matt Robinson, Co-Founder of GoCardless, explains the painful journey that is sometimes necessary to get to this point in the *Explore & Learn* phase:

> When we were struggling to move forward in our early days, Paul Graham of Y Combinator gave us some brilliant advice. He said, "Stop building these features that are going to take 18 months to complete. Instead, spend a week cold-calling your users. Tell them that you've already got all these features, and

see what happens." That week became the most depressing week of all of our lives. Of the 500 people we called, maybe five were interested in using our service.

> — **Matt Robinson, Co-Founder & Board Member,**
> **GoCardless**

At this point, the GoCardless founder team had no choice but to either quit or pivot to turn their business model around. Their approach is an excellent example of how to use the insights from selling in the *Explore & Learn* phase to get where you want to be:

Really go deep. Try and figure out how that business works. What is their role in that business? Put yourself in their shoes: What decision would I make if I was them? Would I use this product? And why? And what would it do for me?

We didn't start out with a problem. We tripped over one when we found someone who had a problem, and listened to them. Afterwards, we went and looked for 10 more people that looked like that. We assumed, if these 10 have a problem, there must be 100 other people that have that same problem. And then we went off to look for those.

> — **Matt Robinson, Co-Founder & Board Member,**
> **GoCardless**

What B2B sales looks like in this phase

Approach the *Explore & Learn* phase as systematically as any other challenge you're facing as a founder.

Reading this book cover to cover is an excellent first step to learn how to sell your B2B product. If you encounter any specific challenges along the way, take a deep dive into the topic – there's quite a few great sales books, blogs and presentations out there (see our Suggested Reading section at the end of the book).

Still, operational experience is worth a thousand books (which is why we have included so many founder stories from our network). Speak to founders in B2B startups who are two or three years ahead of you. Make sure to select investors or advisors who have operational experience in sales that they can share with you, too.

Having said that, you'll be most successful if you approach the search for your first customer "organically" in this phase.

Your existing network, word-of-mouth, and inbound leads (where connections or press articles point customers to you) are the most promising channels to find customers in the *Explore & Learn* phase.

In many cases, you won't have any connection to a potential customer. Nevermind that – there's a lot of opportunity in cold approaches too! Just make sure to research them well and are specific about your benefits for the customer. Few executives ignore a cold call from someone who identifies one of their pain points and offers a compelling solution!

Most founders first develop a technology and then set about finding customers for it. Eventually, because they don't know what their customers actually want, they end up doing a lot of customization for every single one – a complete waste of time. So I do it the other way around: I start to sell as early as possible. By selling to customers, I get to understand them, their use cases, and their people, and can develop my technology accordingly.

— Avinoam Nowogrodski, Co-Founder & former CEO, Clarizen

Because finding the right customer is your first goal in the *Explore & Learn* phase, you'll spend lots of effort and many iterations on segmentation and ideal customer's profiles (ICPs).

Don't underestimate the thought and hard work that go into just finding out *who* you want to sell to before you even start selling anything.

Many founders intuitively get that it makes sense to segment the market by industry, size, or geography. There are many other criteria, though, that founders often neglect. For example, have you considered the age of your customers' typical employee? In our experience, this factor impacts the likelihood of them adapting to new innovations.

Finding your startup's ICP is complicated – that's why sticking to a fast, iterative working mode and mindset matters in the *Explore & Learn* phase.

There will be internal trade-offs – deal with them fast and professionally.

We often encounter startup teams where the developer, the product manager and the sales founder all do a great job on their own – and the team still hasn't gotten anywhere. Why? Because the founders don't deal with the inevitable trade-offs between development, product, and sales that come up in the *Explore & Learn* phase.

For example, the founder primarily focusing on sales has spoken with several customers who all want different features in the product. There is never any internal conversation on prioritization. As a result, the developer is stuck in the lab for months, working on a long list of features – when maybe there's just *one* feature that *all* customers are eager to pay for right now!

Your success in the *Explore & Learn* phase depends on a combination of your founder's charisma and your deep product and customer knowledge.

If you have prioritized things right, you're selling just a rough prototype, or even just a mockup in a slidedeck in this phase.

Your initial customers will therefore be sold on you – the founder – rather than your actual product. Like startup investors, they will need to believe in you and your background, as well as in your new approach to solving their problem. In turn, no customer will trust in sales employees in this phase without your involvement as a founder.

Having detailed insider knowledge and experience about your customers' problems – and knowing how to talk about them on their terms – is an absolute must. But you also need to navigate the complex dynamics of their decision-making unit, with many different and sometimes conflicting individual goals within the customer's organization.

Be prepared for a steep learning curve. You cannot outsource founder sales while in the *Explore & Learn* phase.

Identifying your customers' price sensitivity is detective work – and a key lesson in the *Explore & Learn* phase.

Avoiding discussions on pricing or failing to actually charge money for your solution out of fear that your product is "not finished yet" is one of the most common mistakes we encounter with founders in the *Explore & Learn* phase. You won't know if you actually identified a relevant pain point if your customers don't pay for your solution.

An exception – the *only* exception – to this rule are arrangements that involve short-term co-development or co-innovation projects aimed at further product development and gaining credibility. In this case, the customer "pays" for your product by helping to build the product and by providing a powerful reference for future prospects.

At the end of the *Explore & Learn* phase, you will have signed deals with the first ten to thirty customers.

Ten customers are better than one. But not just because ten customers promise higher revenue.

If you engage with at least ten customers in parallel, you have a better chance of understanding your target customers' overall needs, what solutions they use, and so on. Then, knowing the overlap between your customers, you can determine which parts of your product to focus on.

If you just deal with the needs of one or two customers, you run the risk of building a highly customized product tailored to these customers' individual context, not the greater market. In this case, you end up a consultant rather than a startup founder!

One startup in Martin's incubator was hit especially hard by this insight: The team was developing a product for municipal utility companies. The first utility company they contacted was enthusiastic about their product, which led the team to fully commit to their product. It turned out, however, that the second to 40th utility did not share the first customer's excitement. Eventually, they had to drop the business idea entirely.

The Standardize & Optimize phase

What this phase is about

While the *Explore & Learn* phase is all about the market, the *Standardize & Optimize* phase is all about your company.

The goal in the *Standardize & Optimize* phase is to build your sales organization into a stable, well-oiled machine.

You will know that your sales organization has become a machine when it *predictably* converts inputs like marketing expenses and sales calls into outputs like revenue and profit. In other words, when your output is no longer a matter of trial and error. If you have reached that point, congratulations – your startup is ready to scale.

Because the machine will likely require more fuel (or battery power) to pick up speed, this is also the point where you need to start talking to larger investors who can increase your inputs.

Your key task in the *Standardize & Optimize* phase is to make every single aspect of your sales machine repeatable and scalable.

This task requires hard work and a critical look at every part of your company. Standardizing as many processes as possible is a big step toward scalability. Beyond that, you need to determine better ways to identify a larger number of customers, engage with, and sell to them. There are a myriad of ways to optimize the management of these processes, many of which we will discuss in this book.

> Most of the things you're doing now won't work at your future level of scale. So you have to think about both things at the same time: what's driving the quarter and the year versus what's going to multiply both the logo acquisition and the average order value on the upsell in 12 months' time.
>
> **— Chris Tottman, Co-Founder & General Partner, Notion**

The structure of your organization also reflects your company's growing sophistication in the *Standardize & Optimize* phase. Step by step, you will delegate responsibilities and accountability to other team members beyond the founder team. Your sales organization becomes more specialized, too – which is not to say that you don't play a role in sales anymore. The founder's role in sales becomes a different one, but one that is just as important.

Other than the initial *Explore & Learn* phase, the *Standardize & Optimize* phase is open-ended.

Ideally, you will never stop to hone your machine into an ever-faster race car. But iterations are not happening as fast as in the first phase;

given the size of your growing operations, it is more practical to iterate on a monthly or quarterly basis.

> My advice to founders is to constantly validate and reevaluate the fundamental pillars of your business by engaging with your customers. For example, our customers have strengthened our conviction that investing in sustainability pays off – because they told us that it has also become a much more relevant criterion for them over the past years. In other areas, they have made us change our mind: we thought we could achieve scale by mass producing one battery form factor – but many of their customers wanted their own form factors. As a result of this feedback, we needed to redefine our portfolio and consider other strategies.
>
> **— Peter Carlsson, Co-Founder & CEO, Northvolt**

What B2B sales looks like in this phase

In the *Standardize & Optimize* phase, you know which customers you want and which you don't.

At this stage, you already have a granular picture of your ideal customers. Your ICP allows you to focus outbound sales on those customers who fit your criteria. Equally importantly, it lets you quickly qualify incoming leads into "Yes" or "No," because you know what questions you need to ask them.

Nevertheless, there is always room to evolve and improve. Using the growing amount of data you're gathering, you will constantly sharpen your ICP and the criteria for lead qualification – about every half year.

Instead of waiting to be found, you will use your growing experience to actively hunt for those customers with the largest revenue potential.

Before, you were often found by customers through various inbound channels. These early customers were excited about your product, but the average revenue per account (ARPA) they brought in tended to be rather small.

This changes in the *Standardize & Optimize* phase. Now you're able to actively use your ICP to create a list of high-potential customers you want to have onboard. The references you have gathered from your enthusiastic early adopters are helping you power up your outbound sales to hunt the big fish.

The increasing volume of your sales pipeline starts to require systematic management.

In the *Standardize & Optimize* phase, your leads and customers become too many to deal with on a case-by-case basis. From pipeline management to reporting and contracts, you need to make a big push for standardization across your entire sales process. This is key to keeping your machine under control and steering it in the right direction.

Keeping all systems in balance is the big challenge in the *Standardize & Optimize* phase. For example, there's no point in generating a huge amount of leads at the top of the funnel if you have no efficient process or not enough resources to qualify and convert them.

To keep the balance, you need to be aware of the interconnections between your system's diverse parts – such as the stages of your pipeline, the companies in it, the performance of your team members, and so on. Your reporting system needs to be granular enough to serve this purpose, but not too detailed as to lose yourself in a myriad KPIs.

As your sales processes increasingly standardize, your role as founder gradually transitions from doing to managing and optimizing.

Once you know what a typical sales process looks like, you can begin to delegate parts of the process to sales professionals. In the beginning, they will help you identify and qualify the increasing number of leads, while you focus on converting and closing them. Eventually, you will also transition this part to your account executives and focus on continuously optimizing the overall process.

Many founders find that recruiting and hiring the right people for their sales organization is the biggest hurdle in this stage. Defining the right criteria for the new hires is paramount for making this transition a success.

Throughout the transition, you need to make sure to institutionalize the continuous exchange between sales, product, and technology beyond your founder team.

No matter how mature your company becomes, sales will always remain the key source of feedback on your product, and there will be new trade-offs between sales, product, and technology. You'll need to make sure to implement a regular process with the responsible team members outside of your founder team to ensure that these decisions continue to be made!

Overall, along the lines of *standardization*, the overlapping requirements of a defined set of similar customers within your ICP continue to be the guiding light for developing your product. But don't neglect the potential for *optimization* that comes from developing a second set of key features that drive lock-in, user expansion, and upselling – all of which can increase your revenue at a great cost-benefit ratio.

If you're successful in your efforts, you will see the results materialize in the numbers.

An initially smaller customer will upgrade to your first €100,000 contract – a watershed moment. Or a big-brand customer will knock on your door because of the excellent references of an existing customer. Or you'll sign more and more multiple-year contracts because your customers love your solution and can't live without it anymore!

With the continuous standardization and optimization of your sales machine, your company will move forward faster and faster.

In the following chapters, we'll show you how to actually get there – from *Explore & Learn* to *Standardize & Optimize* – step by step.

3 - MARKET SEGMENTATION

How to find your perfect target company

In many startup pitches we hear as investors, the founders try to impress us by advertising their product as a silver bullet: "It's so useful, basically *everyone* can benefit from it." Then they rattle off a long list of use cases in all kinds of different industries. More often than not, the ideas on these use cases come from people not actually working in any of these industries.

Thinking ahead about expanding your market in the future is good. But the assumption that everyone can and will use your product is dangerous.

If you're not crystal-clear about who your (initial) target group is, you risk tearing your product apart to fulfill radically different customer needs. Similarly, you'll waste a lot of resources trying to simultaneously get a foot into the different industries you're aiming to sell to.

How to achieve product/market fit

Especially for technology-driven startups, getting product/market fit right is one of the most challenging milestones of the entrepreneurial journey. And for B2B products where feedback cycles are longer, getting product/market fit right while you're under pressure to deliver first results can be particularly nerve-racking.

Felix Reinshagen, co-founder of NavVis, attests to this when talking about the team's first attempts to find a market for their indoor mapping technology:

> NavVis started out as a technology-driven university spin-off in 2013. At the time, everybody was convinced the technology was great – but we had no idea what would be the most profitable use case for our technology. Every time we found a new customer, they would pull our technology in a new direction – and we didn't know if this market was actually the right one. However, we needed to find paying customers to demonstrate traction to our investors. It was a constant tightrope walk between making revenue and finding product/market fit.
>
> **— Felix Reinshagen, Co-Founder & CEO, NavVis**

Because it is such a daunting challenge, founders with little experience in sales may be tempted to delegate the search for a fitting market to "a sales professional." Felix explains why this doesn't make sense:

> If you have a hammer, everything around you looks somewhat like a nail. You start pounding all around you in the hopes of hitting those nails. But then the porcelain shatters, and you figure out what you hit wasn't a nail at all. There's no way around it, though: you need to keep pounding in order to find the nail. That's why early sales is the founders' job. Before you have found your nail – clear and consistent market resonance to your product – there's no point in hiring a sales team.
>
> **— Felix Reinshagen, Co-Founder & CEO, NavVis**

Felix's story makes it clear once more why sales is such an essential task for founders, especially in the *Explore & Learn* phase of their startup:

Sales is the link that connects the product with the market in practice.

If you think about it, all successful concepts for achieving product/market fit – Lean Startup, Disciplined Entrepreneurship, the Mom Test, etc. – essentially describe the typical sales process in the *Explore & Learn* phase:

- Talk to many potential customers in a methodical way to get meaningful input and feedback.
- Iterate development cycles often and test your product with real customers.

It's easy to see that the feedback you get through your sales process will help you develop the best product for a specific market. But which one is the "specific market" in that equation?

Product/market fit means that you have defined not only a product you want to sell, but also a market that you want to sell to.

In the following, we will help you find this "specific market" you're optimizing your product (and sales processes) for. In Felix's terminology: We will help you shatter less porcelain and find the nails for your hammer faster.

Do's and Don'ts in market segmentation

Being able to sell repeatedly and successfully is the essential growth engine of your business.

For that growth engine to run smoothly, you need a group of customers that

1. Will use the same product
2. Can be reached by the same sales processes
3. Will look at each other as references

References are the grease that lets your growth engine kick off much faster. If your customers know and trust each other, their word-of-mouth references will create viral effects that cost you nothing and are powerful marketing factors at the same time.

A group of customers that fulfills all three criteria is called a **market segment.**

In comparison to all the engineering you need to get the complicated features of your high-tech product right, defining a market sounds pretty easy, right? But here's the catch:

Almost all startups get market segmentation wrong initially.

To some extent, that's because startup founders tend to be experts in another (often technical) field and lack the experience to evaluate a market. But there is another explanation, too: the symptoms of bad market segmentation are less obvious than software that doesn't do its job. In fact, many startups appear successful at first, only to run into problems later.

3 typical mistakes in market segmentation

To give you a better idea of the pitfalls to watch out for, let's have a look at some typical mistakes founders make in market segmentation.

1. Never choosing a segment (or: Death by Many Pilots)

Of course, some experimentation with different market segments in the beginning is okay, and we actually recommend this to founders. But when the arbitrariness continues beyond the *Explore* phase, it becomes a problem.

Never choosing a market segment leads to what we call "Death by Many Pilots." This error mode is highly devious, because it initially looks like the startup is highly successful.

A B2B startup slides into "Death by Many Pilots" when it sells pilot projects to a number of customers from different market segments, but then fails to focus on a single market segment after the conclusion of these pilots. With the conversion of each pilot into a paying, long-term customer (the outward success), the startup is spread thin between the different demands of the diverse industries and its value proposition becomes more and more diluted.

Eventually, this situation will result in the development of many different products instead of one standardized core product that can be sold again and again in the future. In other words, the business doesn't scale (and remains, in effect, a consultancy).

2. Letting your market segment choose you

Of course, it's a good sign when potential customers show an interest in your product. But without any qualifying criteria from your side, being chosen instead of actively choosing your market is just another road to a Death by Many Pilots.

We see this happen most often to founders who hesitate to actively focus on sales. Sometimes they have little experience with the job and don't know how to start. Sometimes they (subconsciously) try to avoid it. If they then come across a customer by chance, they take it on without considering its contribution to achieving product/market fit.

Other circumstances can contribute to a situation of "being chosen," too. Ben Stephenson, co-founder and CEO of Impala, describes a typical dilemma in the early days of a startup:

When you're just starting out, people are trying to help you by referring all kinds of contacts to you. That's nice, but can actually be quite harmful. Because of your common friend, these contacts take the time to sit down and talk to you. But they'll give you a bunch of problems, and a bunch of feature requests – and then, even if you solve their problems, they're not buying your solution. Because they are customers for a later stage, from across the chasm.

— Ben Stephenson, Co-Founder & CEO, Impala

Sometimes it is the prospect of a shiny logo on their own website that tempts founders to accept customers regardless of their market segment. Tai Alegbe, CEO and co-founder of Contingent, describes this pitfall:

As a startup, it's easy to get sucked into a sales cycle with a big name customer. And then, 6 to 12 months into the sales cycle, you realize it's not the customer you want to talk to right *now*. A clear idea of the opportunity in each customer segment helps you to avoid this.

— Tai Alegbe, Co-Founder & CEO, Contingent

3. Prioritizing product fit over market fit

Like NavVis's Felix Reinshagen, many startup founders who love their product start seeing nails for their hammer everywhere. Especially platform startups that are not industry-specific often have more *use cases* than business cases. Their major challenge is not to find use cases, but to determine whether these market segments also offer a *business case* for the startup.

Sometimes, ideal use cases simply don't make good business cases. Consider, for example, a software that would improve business processes in hospitals. Hospitals might benefit greatly from improved business processes – but in practice, they are also often extremely risk-averse and slow in taking decisions. If you factor in the high cost of sales and the low willingness to close, you'll have to say "No" to those customers – no matter how valuable your product might be in their industry.

Product fit and market fit are not as closely related as it seems. Arun Srinivasan, co-founder and CEO of Clarisights, describes the archetypical problem with segmenting for product fit before market fit:

> In the beginning, we thought that our product was ideal for SMBs [small and medium businesses]. Indeed, they did the pilot and had great use for our product – but then had no budget to pay for it.
>
> **— Arun Srinivasan, Co-Founder & CEO, Clarisights**

In this context, it's extremely important for founders to learn to differentiate between a customers' excitement for the product and their actual potential as a paying customer.

> Unfortunately, the users themselves have no idea what they want. Some of the first users who approached us were museums. They were so excited about our technology. But it turned out that they typically don't have the means to pay for it, and that the people in this sector are not that tech-savvy overall. In contrast, there were other organizations that weren't too excited at first, but eventually turned out to become our paying customers.
>
> **— Felix Reinshagen, Co-Founder & CEO, NavVis**

No matter the reason, the lesson is this: a good product fit in a segment doesn't mean that the market segment is good for your business.

Make hypotheses and learn from your mistakes

Founders sometimes hesitate to make a conscious choice for a market segment because they are afraid to make a mistake and not sell anything.

We refer hesitant founders to Peter Thiel's story about PayPal in his bestseller "Zero to One." The PayPal team initially targeted users of Palm handheld devices as their market segment, but soon found that this group had no inherent need to send money back and forth among each other. Only after refocusing on Ebay powersellers, the product started to deliver both value to their customers and revenue for the startup.

Remember, it only looks as though other successful startups' products were meant to be used in their market. In fact, it was the other way around: only after they have found the right market segment through exploration and learning had they achieved the product/market fit.

While you are in the *Explore & Learn* phase, having chosen a bad market segment is not a failure – it's a learning experience.

While you are still actively searching for a market, any market segmentation is a hypothesis rather than a fixed variable. As long as you learn from them, bad choices are just intermediary steps rather than dead ends.

What a good market fit looks like

The great thing about a good market fit – a market segment that ideally fits your product and is a good business case – is that you can usually recognize it once you see it. You gain traction with customers, and your growth engine starts to speed up almost naturally.

Martin tells the story of how one of his investments, Kinexon, took off once it found its market segment:

> Kinexon uses sensor technology to measure 3D position and track distances between individual units. From the start, the founders had the hypothesis that beyond improving processes on industrial shop floors, its solution could also be applied to analyze the movement of athletes on a field. To test this hypothesis, Kinexon presented its technology at the MIT Sloan Sports Analytics Conference for the first time in 2016.
>
> Soon after the conference, Kinexon was invited to demo their solution to the Philadelphia 76ers, who they eventually won as their first customers. The team's athletic director immediately started talking enthusiastically about the benefits of the technology at events. Kinexon won further positive press when ESPN covered its solution in action during a Houston Rockets pilot training. That's when the bowling pins started falling.
>
> Today, Kinexon is the market leader in the NBA with more than 75% of NBA teams using its solution for training purposes. And the market is still expanding, as the NBA has recently purchased Kinexon products for maintaining safe distances between players and teams in light of COVID-19.

Sales through word-of-mouth and references are great indicators that you have found your market.

The case of Kinexon highlights the "strike" feel of hitting the right market segment. Your pilot customer is the first bowling pin in a market segment – and this pin falling triggers a chain reaction that brings in many similar clients from the same market.

Another example of a team that aced its market segmentation is Isar Aerospace, an alumnus from Martin's incubator that builds rockets to launch satellites into orbit.

> Development times are extremely long in the space industry – easily four or five years. And you have to decide on a particular system in advance, because the development work is not easily transferable between different systems. This means that we had to bet on a market segment at a very early point in time. In retrospect, it looks like we knew what was coming – but in the end, it was an educated guess from looking at the trends for satellite systems, analyzing what our competitors were working on, and asking our customers what they were planning.

— **Daniel Metzler, Co-Founder & CEO, Isar Aerospace**

How to define your ideal market segment

The math of segmentation

Before selecting the criteria by which you want to define your market segment, you need to consider an important question: How many customers do you need in your market segment?

Answering this question is important because the market may be endless, but your sales resources are not. You need to whittle down the millions of potential B2B target customers into manageable chunks, or "segments."

How many customers your target segment needs to include depends on the size of your deals, or more precisely, the average revenue per account (ARPA).

To illustrate this, Christoph Janz of Point Nine Capital uses animals to represent customers with different ARPA, starting with **Mice** ($100/year) and continuing with **Rabbits** ($1,000/year), **Deer** ($10,000/year), **Elephants** ($100,000/year) and **Whales** ($1,000,000/year).

Depending on your typical deal size, the number of animals that you need to hunt to achieve your target revenue for a given year differs dramatically. The number of available prey also varies greatly, as there are many more Mice than there are Elephants or Whales.

Five Ways to Build a $100M SaaS Business

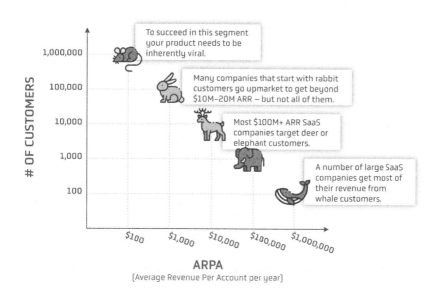

As we will explain further in the rest of the book, whether you target Mice, Deer, or Whales has a profound impact on your sales approach: you just cannot spend the same resources on hunting each of a thousand Mice that you would on hunting a single Elephant.

What is an ARPA that B2B startups typically target?

Most B2B startups we have seen have initially built their business with Deer or smaller Elephants, i.e. customers with an ARPA in the range of $10,000 to $100,000.

The spoils (or logos) of your first successful Deer or Elephant hunt will demonstrate relevant traction to investors. They also make for a tangible and motivating success to celebrate with your employees!

In contrast, tiny Mice and Rabbits just won't pay for the individualized sales efforts most B2B products require, especially if you consider that a certain percentage will never convert into paying customers. At the other end of the spectrum, the decision processes of large Elephants and Whales are so complex and lengthy that young startups risk starving before closing a deal. These animals are better targets for a later stage of the company's development.

Further criteria for segmentation

Let's assume that you have a B2B SaaS startup with a typical ARPA of $10,000 to $100,000 and operate from Germany. From initial experiments, you think that your sales process will generally last between two to six months and will require multiple contacts with your targets.

Taken together, you conclude that it makes sense to go after Deer or small Elephants. Still, there are tens of thousands of these in Germany, let alone all around the world – way too many.

How do you select a manageable market segment (500 to 1,000 Deer or Elephant companies) to target in your sales process?

Classic criteria

Some classic criteria for market segmentation are company size (by revenue or by number of employees), industry, and geographical location. The advantage of these criteria is that there are excellent data sources available that you can easily filter to arrive at a list of target companies.

Company size - Size creates a lot of similarities in organizational structures, budget limits, length of sales cycles, and so on. Revenue or number of employees are highly correlated measures for company size, so both are suitable proxies.

As the data in the following figure shows, of the 3.5 million companies in Germany, the great majority of 3.4 million are small, with less than 50 employees and typically less than €10 million in revenue.

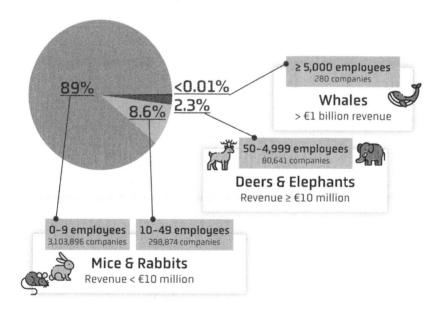

Just by focusing on medium and larger companies, you will have narrowed down your target market immensely.

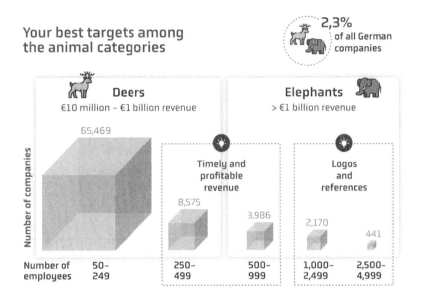

Segmenting based on size can also be a great way to grow along with your customers, as Michael Wax of logistics startup Forto explains:

The logistics market is very attractive because it's so fragmented. The smallest of our buyers were 16-year-olds who were importing cat scratching trees from Thailand to sell them on Amazon. And on the other end of the continuum, we talked to IKEA, Volkswagen and Coca Cola. We worked our way up the long tail of the market: we started with the solopreneurs who imported one or two containers per year in order to prove traction and experiment with our services. Now more than 90% of our revenue comes from customers with more than 500 containers annually.

Our revenue comes from three clusters of customers:

1. Customers up to 10-20 containers/5-digit tickets: The extreme long tail, individual Amazon FBA sellers. Their priority is usability and customer experience. Some of them syndicate their shipping over social media groups. This is also where we found a lot of our first customers.

2. Customers from 10-500 containers/6-digit tickets: SMB customers, online shops. They are a slightly more price sensitive, but still value usability. You sometimes have to meet them in person to finalize the sale.

3. Customers from 500-10,000 containers/7-digit tickets: Mid-market upwards. Our biggest customer imports fridges, about 25,000 containers per year. This is traditional canvassing: We actually have to get into the car and drive around to build a personal relationship with the customer.

— Michael Wax, Co-Founder & CEO, Forto

Industry - Depending on your product, the industry of your targets can be a natural segmentation criterion. If your product improves industrial processes on the shop floor, for example, you need to identify which industries actually have a shop floor (as well as the problem that your solution fixes). In contrast, segmenting by industry is less useful for solutions that address more generic business challenges, for example accounting or HR.

Geographic location - Geography matters for segmentation in multiple ways. For practical and for legal reasons, it makes sense to initially focus on a single country as a target market – usually your home country, because you are most familiar with its cultural customs and regulations. However, depending on where your startup is based, it can be smart to start with a bigger market. Many Israeli startups, for example, launch their product in the US from day one, as their home market is simply too small.

For other startups, geography is an important factor because it is tied to regulatory and political concerns, as Isar Aerospace co-founder Daniel Metzler explains:

> The space industry is a very political business – after all, it's a core technology that can't just be sold across borders. That's why geography plays a role for us, too.
>
> **— Daniel Metzler, Co-Founder & CEO, Isar Aerospace**

Language is also a crucial factor, both for localizing the product and for the sales process. Felix Reinshagen of NavVis summarizes a lesson that many startups had to learn:

> Localization turned out to be crucial: if we send a German speaker to France, they won't sell anything.
>
> **— Felix Reinshagen, Co-Founder & CEO, NavVis**

Custom criteria

The power of market segmentation becomes most visible with startups that have developed custom criteria to move even closer to perfect market fit.

Tai Alegbe explains how Contingent chose "organizational sophistication" as the most important segmentation criterion:

> We segment the market not by industry, but by the sophistication of an organization. For one, the level of sophistication determines the organization's buying process and length of the sales cycle. More importantly though, it determines the customer's

need for our solution: a highly sophisticated organization has probably found its own processes to solve the problem, while an organization with low sophistication might not even see the problem. That's why we're going for "semi-sophisticated" organizations.

— Tai Alegbe, Co-Founder & CEO, Contingent

For Christoph Janz's portfolio company Zendesk (a cloud-based customer service platform), practical criteria were crucial in differentiating the low-hanging from the high-hanging fruits:

For Zendesk, it was a very good indicator if the prospective customer used Salesforce. If they didn't, it was likely that Zendesk would be the first SaaS software the customer would be using. And they didn't want to be the ones who had to explain to them what the cloud is.

The prospective customer's software stack is a valuable signal on whether the company is an Early Adopter, and is more likely to use new tools than others with a more old school mindset.

**— Christoph Janz, Co-Founder &
Managing Partner, Point Nine Capital**

As with most lessons in startup life, the criteria that work best weren't developed at the whiteboard but come from experience. If you have worked with a customer before that was a perfect match, find out why it worked out so well to define your segmentation criteria. This is what Arun Srinivasan from Clarisights did:

To pin down our ideal target segment, we tried to identify which factors had made our first big customer, Delivery Hero, such a good fit. For example, its business was data-driven, not brand-driven. And it was operating in a low-margin market, so it had a greater need for efficiency-increasing solutions like ours. We also tried to learn how its teams were typically structured, and what the tools were the company was using before. Eventually, we converted all this information into criteria that we used to identify new leads.

— Arun Srinivasan, Co-Founder & CEO, Clarisights

Which custom criteria you apply to find your ideal market segment will be specific to your context and company. To fuel your creativity, we have collected a number of examples for criteria and the hypothesis behind them in the figure below. (Keep in mind that your hypothesis might be different even if you use the same criteria. It depends on your product and business model.)

Segmentation criterion	Hypothesis
Is located in a geographic region with a higher affinity for digital innovation (US, UK)	Has a higher affinity for modern software propositions
Operates in an industry with low margins	Has a higher affinity for cost-saving value propositions
Is privately held/family-led	Has a higher affinity for innovation
Has a young employee base	Has a higher affinity for innovation
Faces certain challenges (growth, internationalization, layoffs…)	Has characteristic needs

Has high organizational complexity (number of offices, teams, countries...)	Has a higher need for simplifying solutions
Uses specific software/machine/ process stack	Has specific requirements for software integrations and plug-ins; has a higher affinity to innovation if they have a modern software stack
Employs/is hiring domain-specific job titles	Already has budgets dedicated to specific product domain
Participates in domain-specific events and PR	Has an affinity to the product domain

Strategic considerations

In the beginning, when you are still working on your product and looking for your market niche at the same time, getting a foot into the door is all that matters. In this stage, it may be more helpful to segment your market by strategic rather than statistical criteria.

Ben Stephenson, co-founder and CEO of Impala, describes how the customer's open-mindedness was their main selection criterion in the startup's early days:

> In the very beginning, target the low-hanging, early adopters who *want* you to succeed. In our case, that included a 10-bedroom hotel in far West Wales, where you need to take a train, two buses and a taxi to get there. Anyone who is willing to talk to you and give you a chance! Watch out though to not stick with the early adopter segment for too long. Use them to operationalize your business, build a product and a revenue machine, and then target larger customers.
>
> **— Ben Stephenson, Co-Founder & CEO, Impala**

Note how Ben stresses the temporary nature of this "soft" criterion (beware the Death by Many Pilots!). His point is to use the early adopters as a means to a purpose (developing the business model and product) and then move on toward more profitable market segments.

Veronika Riederle, CEO of Demodesk, underlines the importance of strategically choosing your first customers:

> Our first customers were mainly startups from our network, like participants in the startup accelerators we participated in. They supported us a lot by giving us feedback on our product when it wasn't at the stage that anyone would've paid anything for it yet. I think that's often the case for startups: you sell to your network. It's all about who knows whom, personal introductions.
>
> **— Veronika Riederle, Co-Founder & CEO, Demodesk**

Ognyan Vasilev from Salesforce stresses the power of references from an easier-to-crack market segment as a stepping stone toward larger prey:

> In the beginning, it's better to segment customers by duration of sales cycle or propensity to buy. By targeting medium-sized companies where cycles are faster, founders can get the necessary references to approach the big customers (and to prove traction to their investors!)
>
> **– Ognyan Vasilev, EMEA B2B Industries Advisory and GoToMarket, Salesforce**

In later stages, when the business model has already proven itself, strategic opportunities become more important than references. Tai Alegbe of Contingent describes how the criteria of scalability and opportunity guide the company's evaluation of new market segments:

When we choose a new market to address, we ask ourselves a number of questions, including: Which market can we dominate quickly? Which one can we use to conquer adjacent markets? It's all about eventual opportunities. In contrast, brand names don't matter much to us. We are looking to learn how we can sell to 1,000 companies in the same way, not to get a single brand name on board.

— Tai Alegbe, Co-Founder & CEO, Contingent

The characteristics of your target customers often change in a predictable way as you penetrate deeper into a given market. Geoffrey Moore ("Crossing the Chasm") provides a useful framework when he suggests thinking of your target segments along the lines of openness to innovation and sorting them into:

- Innovators
- Early Adopters
- Early Majority
- Late Majority
- Laggards

Targeting each part of the successive profiles may require some adjustments to product and sales processes. Moore's framework predicts the biggest need for adjustment (the "chasm" to be crossed) is between the Early Adopters and the Early Majority.

Your Ideal Customer Profile (ICP)

As the result of your segmentation process, you will have a number of criteria that create a clear picture of the kind of company you are going to focus your sales effort on.

This collection of criteria for your target companies is called Ideal Customer Profile (ICP).

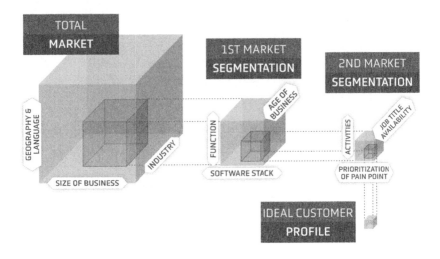

Arun Srinivasan of Clarisights, who had to change his startup's ICP after finding that small businesses had not enough budget, came up with this definition:

> Our target segment are enterprise customers who already had a business intelligence officer and a reporting solution – both of which did still not solve their problem – and who had a big marketing budget. It's definitely harder to sell to larger organizations, but at the same time, you get more money.
>
> **— Arun Srinivasan, Co-Founder & CEO, Clarisights**

Arun's example illustrates two important indicators for a good ICP choice: these companies have both a problem *and* a budget, making them a profitable market segment for the startup.

Jörg G. Beyer, co-founder and former Co-CEO of LeanIX, described the company's ICP in the startup stage as follows:

- Industry: Impacted by digital transformation
- Geographic coverage: Wherever possible
- Size: >€1 billion in annual revenue
- Company employs an Enterprise Architect

Note how LeanIX used a mix of classic, custom and strategic criteria to arrive at its target segment – large companies with high organizational complexity. Particularly interesting is the existence of a role like "Enterprise Architect" as a criterion: Jörg and his team used this person as proof that the target company is already aware of the challenge their solution was addressing (and then also used the person as an entry point to sell their solution into their targets' large corporate organizations).

HOW TO

Create a list of companies within your target segment

1. **Get creative** - Arun Srinivasan describes how Clarisights used publicly visible data on social networks and job portals to identify (and later contact) potential targets within its ICP:

   We actually found a lot of the information we needed on LinkedIn: how big their marketing teams were, whether they were operating in multiple geographies, and so on. Job ads were also an excellent source of information – they often contained detailed lists of their existing marketing channels. Even better, if we saw that a company was hiring a marketing analyst, we used that in our messaging: "You're trying to hire a marketing analyst – with our platform, you won't need that person."

2. **Buy the data** - Many great data sets are available for free, such as the FT 1000 (Europe's Fastest Growing Companies). For those that are not, use the trial option of local and international data and enrichment providers to test out the availability of search criteria as well as the data quality. Ideally, the lists include data such as last year's revenue, number of employees, sector etc. If you've found a good list: simply buy the data. The expenses for purchasing high quality data sets are minimal compared to the follow-up cost if you have to work from a low quality data set.

This played out well for Munich-based unicorn Flixbus. When they launched their long-distance bus service, they decided not to own busses themselves, but to aggregate many mid-sized bus companies. They got an excellent start when they acquired a CD-ROM with 5,000 addresses from German bus companies – the entire universe of their market segment!

3. **Use your tech skills** - Sometimes tech teams can scrape their own data. If the information is publicly available, but not in an existing data set, this can be an efficient way to aggregate and filter the market data you need.

For developing and refining your ICP, follow an "assume & test" approach rather than practicing "trial & error."

Treat the development of your market segmentation like an ongoing science experiment. State your segmentation choices as hypotheses. Then design quick but meaningful tests of those hypotheses to find out whether your ICP selection brings you closer to success.

Your ICP hypothesis could be, for example, that mid-size companies from the tourism industry have high demand for your product. To test this hypothesis, attend an industry conference and talk to at least 20 potential customers from this group. If you get less than five good leads out of this test, you should probably look to modify your ICP.

As the example illustrates, to get actionable results you need to decide on your hypothesis and the criteria for success and failure *before* conducting the experiment.

By the way: doing experiments based on hypotheses is also a great method to make informed decisions on all the other questions we address in the following chapters – which persons or business units to target in your sales process, what pain to focus on, which revenue model to choose, and so on.

4 - DECISION-MAKING UNIT

How to find your customer within your target companies

The challenge in B2B sales is that a company is not a single entity, like an actual human. It's not the company that decides on buying your solution – it's the humans within the company. And these humans can have conflicting interests and perspectives regarding your product.

In order to successfully sell to your target companies, you need to understand how the humans within the companies typically make purchasing decisions.

How to find the decision-making unit

A subconscious bias in the minds of many founders (and indeed many sales trainers) is the idea that you just need to know how to lead successful "sales conversations," that is, how to talk to people to convince them to buy your product. But as Robert B. Miller and Stephen E. Heiman already pointed out in their classic "Strategic Selling": your strategy can only begin once you know who the players are.

In order to identify the relevant players in their specific context, Martin regularly refers the startups in his incubator to the "decision-making unit" framework by Bill Aulet, entreprencurship professor at MIT Sloan and bestselling author of "Disciplined Entrepreneurship."

The three primary roles in the decision-making unit

When analyzing your targets, look for three primary roles: End Users, Champions, and Primary Economic Buyers.

- The **End User** is the person who will actually use your product or service. The End User always plays a significant role in the buying decision.
- The **Champion** is the person who wants the customer to purchase your product. He may be the End User, but not necessarily so.
- The **Primary Economic Buyer** is the person in the company who can sign off on the money required to purchase your product.

Source: Bill Aulet, Disciplined Entrepreneurship

In practice, the constellation might be a bit more complicated, as the example of Algolia illustrates. For selling the company's "search-as-a-service" technology, Nicolas Dessaigne's team needs to consider three different kinds of End Users:

We optimize the product for three groups: 1) the user, who is the developer who's going to implement our product, 2) the end user, who is actually the consumer who is using the search, and 3) the business user, who is someone who's going to optimize the search for impact on conversion.

This means we can sell through development teams but also through business and marketing teams. And we have found that we have the best win rate when developers are involved. Why? Because they are the ones implementing the product.

Even when they are not the buyers, they have a strong say in the choice of technology. They are our true champions.

**— Nicolas Dessaigne, Co-Founder &
Board Member, Algolia**

For identifying the decision-making unit, zoom in to your target segment. The basic assumption is that all three primary roles exist in one form or the other at every potential customer.

Your task is to do the detective work and find out the typical pattern of roles within the companies of your target segment.

Work your way through this in two steps:

1. **Company level** - In each conversation you're having with a potential customer, try to identify who occupies the Champion, End User, and Primary Economic Buyer roles at this specific company.
2. **Market segment level** - Identify the most typical constellation of the three roles to develop a standardized sales approach for your target segment.

Knowing the typical pattern of the three roles within your target segment gives you a great starting hypothesis for approaching potential new customers.

HOW TO

Find out the decision-making units in the companies within your target segment

1. **Ask questions** - Bill Aulet gives simple but powerful advice:

Once you have a first person at a target excited, leverage the opportunity to ask them your questions:

- What would we need to do to bring our product in for a test?
- Who besides you would be involved in the decision?
- What could stop this from happening?
- Who controls the budget?

2. **Be straightforward** — Ognyan Vasilev from Salesforce encourages founders to not beat around the bush:

If you're not sure whether the person you have been talking to has the power to actually make a purchasing decision – just ask them. In most cases, they will give you a straightforward answer: "We need this one manager to be involved to decide."

Champion and End User

The person you expect to be your Champion should be the first target to contact within a prospective customer.

Identifying your Champion's typical role

Often your Champion will be an End User with a direct interest in the solution you are proposing:

It turned out that the person with the biggest pain was the easiest to approach. So we always tried to enter the organization bottom-up by finding a Champion for our solution.

— **Jörg G. Beyer, Co-Founder & former Co-CEO, LeanIX**

However, the relationships aren't always as straightforward as this rule implies, as Nicolas Dessaigne cautions:

A lot of our sales to big companies initially happened bottom-up, from the product. Their people found us somewhere, and signed up for fifty bucks a month just to test our solution. Their development team implemented it, and it was working exactly the way they needed it to.

But sometimes, we also have developers against us. These are the ones who want to build what we offer themselves.

— **Nicolas Dessaigne, Co-Founder & Board Member, Algolia**

It helps to have a clear role description of the person who will be using your product. It's even better if this description is summed up in a typical job title, e.g. "Business Intelligence Officer." In a deeply practical sense, knowing what title to ask for helps you to get to the right person when you are calling the company. And reversely, finding out if this title exists helps you qualify whether the company you are targeting actually has any use for your product.

It is good practice to describe Champions and other roles in a comprehensive "persona" an illustrative description of the target person that describes his or her typical hierarchical position in the organization, their responsibilities, their targets, job titles, needs and fields of interest. Creating personas will help you, and later your team, to search for and recognize the right kind of contacts within a larger organization.

> We only contacted companies who had a job title called "Enterprise Architect." For us, this was the clearest indication that the company paid enough attention to their IT architecture to afford our product.
>
> **— Jörg G. Beyer, Co-Founder & former Co-CEO, LeanIX**

Finding the right person in a specific company

Traditionally, calling the company headquarters and asking who might be the right person to talk to about your product was the #1 approach to get in touch (and it's still a great idea). Especially for more traditional industries with a lower degree of digitization, asking your way through the phone chain might be the only way to identify your Champion or End User.

Today, many employees especially in high-tech and digital industries are active on LinkedIn or similar professional networks. You can leverage these networks to directly identify your Champions and send them a message. In fact, LinkedIn offers a specific solution to filter for the right contact persons.

At times, it even makes sense to start your research for leads with the individual contact and the characteristics of the buying persona instead of the company and its characteristics. If individuals within the company become aware of a specific need of the organization, they often start to look for solutions themselves and compare these against each other. You can use the publicly traceable data from their research activity, for example, their comments on LinkedIn posts or their whitepaper downloads to reverse-engineer a list of companies to target – the right person to contact is already included.

The point is to become creative in your detective work:

> For our first customer, it was important to understand their particular organizational structure. As a big corporation, they have unique roles and management levels. Some of the names at the top level were publicly known. We had also found a career website where they described their career levels, which we then compared to the job titles in the email signature to find out what level we were talking to. This is how we worked us in from the bottom up and from the top down at the same time.
>
> **— Gregor Stühler, Co-Founder & CEO, Scoutbee**

The strategic importance of Champions

While the Champions and End Users do not eventually make the actual purchasing decision, our experience shows time and again that the advocacy of these stakeholders can make a real difference in "winning the war," especially if there are conflicting interests within the company:

> We try to onboard everyone in the marketing teams during the pilot period. Once they do that, the chance is very low that they go back to their old solution because they've seen the value we deliver. It's crucial for us that we have everyone in marketing onboard, as the marketing teams are the ultimate users of our product. In fact, we wouldn't have closed our first big deal without a marketer as the internal champion for our product. He was so pained with the status quo that he gathered his team and went to war [with an opposing department] for us!
>
> **– Arun Srinivasan, Co-Founder & CEO, Clarisights**

Getting your Champion on the team is also important for Scoutbee's sales process:

The main criterion in lead scoring for us is that we have a Digital Champion internally, or that we can build one. Procurement in itself and the procurement leadership isn't typically very digital. We try to find someone who might even tie his or her career to this. There typically aren't many rapid ways to advance your career in procurement, but this kind of side project makes our Champion shine and gives them a chance to advance internally. Once someone has tied their career progression to us, we have so much more punch internally than we would on our own.

— Gregor Stühler, Co-Founder & CEO, Scoutbee

In adding to the strategic component of identifying a Champion, Stephan Rohr of TWAICE further expands on the aspect of "emotional connection" to your Champion and highlights it as the crucial component of your sales effort:

I believe that you'll always close your first deals based on the relationships you've built. In the end, the customer is a human. Often, it's a tech person who is excited about you and your solution. But the crucial point is that you have to have a relationship with them, or they won't buy.

Particularly in B2B, you need a champion who you're having an emotional relationship with. He or she will have to overcome internal hurdles. And he or she wants to be able to sign your deal without having to worry that their head will be the first to roll because something went wrong. Especially when in the beginning, there won't be any references with other big clients they can hide behind.

— Stephan Rohr, Co-Founder & CEO, TWAICE

Primary Economic Buyer

Ognyan Vasilev of Salesforce points out a typical pitfall for founders, especially in startups with highly technical solutions:

> Startups often find it easy to connect with experts who understand their product and are excited about the tangible improvements it brings. However, these are often not the ones that will take the final decision on adopting the solution.
>
> **– Ognyan Vasilev, EMEA B2B Industries**
> **Advisory and GoToMarket, Salesforce**

For this reason, never focus solely on working with technical experts and R&D teams. After getting a foot into the door on the technical level, always try to get introduced to the economic decision-makers.

Keep in mind, too, that there are different levels of decision-making power within the same organization. Trying to sell a product of €100,000 to a department head who is not authorized to make this decision is a waste of time – and one of the most common mistakes founders make.

Identifying the typical Primary Economic Buyer role

If you are trying to find out who the Primary Economic Buyer of your product is, it helps to look at the organizational chart, as budget control is typically closely related to hierarchy. This will also help design the right marketing messaging for convincing the stakeholder at the relevant decision-making level.

The following table summarizes the relationships between budget responsibility, contract signing capability, marketing message and other teams involved in the purchasing decision.

Title	Revenue & budget responsibility	Contract signing capability (Target ARPA)	Marketing message	Involved teams
CEO	€1 billion	€10 million	10 year vision, P&L impact in €, competitive advantage	Board/ Shareholders
CXO	€100 million	€1 million	P&L impact in €, competitive advantage	CEO, Purchasing, Legal, IT
SVP/VP	€50 million	€500,000	Competitive advantage, revenue gains, cost efficiency in €	Purchasing, Legal, IT
Director	€10 million	€100,000	Cost efficiency in €	Purchasing, Legal, IT
Head	n/a	€50,000	Product benefit	Purchasing
Manager	n/a	€1,000	Product benefit	
R&D/ Innovation		€25,000- 50,000 (pilot only)	Innovation	

Additional roles

Additional roles in the decision-making unit

While the primary roles are quite intuitive, it is important to understand additional roles that you may encounter. These are:

- **Influencers** - These are people who have the power to influence other decision-makers, based on their experience or standing within the company. They can reside either inside the company or outside; for example, in media publications, industry groups, or consultancies.
- **Veto Powers** - These stakeholders are particularly dangerous for you. In corporate settings, veto power can be based on hierarchy, but also on function. For example, the IT department may have veto power over any software or hardware purchase.
- **Purchasing Department** - Starting from a certain corporate size, you will encounter this department. It is focused on handling the entire purchasing process and famously aims to drive prices down. In general, think of them as a link in the chain that you should neutralize, but not actively sell to.

Source: Bill Aulet, Disciplined Entrepreneurship

In your sales process, you may encounter Influencers on both sides. In the best case, they fight for you because they believe in your solution or the benefit of innovation in general. If you are less fortunate, they fight against you. The worst case is when the Influencers hold Veto Powers at the same time.

Influencers can be personally motivated – like the head of the 10-bedroom hotel who wanted Impala's young founders to succeed

– but also act from their role within the system. In the latter case, it's important to develop a strategy to either leverage or, as in Clarisights's case, deal with them:

> As SMBs grow, they tend to hire a Business Intelligence Officer who wants to centralize reporting under themselves instead of letting everyone in marketing use our reporting platform. So we always reach out to the marketing department and try to avoid an immediate referral to business intelligence, because these people are typically worried our automation solution will eliminate their jobs.
>
> **– Arun Srinivasan, Co-Founder & CEO, Clarisights**

The larger the corporate animals you are hunting, the more complicated (and time-consuming) the entire decision-making process becomes. At the other end of the spectrum, the purchasing department becomes merely one of the many decision-making units who need to sign off on your deal.

Taking all of the possible roles within the decision-making unit together, the end result of your research within the sales process may look something like this:

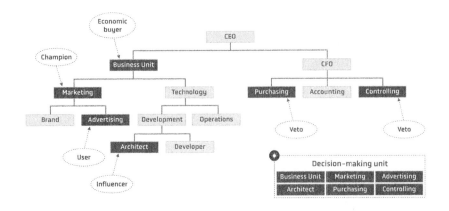

In the remainder of this chapter, we'll illustrate the process using the real example of LeanIX.

Case: How LeanIX dealt with the decision-making units of Elephants

Jörg G. Beyer, Co-Founder and former Co-CEO of LeanIX, used a framework similar to Bill Aulet's to find their way through their customers' decision-making structure and design a successful sales process. Because LeanIX's early target segment was Elephants – ticket sizes of €30,000 to €200,000 from companies starting at €500+ million in revenue – with complex corporate structures, it's an excellent example of how to successfully navigate corporate decision-making.

Step 1: Identifying and convincing the Champion and first-level Economic Buyer

Jörg and his co-founder initially selected their target companies by checking for the existence of a job title called "Enterprise Architect." This role was their first point of contact and their entry point into the organization. They knew that this person would understand the problem and appreciate the solution. Because this person had the biggest pain and LeanIX could help solve it, it wasn't hard to win the Enterprise Architect as their **Champion** (and End User). To convince them, they used messages revolving around ease of use, time savings and innovation.

At the same time, Jörg was aware that the **Economic Buyer** position rested higher up in the organizational chart, typically with some CxO. To convince this Economic Buyer, they needed another story, typically focused on economic improvements in terms of higher revenue, lower cost, higher speed and lower risk. To figure out the right angle, Jörg worked closely with the Champion they had won:

When it came to talking to the Economic Buyer, some Champions took on the task themselves, saying "I know exactly how to talk to my boss." Others appreciated any support we could give them, so we created an individual slide deck or a short business case for the Economic Buyer.

— **Jörg G. Beyer, Co-Founder & former Co-CEO, LeanIX**

Step 2: Identifying and convincing the top-level Economic Buyer

With a smaller company, the story would have ended there with a successful sale. However, within Elephants, the CxO is only part of a larger organizational puzzle with national, regional and global decision-making units. And LeanIX's product only unfolds its full potential if it is applied to the entire organization, not just an individual department.

For this reason, Jörg needed to zoom out and start the process all over, this time with the CxO as LeanIX's Champion.

Step 3: Navigating all the additional roles within the procurement process

Once Jörg had won over the top-level Economic Buyer of the organization, his job became to manage all the additional roles that were involved in actually implementing the closing of a deal.

As is expected with a large corporation, the bulk of the negotiations and discussions on specific conditions took place within the Purchasing Department. However, because LeanIX's product is attached to the backbone of the company's IT structure, there were Veto Powers in the Corporate Audit and Security Department that Jörg needed to pass as well.

Even LeanIX's Champions inside the company often didn't know all the details of the procurement process. In guiding them through the rules, regulations, standards and compliance requirements, Jörg likened his job in sales to that of a "service dog":

In companies the size of our target customers, the Economic Buyer herself is also embedded in a governance structure. Calling this structure a "Buying Center" is unsuitable: it's not a center, but a lot of individual stakeholders with their own distinct rules, processes and requirements. When the negotiations start, the real challenge begins: you need to follow the rules for procurement procedures, convince the purchasing department, pass security requirements, coordinate logo usage and press releases with the communications department, etc. etc. Our role is to help the Champion navigate the process and support the Economic Buyer in their decision to buy the product.

— Jörg G. Beyer, Co-Founder & former Co-CEO, LeanIX

5 - PAIN

How to use pain to connect with your customer

Here is an essential truth: corporate organizations don't care how cool your product is. They aren't eager to change their way of doing things. And they don't like spending money.

You have only one chance to break through and get them to do all these things they don't like to do:

You need to make your customer aware of a pain that hurts them enough to merit their attention – and then prove to them your ability to make an impact toward its solution.

Note how both of these requirements are independent of what *you* think would help your customers. Instead, you need to strategically influence what *your customer* thinks about the status quo.

What is pain?

Pain is an unmet need – either a hidden problem or a problem for which companies haven't found a solution yet.

The archetypical business needs revolve around money. Since businesses want to be as profitable as possible, they strive to find ever more ways to cut costs and/or increase revenue. This is an ongoing pain. At least we never heard any successful company CEO say, "More profitability? No thanks."

All other pains companies experience are a derivation of this need. Many startup solutions increase efficiency – this typically translates into "money" as either higher throughput or lower costs for machinery and personnel. Similarly, the need to differentiate against the competition or prevent unhappy customers from leaving are based on the fact that these factors will, in the end, cost the company money.

Note that some authors also use the concept of "gain" to illustrate the opposite of pain – when you help your customer make more revenue or better margins or gain more time. Essentially, it's another way of saying the same: if a company could earn more, but doesn't do so, it is basically "losing" money. The underlying idea is the same, if you consider the concept of opportunity cost.

For psychological reasons, we advocate for using the concept of "pain" rather than "gain" when considering your messages toward your customer.

Experiments in behavioral economics (Kahnemann's "Thinking Fast and Slow") have shown that the avoidance of pain is a stronger motivator than the outlook to achieve a similarly sized gain: people fret more about losing €50 than they are happy about gaining €50.

Applied to B2B sales, this means it's more powerful to tell your customer "Using our solution, you'll save 50% of the costs" than to frame it as "With our solution, your operations will be twice as efficient."

The pain formula

The formula that defines your sales momentum is:

**Sales Momentum =
Perceived Pain * Perceived Quality of your Solution**

If you fail to convince your customers on either one of these dimensions – perceived pain or perceived quality of your solution – you won't have a chance at selling anything. In turn, if you fulfill both of these criteria, you will enjoy great momentum toward a successful sale.

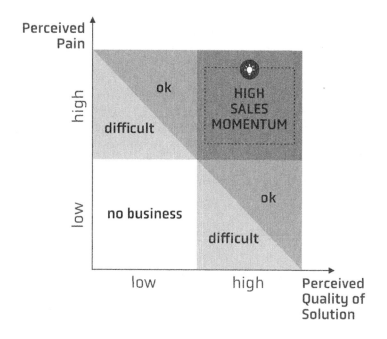

From this logic behind your sales momentum are three challenges you must overcome one by one in order to sell, starting with the most important one:

1. You need to identify customers with a pain that is large enough that they are motivated to act on it.
2. You need to establish a clear link between your solution and its ability to relieve the customers' pain.
3. You have to prove the superiority of your solution over incumbent solutions or your competitors' offerings (if such offerings exist).

In the remainder of this chapter, we'll address the three challenges in detail.

How to identify a sufficiently large pain

The difference between a product that solves a real pain from a product that's just nice to have is often illustrated as the difference of painkillers versus vitamins:

If you have a really bad pain, you won't think twice about getting up at night and driving to the nearest pharmacy in order to get painkillers. In contrast, if you forgot to get vitamins on your last trip to the supermarket, you might be annoyed that you have to neglect your health regimen for a few days. But it's nothing that keeps you up at night.

The consequence for your startup? You'll want to sell painkillers, not vitamins.

Painkiller	Vitamin
Need to have: "If we don't use this, we can't meet our cost targets for next year."	Nice to have: "It would be cool if employees would be able to do this task on their mobile."
Solves unmet needs: "This solution helps the marketing department to access data that they would never have found otherwise! This enables a much better targeting of their campaigns."	Improves an existing solution: "This solution helps us to gather the data a bit faster than our current solution."
Want to use: "This new software saves our sales team a lot of back office hassle, so that they can spend more time with customers."	Should use: "It says everywhere we should digitize our processes more. Someone should look into this new sales tool."

All of this is not to say that you won't be able to build a business on selling vitamins – many people make a fortune doing just that. However, in B2B sales you can't play with spontaneous buying impulses and emotional appeals as much as you can with actual vitamins.

For this reason, it's much easier to sell painkillers for a real and large pain than vitamins aiming at a vague improvement of the status quo. Having a large and clearly defined pain also helps to get your customer to respond to your propositions, and to charge higher prices for your solution, too.

It simplifies your sales job a lot if your customer's pain is well-known, obvious and quantifiable.

To find out if that's the case for your "target pain," look for the following indications:

- There is a specific budget assigned to address this issue
- There is a job title indicating that someone is in charge of the issue
- The issue is discussed widely in the industry press and at industry conferences
- There are incumbent solutions and/or strong competitive offerings to address the issue (which is great as an indicator for the size of the pain, but, of course, entails other challenges for your business)

These indicators for pain awareness are great segmentation criteria, especially for highly innovative products.

Along with the awareness of the pain, the *degree* to which your target segment feels the pain is a good segmentation criterion, too.

In his book "Secrets of Sand Hill Road," Scott Kapur, Managing Partner at Andreesen Horowitz, tells the story of his portfolio company Okta, a company that helps companies administer multiple SaaS applications. When Okta started out, the team believed that SMBs would be more forward-thinking and faster to adopt the startup's solution than larger enterprise customers. However, it turned out that for enterprise customers, the pain was much more imminent, because they were more likely to have a lot of SaaS applications installed that they needed to administer. Eventually, the larger degree of pain they experienced made them the better target market.

If you are confident that the pain is known and large enough in your target segment, you can move directly to the next step of proving how your solution addresses the pain.

If not, you might need to put in some additional work to help your customers uncover their hidden pains.

Uncovering hidden pains

In many cases, the customer pain is real, but the customer is not yet aware that the current situation is painful. How can this be?

Especially with innovative products, the pain is hidden because it's disguised as a "fact of life."

Before the advent of the automobile and the railroad, no one would have thought to complain about horse carriages being too slow – the natural speed of the horse was just a fact of life. Everyone knew there was no faster way to travel – until there was.

In other cases, the customer doesn't have any process or incumbent solution in place to deal with a certain task. They are only vaguely aware how much things could be better, but their data doesn't allow you to quantify or confirm this in practice:

> We tried to share an efficiency calculation with our customers, where we explain how our scouting solution saves them the

8,000 hours they would have to spend scouting for the same number of suppliers the traditional way. Amazing, right? But then they say, "In theory, that's nice, but we don't do any scouting in practice, so there's no savings."

— Gregor Stühler, Co-Founder & CEO, Scoutbee

If your potential customer is open to this, you might also make use of your role as an outsider and offer to uncover pains for them. For physical processes, you can even offer to go to the factory floor and observe how things are done in order to uncover potential for improvements.

If the pain is unknown or unclear, you need to come up with creative ways to alert your customers that something hurts before you offer them your painkiller.

To this day, Martin still vividly remembers Celonis's first pitch at Vodafone Germany many years ago. At the time, he was in charge of a large call center operation. He was called spontaneously into a meeting that an internal IT expert had set up shortly before. For the meeting, Celonis had prepared a demo of their process analytics tool with real company data from the call centers. Until this meeting, Martin had relied on a number of stellar KPIs and even nationwide awards showing that his call centers were working great for most customers. But in the demo, the Celonis salespeople used the product's analytical capabilities to visualize the longest and most painful journeys that a small but relevant number of Vodafone customers have had to endure when reaching out to the call centers for help.

Martin came away from the meeting quite embarrassed by the ordeals that these customers had had to endure under his watch. It was a deeply personal pain – which he was eager to eliminate as soon as possible by giving the Celonis software a try.

Timing your sales process to match the biggest pain

Some pains are like a persistent itch that's always there, waiting to be relieved. Other pains vanish or get worse at certain times. This means that the same target company may react very differently to the same value proposal at different times.

In the business context, the times where pain is biggest are a window of opportunity for your sales.

In his Workbook for "Disciplined Entrepreneurship," author Bill Aulet describes four typical windows of opportunity that startups should watch out for.

1. Changes in leadership

Changes in a company's leadership, or in the persons occupying the core roles in the decision-making unit (see Chapter 4), are often a good opportunity for selling. New people often bring new ideas into the company, are more open for new solutions, or might even purposefully want to "change the way things are done around here" to make a statement.

While changes in leadership are great opportunities for new business, you should in turn actively protect your existing customer relationships from such changes. So keep a close eye on your accounts. If you learn that your current Champion is changing jobs, take the double opportunity to request a handover to a new Champion at the existing client company and make sure the old Champion recommends your solution to her new employer as well.

2. Rapid growth and crisis

Companies experiencing rapid growth are often promising sales targets because rapid growth increases many pains. Growing companies need to improve all of their processes in order to scale their inner workings.

They are also used to making fast decisions. This makes them more likely to invest in improvements than companies operating in a boring but comfortable steady state. After all, no one is eager to change a running system.

While growth is a form of "positive crisis" (as startup founders will readily attest to), the principle holds even more true for companies in actual crises. Crises are high-pain periods, where everyone is literally aching for painkillers. Companies in crises are hence promising sales targets – as long as you are sure that they will recover from the crisis. There is no win in signing a customer who will soon be unable to pay for your product or service.

The onset of the worldwide COVID-19 pandemic has put a third form of crisis to the forefront: external crises. Even though the occurrence of external crises is beyond the companies' direct control (or yours, for that matter), they are forced to deal with them – and you can sometimes use them to your advantage. Especially for B2B sales with long cycles, the pressure of external crises can add the necessary urgency to close a deal fast that would otherwise have taken months.

3. Seasons

For some businesses, the calendar determines their business year dramatically – just think about your local ice cream parlor or your tax accountant's office. During summertime or "tax season," respectively, everybody in these companies will be extremely busy and will likely have no mind to deal with your value proposition. Keep this in mind when you time your sales activities to these kinds of customers.

4. Budget year

In larger companies in particular, the timing within the budget year strongly influences good and bad times to sell.

For example, the approaching end of the budget year can mean both: Sometimes the departments are in a spending mood, looking to allocate their leftover budgets to avoid budget cuts for the next year. Other times, the end of the budget year means that they have already spent all their money. Especially if you're hoping to sell a large ticket, you might need to actively work with your Champion toward securing the necessary funding in the next budget cycle.

If you feel like the customer is interested, but budgets are an issue, do not hesitate to ask the customer about their budget year and the best timing for a sales discussion. Also, budget years are often different from the calendar year, which is another reason to openly ask about them.

How to establish a clear link between your solution and the pain relieved

Once you have uncovered a real and large enough pain, the next step in selling is to make sure that your product is able to reduce the identified pain, and to prove this to the customer.

Fine-tuning your painkiller

There is a direct linkage between customer pain and your product. Pain and solution have to match to be able to sell successfully.

Founder sales is the only way to create and maintain a match between pain and product.

Before you have achieved product/market fit, there will necessarily be some mismatch between pain and product. It's crucial to understand that even the most experienced sales veteran can't overcome this mismatch. It's up to you, the founder, to fix this situation. Bastian Nominacher explains why:

A founder can sell on an entirely different level to a sales representative, who can only change the product or change the pricing. A founder can change the rules if that helps close the deal.

— Bastian Nominacher, CEO and Co-Founder, Celonis

Every interaction with a target customer is an opportunity to gather essential information about the customer's pain. Feed back this information into your product development process to come up with a better painkiller.

Don't stop to maintain the link between pain and product development once you have achieved a first product/market fit. Remember, both the customers' pain points and the competition are evolving too! In later stages, where sales is delegated to a specialized team, this will require setting up efficient processes for continuous feedback from sales to product development.

Troubleshooting the pain/product link

While you are working on product/market fit, there will be situations where you will discover broken links between pain and product.

Like in medicine, it won't always be obvious what's wrong. Maybe the customer has a different ailment than you thought, so this specific "patient" is just not receptive to your painkiller. But maybe, your painkiller doesn't work so well yet. Or it does, but the customer is slow to recognize it. It requires an open mind to all possibilities to analyze the situation.

Let's have a look at some of the typical cases where the link between pain and product is weak or broken, and how to fix them

Customers don't see the relevance of your solution

If your conversations with customers reveal a high pain with a certain issue, but you hardly manage to sell anything, take a critical look at your product. Is it actually relieving the customers' pain? If not, why not? It might be a lacking functionality, or maybe the implementation is just not as good (yet), or the UI/UX does not fit the skill set of the user, so the customer has more pain from the therapy than your painkiller is actually doing good.

If you are convinced that your product is in fact a great painkiller, and the customer is still not buying it, maybe you need to optimize your selling technique and process. Try, for example, to quantify your value proposition better, so the benefits of your product are easier for you to communicate and for the customer to understand. Also, Proof-of-Concept projects may be useful to let the customer experience the quality of your solution.

The pain is less relevant than you thought

If you have developed a great fix to a problem of many companies, but no one is buying it, critically analyze the situation using the insights from your sales conversations. Depending on how consistently you've heard the word "no," try different customers or a different market segment entirely.

If you've tried playing around with your market and still are hearing "no" to your sales proposition all the time, it's likely your basic product hypothesis was wrong: the pain that your product solves just isn't that big, or doesn't exist at all.

Fortunately, if you did everything else right, you will have gathered enough information from your sales conversations to adjust the product or "pivot" – change the product altogether to solve a bigger pain. Ideally, you can find a new pain point and product that allows you to use a lot of the investment you made into your development, your network, your brand and your employees.

Proving that your painkiller works

For some offerings, it is rather simple to show how much pain your solution relieves. If your solution does the same as an existing solution, but cheaper/faster/easier, it's easy to convince your customer that your solution is the better choice.

In contrast, the merits of your solution are harder to convey if your product solves a pain that has never been addressed before. If it has never been done before, how can the customer be sure that your solution will actually do the job?

The best proof of impact occurs if you successfully quantify as exactly as possible how much your product is helping to relieve the customer's pain.

Fortunately, the main dimensions for doing so – money and time – are perfectly quantifiable. We'll show you some examples below.

But what if you are just starting out and have no idea how much pain your product *actually* relieves? Stephan Rohr from TWAICE recommends to make an educated guess – and then find out the truth together with your customers:

To initially quantify the value of our solution, we took some use cases and tried to quantify them. With these numbers, we then went into our customer meetings. In most cases, our numbers blew up right into our face. But then we asked a lot of questions and were able to find out why exactly they disagreed with our "12% reduction." The thing is, if you don't come up with an actual number first, nobody will tell you why it's wrong.

Nobody will attack you for bullishly stating numbers, even if the numbers are completely off. First of all, you're a young startup and everybody knows you have no idea. But oftentimes, the customers themselves don't even know exactly – especially when you're building a completely new business area.

— Stephan Rohr, Co-Founder & CEO, TWAICE

Quantifying the money saved

The best sales argument you can make is to quantify the value that your product generates in terms of money.

The easiest way to convey the monetary benefits of your solution is to compare it against the customer's current solution and describe how much they will save by switching: "Our solution is just as good, but 50% cheaper."

We're quite lucky that our solution is replacing something. The budget item is already used for running annual surveys. What we're providing is a more innovative, agile way to get the results, so we're not fighting for budget. It's there. Maybe we're trying to increase it, but it's already marked as an item.

— Neil Ryland, Chief Revenue Officer, Peakon

Quantifying your impact in terms of revenue increase – "Our solution helps you sell 50% more" – is a harder sell.

This is not to say that revenue gains are less valuable in general. In fact, the most disruptive solutions often unlock entirely new levels of revenue gains. They are still the hardest to sell because customers have no frame of reference and need to make a leap of faith to believe your story. It's a chicken-and-egg problem: before you have actually implemented your solution, all you have to show for is a chain of assumptions that your customer can either believe – or not.

Quantifying the value your product generates helps you define and communicate your pricing, too.

Describing your pricing as a fraction of the cost saved by the product makes it easy for your customers to understand and accept it. Also, the monetary benefits of your solution are a good guideline to defining your pricing in the first place.

> When we talk to prospective customers it is helpful to quantify the potential value gain resulting from a solution. In the context of our product for COVID-19 contract tracing and proximity warnings, there are two fundamental value drivers, however, only one is easy to quantify. The value of our solution for protecting human health and even lives as the most important good is immediately clear – but still inherently immeasurable. In contrast, a CFO or controller can clearly quantify the financial impact of a possible COVID-19 related factory closure. These risks run up to several million euros, depending on the size of the company. This makes it easy to demonstrate the cost-effectiveness of a product that reduces both the probability and the business impact of a COVID-19 outbreak.
>
> **— Oliver Trinchera, Co-Founder & CEO, Kinexon**

As we will elaborate in more detail in the next chapter on pricing, it's a good rule to set the price of your solution at one-fifth or less of the value it creates in order for customers to perceive the price as fair.

Quantifying the time saved

In some cases, quantifying the time saved by using your solution is just as powerful as quantifying the money saved.

This is especially true for businesses whose profit is directly related to their ability to complete a production process or the provision of a service faster:

On average, Demodesk helps to cut ramp-up time for a B2B sales rep by half, from six to three months. This means that new sales reps achieve their quota three months earlier. You can easily quantify the value this represents for the customer.

—Veronika Riederle, Co-Founder & CEO, Demodesk

In his book "Disciplined Entrepreneurship," Bill Aulet provides a great example for the quantification of time saved through his own startup Sensable Technologies.

Sensable Technologies used force-feedback haptic devices and touch-enabled 3D modeling software solutions to reduce the time from design to availability of a product significantly. For a company racing to get toys matching a surprise blockbuster movie on the market, or to sell a pair of shoes in line with the latest fashion trends, the value of eight weeks in time savings was easy to grasp.

Visualizing how a solution saves time in each step of the process is a powerful tool. Your visualization is even stronger if you quantify the time saved precisely, down to the single weeks and days, in order to make your value proposition as plausible and credible as possible.

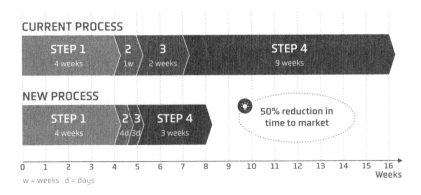

How to prove superiority over your competition

If there is a real and large enough pain, and your product solves it, the only thing that can still crash your sales efforts is a competitor addressing the same pain.

Continuously researching, understanding and benchmarking yourself against the competition is an important task many startup founders neglect.

It relates to pain on two dimensions:

1. **Pain persists, so customers will keep looking for a better painkiller** - Even if you manage to sell your painkiller now, if the pain (and the related business opportunity) is big enough, there will be others trying to relieve it. If you don't keep up with the competition and constantly work on making your product better, in the long run, your customers will switch to the next, stronger painkiller.

2. **The biggest pain is the most important dimension for a sale -** In reality, most customers have not just one, but many pains they are looking to relieve. If your painkiller does solve a specific pain, but does not help with many neighboring issues, your customer may still prefer the "one-stop-shop" solution provided by a competitor.

Incumbent solutions or competitors' offerings that address the same pain as your solution are both a blessing and a curse.

On the one hand, you can skip the part of proving that the pain exists and can be solved. On the other hand, you'll have to prove that your painkiller is better than the alternatives – for example, that your product does the same at a lower price, or that using your solution to complete a certain task typically takes less time than the competitors' solutions (no matter which one the customer is using).

Especially as a startup, having to prove all of the above, often versus established corporations, may appear daunting. But it can be done – even as a group of students trying to build a rocket startup:

> Even though we were basically just a student team at the time, we already had an excellent technical track record. At the time, we had already developed Europe's most powerful cryogenic hybrid propulsion system. Because of this, customers took us seriously – and in fact, their demand was what prompted the founding of Isar Aerospace in the first place.
>
> It was a big credibility booster for us that we had won Bulent Altan, former Vice President of SpaceX, as an investor. That's a name everyone in the industry knows and trusts.
>
> Just by announcing our MOU with Airbus, within two weeks, we had 15 satellite companies calling us about our satellite launches. Their reasoning was: if Airbus had done its due diligence and trusts these guys, we can trust them for sure.
>
> **— Daniel Metzler, Co-Founder & CEO, Isar Aerospace**

6 - REVENUE MODEL AND PRICING

How to earn money from your customers

Your revenue model is one of the basic cornerstones of your business.

In his "Disciplined Entrepreneurship" Workbook, Bill Aulet defines the revenue or business model as "the framework by which you extract from your customers some portion of value your products create from them." Simply put: it's how you make your money.

For your company to survive and thrive, your revenue needs to be higher than your costs in the long run. This is what people mean when they say you have "a business case."

Like a cornerstone of a house, a revenue model is hard to change once the business is up and running. And like a cornerstone is essential for the stability of the house, the revenue model is essential for the profitability of your business. For these reasons, it's important to get this part of your business right from the ground up.

Your revenue model and the pricing of your product can either hinder or facilitate your sales, too.

A good revenue model can even be a source of competitive advantage. Your customers might choose your solution over another if your revenue model reduces friction for them or lowers the hurdles for the adoption of your solution.

How to choose your revenue model

In situations where you bootstrap your startup – grow without external investors – the classic, straightforward revenue model of selling your product or service to a customer for a one-time charge still works best. With a one-time charge, you recover your cost and realize a profit immediately after the sale.

One-time charge

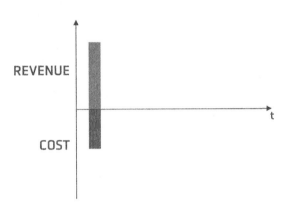

From a sales perspective, however, the one-time charge model has significant downsides, as Moritz Zimmermann explains:

> In the old school model, where you sell a perpetual license or a subscription, you try to sell as much as you can to the customer at once. But this means that the customer might pay for stuff he won't eventually need. And you may give too much discount because you can't precisely define the value your solutions have for the customer.
>
> — **Moritz Zimmermann, Co-Founder & former CTO, Hybris**

In SaaS startups, subscription-type revenue models have mostly replaced the perpetual software license for several reasons:

- **Startups** and **investors** appreciate the higher upside a subscription-type model generates in the long run compared to a one-time charge. Also, it is much easier to predict revenue going forward, which generates more stable growth. For these reasons, investors value startups with recurring revenue models at 10x their revenue instead of 5x for perpetual licenses or 1-2x for one-off transaction models – a formidable difference, and a main driver for founders and VCs to push for recurring revenue models.
- **Customers** often prefer subscription-type models because they require a smaller initial investment. Also, there's a lower risk associated with adopting the new solution. That's why the hurdles for internal decision-making are smaller for subscription-type models.

Models with recurring revenue

While there are countless tweaks and variations to each of them, the most common categories of revenue models based on recurring revenue are the following.

One-time charge plus service contract

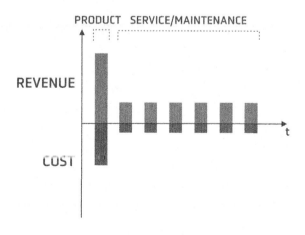

This model is a hybrid between a one-time charge and a subscription model. Startups often use it for more complex products that customers need help with in order to constantly adapt it to their needs. It's also applicable to products that physically change or degrade over time and require maintenance.

For software products, a 10-20% annual fee is typically added to the one-time charge for ongoing maintenance. For hardware, the amount is more variable and depends on the specifics of the use case.

Subscription model

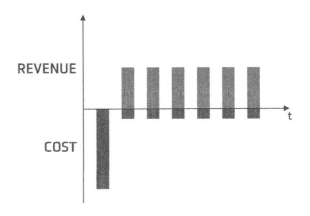

The subscription is the basic model for recurring revenue. Like a magazine subscription that is delivered to your mailbox each month, you receive the product, or access to it, as long as your contract lasts.

The major variables are the length of the subscription cycle as well as the renewal conditions. Typical subscriptions are charged monthly or annually ("annual license fees").

The subscription model is great for getting a foot into the door. If the customer company then grows and buys more licenses ("seats" or other units) for additional users, your revenue grows as well.

From the customer's point of view, subscriptions have the added advantage that they usually include automatic security and stability updates.

Leasing model

The model is most familiar from the automobile industry, where customers pay monthly "rent" for cars, and can turn them in every few years in exchange for a newer model. In the startup world, NavVis uses a leasing model for its laser scanning device business.

As such, the leasing model is the hardware version of a software subscription: Within the leasing model, your customer receives a piece of hardware that they can use, but do not own. Leasing contracts are typically longer than subscription contracts and span multiple years.

From the startup's point of view, a leasing model requires a significant investment to provide the hardware upfront. However, leasing models tend to recover more than the investment over time. If the hardware is expensive, it can be leased out again or be resold after the original leasing period ends.

From the customers' point of view, the investment risk is much lower because the cost is spread over a longer time. Also, because leasing contracts usually include a replacement of the hardware at a certain point, they don't risk investing in a product that will be outdated in a few years' time.

Consumption-based model

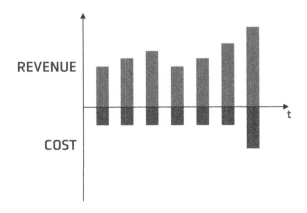

Within this revenue model, your startup provides a certain product or service with a "consumable" component.

The classic example from B2C sales are razors: The razor manufacturers sell their razors at a low cost, and then make their actual profit from the predictable and regular follow-up purchases of razor blades. The same principle can be applied to B2B products. For example, Inveox, a medical technology startup and graduate of Martin's startup incubator, is very successful with selling a piece of machinery that "consumes" sterile capsules also provided by the company.

Software startups enjoy more freedom in defining what is "consumed," but the revenue model is the same:

> Selling seats doesn't make sense for us. Our pricing has always been on usage. In our case, that's search volume. Everything else, data volume, number of queries, is summarized in that.
>
> Our pricing is purely pay-as-you-go. You can start with $1 if your search volume is small. As your search volume grows, you pay more, but less per unit, so there's economies of scale. And

you can also commit to some usage a year in advance to get an initial discount.

— **Nicolas Dessaigne, Co-Founder &**
Board Member, Algolia

In fact, in B2B SaaS companies, using a consumption-based model as part of a "land-consume-expand" strategy is currently becoming a dominant trend. Moritz Zimmermann, co-founder of Hybris, describes why:

In the land-consume-expand model, you use consumption-based pricing. The advantage for the customer is that he only pays for what he uses. Maybe their sales persons use your software daily, but finance only logs in three days per month. This model makes it much easier to get a foot into the door and then expand after you have proven your value proposition!

— **Moritz Zimmermann, Co-Founder & former CTO, Hybris**

Moritz also points out risks and advantages of the model:

The land-consume-expand model implies that your software is "sticky" – the customer stops paying when he stops using your software, so make sure it's useful and switching is hard. But if you incentivize your engineers to increase adoption and consumption, and combine it with functions that allow the customer to measure and use the consumption data, you actually achieve a very high renewal rate.

— **Moritz Zimmermann, Co-Founder & former CTO, Hybris**

Freemium model

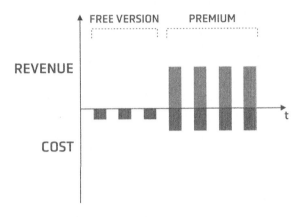

The word "freemium" is a combination of "free" and "premium" – exactly what this revenue model is. In a freemium model, your startup offers two versions of your product: a free version with basic functions and a paid version with additional functions and/or more capacity in terms of traffic or users.

The idea is that a useful free version will incentivize many users to start using the product because the barriers are low. A certain percentage of free users will then convert into paying "premium" users once their needs exceed the limits of the basic version.

Many well-known software companies like Dropbox, Skype, or MailChimp successfully use the freemium revenue model. Many more startups, though, have failed with this approach. It requires the capacity to build a large user base and a well-designed conversion mechanism to work. Also, freemium models are a tightrope walk between creating an attractive free version while reserving enough value for the paid version.

The magic of the freemium model happens in the conversion, not in the initial adoption. Users might sign up in great numbers – but if they don't like your product enough to actually pay for it, your startup is doomed in the long run, leaving you stuck with the operating cost for providing the free service without any revenue to make up for it.

Shared savings/gains

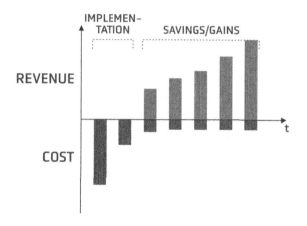

In this model, your startup charges the customer a certain percentage of the cost savings or revenue gains the product achieves.

This model is conceptually elegant because it entirely eliminates the risk for the customer. However, it requires an objective method to measure the exact impact of the product. That's why it is rather hard to implement in practice. Still, some manage to do it:

We enter our sales conversations with an extremely aggressive price point. We say: "No matter what you currently pay – we will cut your current translation costs in half." And that's not because we're cheapos, but because we're using automatization and machine learning technology all the way. 20 minutes into our first meeting, the customer's CFO had only one question left: "Where do I sign?" This of course requires that we're absolutely certain we can deliver. Not just on the price, but also on the quality and speed of our translations.

Our pricing model requires that we get the customer's data on how much their translation expenses are. Only then can we calculate our offer, because it's based on the premise that we cut their original costs for translations in half.

Taking 50% percent of whatever the customers paid for translations before is such a compelling revenue model because it entails no risk to the customer at all. It doesn't depend on anything to generate immediate cost-savings.

— **Philipp Koch-Büttner, Co-Founder & COO, Lengoo**

The model also works the other way around: sharing not the savings, but the additional gains that the customer achieves by using the tool.

Behamics, a startup from Martin's incubator, has developed an e-commerce tool that increases revenue by improving conversion rates and reducing return rates. It uses a revenue model based on shared gains with online retailers.

Behamics meets the challenge of separating the effects of its tool from effects from other factors by creating a control group of transactions for the same shop where the tool isn't implemented. They then compare the sales results of both groups to determine the difference and to calculate their share of the gained revenue.

Advertising and data-driven revenue models

Some companies do not charge anything at all for their main service, but instead use the data they have gathered by providing those services to earn their revenue from third parties.

Google and Facebook are typical examples for this revenue model. By providing their service for free to a massive audience and gathering user data at the same time, they are able to sell "eyeballs" – the attention of specific customer segments – to corporate advertisers.

Other indirect revenue models are based on aggregating data. Those businesses make their revenue from commissions for transactions completed through their site (such as affiliate websites or price comparison websites) or even data-selling (like some apps for period tracking, or certain entertainment apps).

New revenue models

New revenue models have constantly emerged with the rise of digital business models. Apart from your product, an innovative revenue model can be a core differentiator against your competition.

Kai Leppanen, Opera's former VP of Sales for Global Accounts, tells the story of how Opera gained a major competitive advantage through a at the time revolutionary new revenue model he introduced – and what obstacles he had to overcome:

Up until 2005, Opera employed a perpetual license business model, where OEMs paid $0.20-0.30 to be able to use our browser on their devices. This limited our growth, so I invented the Active Use License Fee system for Opera's new mobile browser Opera Mini. Under this SaaS MRR business model, OEMs would pay only if users hit our servers, and we would share the data on browser usage with them.

Eventually, our SaaS MRR model for licensing the Opera Mini mobile browser became a huge cash cow for Opera. But in the beginning, it wasn't easy to convince our customers, the phone

OEMs, to buy into this model. These big companies were not at all used to partnering and sharing – somewhat arrogantly, they preferred to simply acquire software companies. I remember that after buying up another two-year-old browser startup with no users, one particular executive even felt he needed to teach us how to do internet browsers – when we in fact had been doing this since 1995.

— **Kai Leppanen, former SVP, Global Accounts, Opera**

Criteria for choosing your revenue model

Which revenue model do you choose for your startup? Try not to take this decision too lightly. Our glimpse into the big universe of revenue models has hopefully made you aware that the revenue model is a major lever for value generation, both for you and your customer.

When making the decision for a revenue model, ask yourself the following four questions:

1. Does the revenue model reduce pain and friction for the customer?

Paying is a pain. This is as true for corporations as it is for you as an individual. You'll want your customer to feel as little pain as possible, so design your revenue model to reduce potential friction to a minimum. Also, make sure to always connect your pricing to the value the customer receives:

Synchronize payments with value generation. You'll know from your own purchases that it just feels much better to be charged for a product or service at the *same time* or after you've been using it and have gotten value from it.

Especially with products that take time to set up and implement, it might make sense to distribute payments over a certain period via a subscription-based model.

Be transparent about what your customers pay for. This applies if you charge them based on usage rather than time. As long as they actually use your product, seeing their own usage actually reminds your customers of your product's value and a signal for your revenue model's transparency:

> Use a self-compliance tool to continuously illustrate the value your product contributes. This is typically a dashboard or usage notifications that tell the customer where they stand in using your product. Avoid breaking their trust by suddenly charging €50,000 in "usage fees" that they have no idea where they come from!
>
> **— Moritz Zimmermann, Co-Founder & former CTO, Hybris**

Measuring and reporting usage transparently can also be beneficial for the customer because it allows them to separate out the usage between different departments, for example. This way, the organization can precisely allocate the shares of the cost between their respective budgets.

2. Is the revenue model better than your competitors' model?

What revenue models are your competitors using? Can you provide more value to your customer by implementing a different model? In this case, your different model of capturing value might just be the factor that helps you disrupt the market.

Don't just go for the "new is better" fallacy, though.

Sometimes a certain revenue model is simply established in your industry. You would just confuse your customers and create more friction by offering a different one. Carefully evaluate whether the benefits of the model outweigh the costs or whether it makes more sense to differentiate your offering in other aspects instead.

Transitioning to MRR implies an organizational convenience for the customer, too, because they don't have to gather every single translation project within their company first to know how much they'll be spending on translations, and when.

MRR and ARR are not typical revenue models in our market. No matter how big the account is, normally translations are a transactional business: you pay for what you get. We have solved this by selling retainers: for €10,000 per month, you can order translations from us. If you use less, it rolls over to the next month. Still, we need to carefully explain this new model every time.

— Philipp Koch-Büttner, Co-Founder & COO, Lengoo

3. Can you manage the cashflow implications of the revenue model?

Your revenue model has significant implications for your cashflow.

The catch with subscription models, which have a lot of advantages for your sales process and long-term profitability, is that your startup has to be able to afford the delayed cost recovery.

With a one-time charge, you immediately get the entire value of the sale after you have signed the contract. In contrast, it takes some time until a subscription model has recovered the cost of the initial sale and you start to make profit on the customer. Until then, you need another financing source: either revenue from earlier sales, or – more likely in the beginning – an external investment.

The way internal costs occur within your startup also has an impact on what revenue models make the most sense to you.

If you are offering a product that requires a high upfront investment, you need to find a way to cover the cost either through your revenue model or through other sources. A typical example are hardware products (for example battery installations or power generation units) with an investment volume of more than €100,000 per installed device. In other cases, there might be a high upfront cost for customizing the hardware for big projects. Especially for innovative, untested solutions, it will be hard to find a customer who is willing to carry the entire risk for this investment alone. A leasing model might make more sense here.

For software companies, the upfront costs are typically less prevalent, which is why it is easier to start with a subscription-based model. Even if the internal circumstances of your startup hint to a stronger upfront payment (because you're currently struggling to pay the salaries at the end of the month), try to think long-term and consider to cover the cost through a financing round in the meantime.

4. What revenue model would investors prefer?

When it comes to investors' preferences, we can finally give you some straightforward, unequivocal direction: investors love recurring revenue models!

Because it makes your business more predictable, investors prefer a subscription-based revenue model over a one-time charge anytime.

You won't be surprised to hear that investors love revenue growth, too. If you manage to implement a subscription-based revenue model that includes an inbuilt growth factor – like a link between the number of users or the number of transactions handled and your revenue – investors will happily offer their capital to scale your business.

How to choose your pricing strategy

Pricing, in our experience, is one of the most underestimated levers for increasing your startup's profitability.

A price change is by far the easiest strategy to increase profitability. Of course, your increase will have some negative impact on your customer conversion and sales process. However, the effort required to make up for that is often much smaller than trying to gain the same profitability boost through winning new clients or cost-cutting, respectively.

Especially for businesses that operate with small margins, a small change in price will have a significant impact on profitability. Check out the effect for yourself: simply change the prices in your business model spreadsheet and see what happens to your bottom line!

Criteria for choosing your pricing strategy

Your revenue model is hard to change and should stay in place unless it's not working well. In contrast, we recommend that you constantly experiment with and adapt your prices.

Many of the analytical considerations you made when you chose your revenue model will also flow into your pricing strategy:

1. Value created for the customer

From the customer's point of view, your pricing needs to be consistent with the value your product generates. If your price is too high in relation to the perceived value added by your solution, you'll have a hard time selling anything.

In the sales process, it helps greatly to frame your price as a fraction of the value your solution brings to the customer. This is why quantification is so important (see Chapter 5 on Pain) – even if your quantification is just based on an educated guess:

We had a beer with the customer project team after work and asked them casually where they felt our solution could generate value. Afterwards, we took what they had chatted about and did an ROI calculation based on that – granted, a rather short-sleeved approach.

— **Gregor Stühler, Co-Founder & CEO, Scoutbee**

As a general principle, we recommend to start by claiming one-fifth of the value you generate for your customer. Any share higher than that likely won't motivate your customers to adopt your solution. The better you quantify your value, the easier it is to justify your price:

Since we generate a lot of value [with our automated procurement solution], and we can demonstrate a clear ROI, there's never any big discussion on price. Consider the dimensions we're talking about. For example, if we benchmark 10-20 products for the customer, that quickly comes to €200-300 million. By just saving them 5-6% from better offers and maybe 20-30% in process costs, we generate several million Euros in savings. It's pretty straightforward for the customer, and for us, it's a very comfortable situation to be in.

— **Gregor Stühler, Co-Founder & CEO, Scoutbee**

With time, you will be able to raise your price along with your maturing business:

In the beginning, we just made up a price that seemed reasonable. The better we understood the value of our solution versus the competition, the more we could raise our price. After a while, even though our product was still the same, we also leveraged our higher brand recognition and references to further increase the price.

— **Moritz Zimmermann, Co-Founder & former CTO, Hybris**

To further narrow down the value of your solution from the customer's point of view, consider the timing of the value generation, too. As another general rule, value that is generated at a later point in time is worth less to the customer at the current moment. You might either directly reflect this in your pricing or provide other valuable contributions (like free onboarding) to take the value generation timing into account.

Startup founders often fail to understand that the user won't be productive with their product on day one. That's the cost of implementation. Make sure the users know how to use your product to create value. Otherwise, you'll see a lot of customer churn after the first year of your subscription.

– **Ognyan Vasilev, EMEA B2B Industries Advisory and GoToMarket, Salesforce**

2. Value of the customer to you

For most startups, profitability isn't actually the first priority – at least in periods of ample venture financing available for fast-growing companies. Depending on your stage, proving traction to your investors might be the more important goal:

Initially, we just wanted to prove that we could charge customers for our product at all. We asked our users: "What is it worth to you? Pay whatever you can afford." This way, we won our first 10, 20 paying customers. This revenue had more of a symbolic quality, which was fine, because our product was still far from done. But it was enough to be accepted into Y Combinator, and raise external funding subsequently.

— Veronika Riederle, Co-Founder & CEO, Demodesk

Or you might be more interested in winning a specific customer as a stepping stone into a larger market than in extracting the most value from a single deal:

A while ago, we were negotiating with a new customer. The organization was operating in an interesting sector, but the deal was relatively small and the organization wanted to negotiate an even lower price. A purely sales-focused person would ask, "How can we get the most out of this deal?" But in this situation, it was so important to take a step back and focus on the overarching strategic goal. As a founder, I said, "Strategically, this deal can be an enabler to get one step closer to our goal. It might not pay much now, but let's get them on board!" Because for startups, it's not really about sales. It's about building a machine. Sales needs to be approached strategically, not tactically.

— Tai Alegbe, Co-Founder & CEO, Contingent

Generally, it makes sense to lower your price significantly for certain types of customers:

- **"Big logos"** - In general, the reputation boost of showing that a internationally well-known brand is your customer (for example by putting their logo on your website) can be worth more to you than the actual transaction value.
- **Lighthouse customers** - You can use the first customer in a new segment as a reference to convince additional customers in the market (especially if the lighthouse customer is a "big logo").
- **Development partners** - It might be worth a discount if the customer is providing compensation in another way, such as important feedback on a new product.

> In the beginning, we only compromised the price to buy references in a certain market. For example, we closed a €100,000 deal with Toys R Us that would've been worth €5 million, but included other value for us, such as shared PR.
>
> **— Moritz Zimmermann, Co-Founder & former CTO, Hybris**

In this context, we can't stress enough that discounts in general need to be handled with great care. Not only do they reduce future profits from this customer, they might hurt you by spilling over to other customers as well. No customer likes to pay more than others – some even demand a "most favorite conditions" clause in the contract to make sure they always get the best deal. If you have given lavish discounts and they start spilling uncontrollably, this will permanently damage your profitability.

> Our goal was to get one dollar, and we had this sales guy who always went into meetings saying "Well, we could do 80 cents... but 50 would work as well." Most people just don't dare going in with a high enough price. They end up undercutting to win

the deal, because they can't stand the pressure. If you have a value proposition, try selling it right. If your price is 20% too low, you will permanently miss out on 20% of your revenue!

— Alex Meyer, Co-Founder & Partner, 42CAP

3. Thresholds in the customer's decision-making unit

Take into account your lessons about the typical limits in your customer's decision-making unit. Avoid bumping into typical thresholds. This will make your sales process much smoother.

Typical thresholds are:

- **Budget limits for your product category:** Through your interactions with customers, you will soon learn what the typical budget limits for a solution like yours are in your target market.

- **Hierarchy levels associated with budget limits:** Each management hierarchy has a typical limit for what they can spend without asking for permission. Since lower hierarchy levels are usually easier to access, it might make sense to tune your pricing to these limits to speed up your sales cycle.

Staying below a threshold of €100,000 Annual Customer Value seems to help close deals easier and faster. It doesn't involve as many stakeholders within the company, and you can always expand later.

— Jonas Rieke, COO, Personio

In the automotive sector, the budget thresholds are around €9,000, €40,000, €100,000, €250,000 and more than €1 million. We knew that our direct Champion had a signing power of up to €1 million. So we had to limit the price and our offering to an amount below that, so he could sign it off comfortably without having to go through the committees.

— Gregor Stühler, Co-Founder & CEO, Scoutbee

Beware: experience has shown that beyond a certain threshold, the intuitive rule of "lower pricing is easier" actually reverses itself. (This is another example why it is so important to go into the field – you'd have never guessed this from your office desk, right?)

It was a big learning for us to realize that selling at this price level – our Annual Customer Value started at six figures for a license – only works if the price points are high enough. In fact, we increased our prices every single year by a hefty rate for more than 15 years!

**— Moritz Zimmermann, Co-Founder &
former CTO, Hybris**

Choosing a pricing strategy that takes both upper and lower limits into account is a great way to determine the general range of your pricing strategy.

I know there are data-driven models for price setting, value-based pricing and all that… But you can also think of pricing along very simple principles, such as typical budgets in your product category.

— Alex Meyer, Co-Founder & Partner, 42CAP

4. Your competitors' pricing

Analyzing who your competition is (by asking about the current solution for the customers' problem) and finding out what they charge their customers gives you a key reference point for your own pricing.

Be warned to take the publicly posted price lists of your competitors as a benchmark for what their customers are actually paying. Often your competitors actually give big discounts on their list price to most customers. Alternatively, they might make most of their revenue from just one price level, while the other listed levels are merely provided for purposes of marketing psychology. Therefore, make some effort to find out your competitors' real pricing before you start benchmarking.

After all, if you feel that your price is high, but your competitors are charging even higher prices, then those prices might be the customers' reference point. Underbidding them too much might even rouse suspicion about the quality of your product! It is a much better idea to generate ideas for your product roadmap by asking yourself: what would it take for us to be able to charge twice the price of our nearest competitor?

The less competition there is, the more it is your position to define what an appropriate price should look like.

Some startups succeed in defining a new product category and manage to establish an entirely new price for their product. So consider pricing from all sides. It's a lot of tactics, and not necessarily rocket science.

— **Alex Meyer, Co-Founder & Partner, 42CAP**

5. Reputation of your product and brand

The longer you are in the market, and the more customer references or "logos" you can present, the lower is the risk to your customer. This is another good reason to bump up your prices.

> A significant milestone in our first years was to win strong partners like the Big4 firms as KPMG or Deloitte or software vendors like SAP as partner. It helped provide the necessary credibility to get a foot into the door of potential customers. Today, our brand is well-known in the market. That makes it so much easier.
>
> **— Bastian Nominacher, Co-Founder & Co-CEO, Celonis**

5 best practices for pricing

Pricing is a tricky challenge for founders because it touches both on factual and psychological aspects. Here is our advice to avoid the five most common pitfalls in pricing.

1. Never use your costs as a factor

Of course, your pricing needs to be significantly higher than your costs, otherwise you would have no business at all. But have you noticed how we have never used your costs as an input factor when discussing your pricing?

To set a price, many startups initially use calculations based on a multiple of their costs (like 2-3x) or a target margin (like 50%). The problem is that these calculations are typically undervaluing your product: often, your customer is actually gaining much more value from it than 2x your costs! In other words, you give away a lot of revenue you could have well asked for.

To maximize your revenue, it is more helpful to assume the perspective of Pain we discussed in the previous chapter. Put yourself in the shoes of your customer: they don't care about your costs – they care about the value you deliver to their business (and whether the split of value between them and you is fair).

2. Aim high

The experienced founders we interviewed on pricing consistently stressed one point: aim high with prices, and then keep increasing them.

For Personio, customers' astonished comments made them realize that there was a clear potential for higher pricing:

> We started out with a pricing level that was rather low and not very degressive. As a result, our Sales team often reported customers reacting to our price with "Wow, you're really inexpensive!" This and the investment that we put into our product (by now more than 200 people working in Product and Engineering to improve and extend functionalities), made us confident that we could ask for higher prices. Additionally, we changed the packaging structure to provide customers more flexibility for example through add-ons.
>
> **— Jonas Rieke, COO, Personio**

Founders often feel insecure because they don't know the "appropriate" price for their product. They are afraid to be rejected by their customers, so they enter the negotiations with a price that is far below what the customer could have paid. Remember: you need to hit the limit to find out where the limit is – even if going for a crash feels uncomfortable.

Some great advice I've received from an experienced enterprise salesperson: when you feel like your price is outrageously high and you're really uncomfortable with it – triple it and go into the meeting. Because then you will have hit the right price point.

— Alex Meyer, Co-Founder & Partner, 42CAP

It may also help to make yourself aware that price is rarely a showstopper for a deal. If it is, there's usually a mismatch in other aspects of the deal as well.

We've never failed at the procurement stage. Sometimes we lost a single-digit percentage. Most discussions here are on minor issues, like a Service Level Agreement that doesn't comply with their standards. But negotiations have never failed because of the price.

— Gregor Stühler, Co-Founder & CEO, Scoutbee

3. Keep increasing

With every deal you close, and every satisfied customer, several important things happen:

- Your reputation increases through the added "logo"
- Your product improves through the added experience
- Your credibility increases through the industry reference

All of these factors feed back into your pricing. LeanIX's Jörg G. Beyer made this into an internal rule, too:

Right after you close a deal, increase your price for the next customer to find the "real" market price.

— Jörg G. Beyer, Co-Founder & former Co-CEO, LeanIX

42CAP's Alex Meyer adds:

Don't just stick with your pricing because you're lazy and forget about raising it regularly. Yes, that actually happens quite a lot!

— Alex Meyer, Co-Founder & Partner, 42CAP

Because price is such an important lever for your revenue, it's crucial that you don't neglect raising it among all the other points on your busy agenda that seemingly require more "action." Raising prices regularly also prevents you from having to communicate a radical price jump after you have forgotten about increasing the price for too long.

For your existing customers, price increases create the least friction if you agree on regular small increases from the start. In many industries, it's standard to include a certain price increase as "annual inflation adjustment" into your contracts. And yes, the same rule applies: aim high, and wait for the customer to complain about it before you go lower.

Include automatic price increases from the start. I recommend writing something like a 7% annual price increase into the contracts – just try and see what happens.

**— Moritz Zimmermann, Co-Founder &
former CTO, Hybris**

4. Keep it simple

Alex Meyer from 42CAP advises founders to keep your overall pricing model simple. He speaks from his own experience with his first SaaS company:

> Our initial pricing model was catastrophic. We had 1,500 customers with three billing items each, resulting in 4,500 individual billing items. We needed 15 people in debtor management alone. Those people then spent 50% of their time explaining the pricing to our customers – each month! So my advice is to use a simple volume-based pricing model to make sure that your revenue grows when your customers grow. Otherwise, make it simple, or your customers won't understand it. Even your salespeople won't understand it!
>
> **— Alex Meyer, Co-Founder & Partner, 42CAP**

5. Create product packages that allow for price differentiation

When we talk about "your product" throughout this book, we are aware that you are likely not just offering one product, but different packages with a different amount of features, services, or consumables included.

In regard to pricing, make sure that you are bundling these packages in a way that they allow you to also differentiate your prices meaningfully. Your customer should perceive the tradeoff between the price and the value of each package as reasonable. This means, for example, that you avoid huge price jumps between packages and clearly highlight the value added in each higher package and pricing tier.

Creating meaningful packages that build a good basis for pricing is a science in itself. Jonas Rieke has gone through the process at Personio and summarizes the basics in the following "How To."

HOW TO

Use data to create your packaging structure

By Jonas Rieke, COO, Personio

While our first product packaging system and pricing was rather based on an educated guess, this time we took a data-driven approach. Our goal was to use the existing data on our product to create an optimal combination of three different packaging components: Value Metrics, Plans and Add-ons.

- A **value metric** is a single measure that correlates strongly with the value that a product creates for its customers.
- **Plans** are bundles of product verticals, modules or features. Plans should include a well-balanced mix of must-have and nice-to-have features.
- **Add-ons** are a good option to offer your customers more flexibility. Also, it can be a great source for additional expansion.

To find good feature candidates for different packaging components, we first created a structured documentation of all of the components of our product (product verticals, modules, features, sub-features, etc.). Each of these components has different properties: for example, how users interact with it, how users perceive its value and whether it depends on other features. We analyzed this data using statistical methods to identify meaningful value metrics, suitable features and modules for plans, and features for add-ons.

After analyzing our product and evaluating different value metrics, we aggregated our insights and drafted packaging models. Visualizing a prototype pricing page helped to challenge different models with our team. This was also the basis for coming up with reasonable price tags for our packaging components.

Finally, it was important to us that our go-to-market and customer-facing functions were able to tell a comprehensible and exciting story around our new packaging. Thus, the creative and last part of the packaging exercise was to gather a cross-functional team from Product Marketing, Design, Sales and Customer Success and create a profound story around our packaging.

I have described our packaging framework in detail in my 2020 Medium post "A data-driven framework for SaaS Packaging and Pricing."

7 - CONTRACT AND TERMS & CONDITIONS

How to get things in writing

Contractual agreements between businesses describe more than what your customer pays and what they pay it for. In B2B sales, contractual documentation usually contains two parts:

- The **Contract** includes all elements that are specific to this customer in particular scope and pricing. The audience of this document are the Champion and the Primary Economic Buyer within the decision-making unit.
- The **Terms & Conditions (T&Cs)** include all elements that are the same for all customers. The audience for the T&Cs are primarily the purchasing and legal teams within larger companies.

Contract

When your customers ask you for an offer, they are first and foremost interested in two pieces of information:

- The **scope and extent** of your product and services
- Your **pricing and payment terms**

These two factors build the basis for every contract.

Scope and extent of your offering

Whatever you offer: be precise in describing *what* you will deliver by *when*.

This way, you ensure that your customers get what they expect – and you prevent overextending yourself at the same time. Depending on the complexity of your offering, it may also be a good idea to outline what is *not* included within the scope of your offering in order to prevent possible misunderstandings.

When you sell a SaaS product, the scope is pretty straightforward: the customer gets whichever feature bundle within your product architecture they have chosen. In this case, you simply need to make sure that the bundles and their components are well defined in terms of their scope (for example by defining limitations on feature use or data transfer volumes).

When you sell a modular software product, where customers can pick and choose the features they want to order, the contract may get a bit more fragmented. Still, the scope should in principle be easy to outline.

Be careful of hardware and professional services: the cost of delivering what you (accidentally) promised can be extremely high.

This especially concerns professional services required for the implementation of your product, such as training or operational support. When you include these services into your scope, make sure to limit the days or hours of support that the customer can request. Also, limit the services to a particular time period and domain: for example, 10 days of support in training for the first three months of the implementation.

By setting an upper limit to how many service hours are included, you ensure you don't endanger the profitability of this customer for you. Initially limiting your professional support to a basic extent also enables a route to account expansion over time, should the customer require additional services in the long run.

If your business model depends on a low-touch, self-service setup, it's even more important to explicitly exclude in-person customer service and other major cost drivers from your scope. Alternatively, emphasize that these services are only included in higher price tiers (and design them with an included margin).

For SaaS products, it is common practice to upgrade the customer to new software versions without charging them extra. This is often used as a sales argument for moving away from on-premise or permanent license solutions.

To not give away upselling potential in the feature, limit software upgrades to optimizations of the existing functionality. Exclude major feature innovations from free upgrades.

Pricing and payment terms

The pricing and payment terms (see Chapter 6 on Revenue Model and Pricing) are a crucial part of the contract. They will often be the focal point of negotiation.

Again: be crystal-clear in your contract on *how much* you charge for what and *when* you expect the customer to pay.

Besides the actual amount you charge (your pricing), the payment terms (when you expect the payment) are an important lever for your cashflow. Be aware that these two are actually separate issues – which makes an adjustment to payment terms a good concession in negotiations, when you don't want to compromise on the price and can buffer the temporary impact on your liquidity.

We recommend pushing for yearly upfront payments. For you, this payment mode is great because it immediately increases your working capital. But it may even be also in the customer's interest to have one single payment instead of monthly invoicing and payment processes that come with a host of administrative costs and complexity.

For professional services, it's best practice to price them by day (or by hour, alternatively) and separate different tiers based on seniority and role.

For example, you can include different price levels for professional services provided by a Senior Developer or by a Junior Customer Service Manager.

Format

Ideally, your contract fits on a single page. On that page, outline the key terms specific to this customer, refer to the T&Cs as part of the contract, and include space for the signatures of both parties.

There is immense power in the simplicity of a short and succinct document: it shortens the path toward the customer's signature.

> In your contracts, try to use as many standard components as possible. Use conditions that IT and procurement departments are familiar with. For example, use a standard price list where you describe your service offering, and include an order form where you describe what was ordered from the price list, e.g. "15 seats."
>
> **— Alex Meyer, Co-Founder & Partner, 42CAP**

It's ideal if your offer is already documented in the form of this single page, with your T&Cs attached.

Sending out your offer in the form of your eventual contract eliminates any possible confusion about an additional step of "translation" from offer to contract after all elements of the offer have been negotiated and agreed upon. In theory, the customer should be able to sign the offer document and have a full contract as a result.

On the administrative side, it's a lot simpler and faster if your customer is willing to sign your contract digitally.

Ask them to use either your own platform or a signing solution like Docusign or Hellosign. This way, you'll also automatically implement best practices in regard to professional documentation management.

Terms & Conditions (T&Cs)

Those elements of your contract that apply to all customers equally should be aggregated into a T&Cs document. In principle, you can just make your T&Cs available for download on your website. But we recommend to also always send them along as a legal attachment to your contract document.

Despite the standardized nature of the document, it is well possible that individual customers will negotiate about some parts of your T&Cs – for example price increases, contract duration or payment terms.

If you modify your standard T&Cs for an individual customer, describe the modifications in the customer-specific contract document rather than changing your T&Cs document itself.

In the following table, we give an overview of the key topics typically addressed in T&Cs, and add our recommendations for drafting their content. Most of these are standard terms and conditions that require no further consideration. However, we have highlighted topics

- that are especially important from the perspective of a B2B startup (⚠)
- that new customers are likely to negotiate (💬).

Remember, this does not constitute legal advice. Always specify the content of your own T&Cs with a lawyer!

Term	Ideal content	Comment
Software license	Description of the type of license, copyrights, and clear definition of the scope of the product	
Standard price increase	Up to 7% annually	💬
Data usage	Permission to use the data generated by the customer beyond the contract timeframe	⚠️ to enable network effects and further product evolution
Expenses	Travel, accommodation are charged extra	
Professional services	Development, customer service, training etc. are charged extra at a given minimum rate	
Duration of contract	24 or 36 months (minimum: 12 months)	💬 should increase after the first period
Renewal	Automatic renewal for twice the initial contract length (minimum: for the initial contract length)	💬 should increase after the first period
Cancellation	Only in the 3rd month prior to the end of the current contract duration	

Term	Ideal content	Comment
Termination	Conditions for termination and refunds	
Payment terms	Upfront payment for yearly software subscription and retainer for professional services, with due date = date of invoice	
Penalties for late payment	Interest or penalty payment	
Warranties, remedies and damages	Allocation of risks between vendor and buyer	⚠ to prevent existential threats
Limitation of liabilities and indemnification	Limitation to the contract value of the last 12 months at maximum, exclusion of indirect damages and loss of profit	⚠ to prevent existential threats; buy insurance, if needed (and share cost with buyer)
Reference	Permission to reference the customer and use their logo	⚠ to enable best in class marketing
Customer T&Cs	Should not be applied (or only in certain parts)	
Invoicing medium	Digital invoicing only	
Confidentiality	Applicable to all information and material	
Intellectual Property	Resides with the Licensor only	⚠ to secure basis of differentiation

Term	Ideal content	Comment
Customer obligations	Customer is responsible for damage resulting from illegal content, virus, defects	
Jurisdiction	Based on your company location	

Strategic advice

Always propose your own contractual documentation

As a general rule, it's best to propose your own contractual documentation.

Include a tight definition of scope and timing, set your pricing in the top quartile of the market, and attach T&Cs that are only slightly biased toward your position as the seller. In our experience, the majority of your customers will accept your documentation. Negotiations will be limited to the price and possible high-priority elements for each party.

Also, because of the legal implications of any contractual documentation for your business and the deals you are going to make, ask a lawyer to draft your contract and T&Cs documents.

This is also true for any changes in the documentation that result from negotiations in the sales process. For your largest and most complex deals, we recommend to have your lawyer accompany you in the background of the negotiations, if possible.

In your sales process, both your proposed contract and your T&Cs are subject to negotiation. Typically, the emphasis in the early part of the sales process is on the commercial issues that are included in the contract part (such as scope and price).

However, the T&Cs may also become part of the negotiation. This typically happens once the documentation moves to the specialized legal and procurement departments within the customer's organization.

Even individual terms and wordings are sometimes part of the negotiations and should be handled rather pragmatically:

> It really helps to frame your contract in the dimensions your customer is familiar with. I talked to a purchasing lady from a big corporation once and she didn't know what "Software as a Service" was. And they didn't have a procurement process for this. They only had their "man-days" and "license fees." Eventually, we decided to simply reframe our offer with a new wording. Now they have their "yearly license fees" with "professional services," we have our ARR, and both sides are happy.
>
> **— Stephan Rohr, Co-Founder & CEO, TWAICE**

Treat pilot projects with caution (and never make them free)

Pilot projects, or Proof-of-Concept projects (PoCs) only make sense to you if they serve to prove your value proposition and generate trust. This is typically necessary in the *Explore & Learn* phase, where you are still working on product discovery. However, in recent years, the link between pilot projects and follow-up business has become increasingly thin. This is a real problem for startups, as VC partner Alex Meyer warns:

> Until five or 10 years ago, PoCs were a great concept. The customer paid €5,000 or €10,000 and you knew they were serious about eventually buying. These days, every company has their digitalization department, and their only job is to do PoCs with startups – without any intention of ever buying. If your only customers are digitalization departments without any line managers involved, that's a problem.
>
> **— Alex Meyer, CEO, 42CAP**

To avoid this pitfall, treat pilot projects with caution: do only a limited number of pilots in order to learn, and always have your customers pay for them to validate their interest.

HOW TO

Conduct a successful pilot project

By Miki Yokoyama, Managing Partner, TechFounders

1. **Pitch your pilot** - Pitch your pilot project with the customer's use case in mind. Be transparent about the development status of your product, but make sure you clearly communicate the value of the project's outcome. Also, indicate the intended scope of the project and the resources needed for implementation. Pricing is important, but it only works, of course, if you've established a solid product/market fit and if you are solving a pain point for your customer. Generally, selling a pilot project is no different from any other selling.

    Even if you have found a suitable cooperation partner, be prepared to wait. Sometimes it takes weeks or months before all signatures are gathered and the budget is approved – corporations move slow.

2. **Agree on the parameters of the cooperation** - Too many pilot projects fail during the implementation phase because the cooperation wasn't clearly defined. Therefore, at the beginning of your project, discuss and document the following parameters:

- **Goals and expectations:** What is the desired outcome of the project? When will each party consider the project a success? If at all possible, define a clear path to a permanent engagement including the commercials after the pilot.
- **Milestones and deliverables:** What are the milestones that your startup has to deliver along the way? But also: What are the deliverables on the corporate side? You don't want to end up in a situation where your milestone is to do a data analysis by the end of the first month, but the data required is stuck for two months in a release approval process.
- **Working mode:** Startups and corporations have very different ways of working. An agile, iterative working mode can easily look unreliable and erratic to someone who is used to a sequential way of planning and communicating. Address this aspect directly to avoid confusion and friction.
- **Contact person:** Who decides on whether the milestones are reached? Who is the person to go to for operative questions or data? What is the process for receiving payments?

Don't separate your trial contracts from your long-term contracts

In contrast to pilot projects, trials and trial periods are more common in later phases. They allow potential customers to test-drive your product before committing to a long-term contract.

From the customer's point of view, implementing a new product or solution always entails a certain kind of risk – especially in B2B sales, where it can take some time until the product starts to deliver value. Until then, the customer buys the figurative pig in the poke. For this reason, it's common to include a contractual trial period as part of the overall contract and hence give the customer the option to cancel the contract if your solution does not hold up to its promise.

Because it builds on your standardized product, a trial should not incur significant cost to you (as a pilot project might). This means that you should not offer to customize your software for your trial customer. If it's possible at low cost to you, however, you might include your potential customer's data to create a stronger demonstration of your product's value to them.

For small contract values, don't include a trial period at all. Or make it brief, like one or two weeks.

For software-only propositions with low annual costs (e.g. less than €1,000), adjusting your contract to this is usually not necessary. Because your product is significantly more standardized, it's easy for your customers to determine its value. And even if it doesn't work at all, the financial loss is small.

For bigger contract values, avoid separating trial contracts from your long-term, operational contracts.

Customers with larger contract values – who purchase more complex and customized solutions from you – often request more elaborate trial conditions from you. For example, they ask you to trial your solution in a single department or country before they consider rolling it out across the entire organization.

If the conditions for this trial differ strongly from what you actually want to sell and from your typically recurring pricing model (because the customer wants to pay a fixed amount for a certain period), it may be tempting to set up a separate contract for the trial. Don't do this!

Integrate the pilot contract and the long-term contract into one single contract with two phases.

In this single contract, avoid speaking about "trial period," "proof of concept," or "pilot projects" altogether. In our experience, this will often trigger the above-mentioned impulses to separate contracts within your customer. Instead, simply call them "implementation phases":

- Phase 1 - Implementation and validation (e.g. in month one)
- Phase 2 - Operational roll-out (e.g. from month two onwards)

Integrating trial and long-term contracts has two key advantages.

1. **It forces both you and the customer to discuss and agree on all key terms of the long-term contract.** This way, if you cannot agree on a long-term contract, neither of you wastes their time with the trial period.

2. **It avoids the breaking point of a second required signature.** Every signature you have to get entails an additional risk of hold-up and broken momentum. If you integrate both trial and operational contract, but still include the option to cancel after Phase 1 (Implementation), there's no risk to the customer, and you eliminate the risk that you won't get that second signature for any reason.

Successful entrepreneurs like Josef Brunner from Relayr don't do any PoCs anymore without a revenue potential of at least €10 million. They do this by reversing the PoC concept and saying "Here's the contract, you can quit anytime after three months." Risk-wise, it's the same for the customer, but this way, they get the commitment that the customer will set up the project for real

— **Alex Meyer, Co-Founder & Partner, 42CAP**

A final note on trial periods (that we have already touched upon in Chapter 1, but is such a common mistake that it's worth mentioning again):

Never engage in trials for free or for too long.

Some companies suggest that you do a free trial in order to prove your solution's value. Even if your startup is in an early stage, never do a free trial – unless you gain as much in non-monetary value (access to data, domain experience) from explicitly designated co-development projects.

There is simply too much risk in providing a free (or heavily discounted) trial in the hopes of gaining a long-term contract afterwards, in particular if this trial comes with significant operational cost to you. Too often you'll successfully complete the trial – and then another person, who is the decision-maker for the long-term contract, says "No." Or you find out that your *actual* pricing was never acceptable for the customer from the start.

Be pragmatic about the T&Cs

Large customers often propose that you use their Buying T&Cs instead of your own T&Cs. This makes signing the contract easier for them, but naturally shifts most of the contractual risks toward you.

Should you fight for your own T&Cs or accept the rules of the bigger fish? Gregor Stühler from Scoutbee and Alex Meyer from 42CAP have some solid advice:

So far, we've always accepted the customers' T&Cs. At least today we have our own corporate lawyer. Before that, we just went in rather hara-kiri: we accepted everything and hoped for the best. All of those contracts we had to clean up at a later stage to be more fundable.

The issue of software licensing is extremely important to us – specifically, to make sure customer-specific code adjustments belong to us. These are pitfalls that you need to watch out for, because they disappear in the fine print otherwise.

The question is always: what liability scenarios are we talking about, actually? If our software was ensuring the stability of their production, I'd worry like crazy and hire the very best lawyers to avoid possible liability cases. But in the end, we sell a recommendation engine, where the customer is the one making the final decision. Our liability risk is relatively limited.

— **Gregor Stühler, Co-Founder & CEO, Scoutbee**

Enter contract negotiations with a healthy pragmatism. Once the contract is signed, the paper disappears into some drawer and is almost never consulted again. Very few issues actually end up in court – most disagreements can be resolved by a civilized discussion between business partners. And if you really run into serious conflict, the most common solution is to just dissolve the contract and leave.

— **Alex Meyer, Co-Founder & Partner, 42CAP**

Alex Meyer confirms our experience both from within big corporations and from our startups: if you don't mess up *badly* or your deals go high into the 7 or 8-digit range, the only time anyone will look at the contract again – if at all – is at renewal time. Because legal fights are so costly, unhappy customers usually just terminate the relationship, and maybe withhold any further outstanding payments.

There's one exception: those clauses that actually hold existential risk for you.

The customer's Buying T&Cs often include other clauses than yours: guarantees, escrow, most favored customer, or assignment clauses. We won't go deeper into those here – instead, we'll close this part with an excellent rule for evaluating the clauses of the customer's Buying T&Cs by Alex Meyer:

> The only thing you should be careful about are high penalties that exceed the revenue and have the potential of endangering your entire business.
>
> **— Alex Meyer, Co-Founder & Partner, 42CAP**

Regarding your own T&Cs, we have already highlighted those that are especially relevant to B2B startups above. In sum, you need to make sure to include the clauses on Intellectual Property (IP) and the Limitation of Liabilities, to protect the basis of your business and prevent bankruptcy through high liabilities.

8 - SALES PROCESS

How to get from first contact to a done deal

Sales isn't about talent or magic. It's about having a strong grip on the entire journey, from first contact to signing the contract. This is what you achieve by defining a sales process.

The goal in designing a sales process is to standardize the sales activities that work best for your company and your product, and to put them in the sequence that leads to the desired results the fastest.

Why you need a sales process

A sales process allows you to manage your limited resources better.

By pre-defining process stages with specific outcomes and specific timeframes, you will be able to separate promising from unlikely candidates among your potential customers much faster. Sorting out the bad ones will save you time you can then spend on more promising leads instead.

A sales process makes sales repeatable and revenues plannable.

Once you know what the typical sales journey looks like, you will be able to make predictions and forecasts on the basis of your status quo. For example, if you know that 10% of prospects you contact today will sign a deal worth €50,000 in 3-6 months, you can estimate what you need to do to earn €1 million in revenue by the end of the year.

In this chapter, we will give you an overview of how a typical sales process looks like before we dive deeper into its different aspects in the following chapters.

How to structure your sales process

> The real creativity in sales is not in selling itself. The creativity comes out in sales operations, where you design the structure of your sales process.
>
> **— Ben Stephenson, Co-Founder & CEO, Impala**

From a bird's-eye view, all sales processes are somewhat similar. They simply describe the typical steps through which a relationship with a potential future customer evolves.

Once you zoom in closer, you begin to see greater details and more differences between sales processes. These differences are there for a reason: because your product is easier or harder to explain, your target organizations are smaller or larger, or your ACV is higher or lower.

You need to customize your own sales process according to your product and target segment.

We have listed a few examples for differences and the reasoning behind them in the table below. Note that the list could be extended much further.

Variable	Reasoning
Quantity of leads/contacts	Smaller ACV → More leads
Length of a typical sales process	Higher ACV or larger customer organizations → Longer lead times
Ideal approach and medium toward the customer	Higher ACV or more traditional target segment → physical meetings rather than (video) calls
Timing of a product demo	Product value can be demonstrated without lots of customer data → Time demo early in the process
Number of interactions required for a customer to be ready to buy	Larger customer organizations → More interactions
Number of people involved in the buying process on the customer side	Larger customer organizations → More people involved
Existence of a trial period and length of that period	Higher ACV → Trial required Lower ACV and hence limited risk → No trial necessary

Be aware that every sales process is an ongoing work-in-progress.

With growing revenue and your growing salesforce, you will need to make incremental changes to the respective stages and activities within those stages.

Tuning your sales machine requires constant attention. While you do founder sales, you'll do it automatically. Later on, you'll need to establish regular occasions to do so with your team.

We recommend conducting a quarterly process review, where you look at the last quarter's sales activities to identify potential improvements. In your review sessions, pay special attention to those cases that did *not* go well, and try to find out why these contacts haven't progressed further in each stage. Again: it's all about identifying patterns and changing them to your advantage.

> In the beginning, it was trial and error for us, and not at all standardized. But as soon as we could, we analyzed what worked and what didn't.
>
> **— Bastian Nominacher, Co-Founder & Co-CEO, Celonis**

As your startup, product and market evolve, so will your process to tune the sales machine to maximum efficiency. In sales, as in startup life in general, getting better requires constant, never-ending iteration and refinement.

HOW TO

Use tools to manage your sales process

- **Start simple** - In the beginning, setting up any tools is a waste of time. You need to get the rough outline of your sales process right first, so just start with an excel spreadsheet, define a basic process and iterate on that process. Take special care to clearly define the respective entry and exit criteria (or inputs and outputs) for each process stage. The more detail you can add from bottom-up trial and error, the more time you'll save later on.

- **Upgrade to a lean CRM** - Once you have found a sales process that works for you, upgrade to a simple self-service CRM (customer relationship management) software. There are a number of them out there at €1,000 to €2,000 per year, such as Streak, Salesflare, Pipedrive, Hubspot, Close, Agile, Base... Pick whichever you like best; it doesn't make a huge difference.

- **Upgrade to Salesforce** - As soon as you have your Series A financing in the bank, upgrade to Salesforce. It's the market standard and whether you like it or not, it's the most powerful tool out there – if only because the best tools are built on top of the Salesforce platform. Depending on your team size, the migration and the initial customization toward your process will cost around €10,000-30,000 and the ongoing cost will be €3,000-10,000.

- **Build your sales software stack** - Once you've established your core sales process and CRM, use advanced tools to optimize your process and activities and to support your sales team.

One of the most sophisticated stacks we know was built up by Neil Ryland at Peakon:

- Salesforce - CRM
- Clearbit - lead enrichment
- Marketo - lead management
- Chili Piper - lead scheduling
- SalesLoft - sales orchestration
- Drift - sales personalization
- Tableau & Microsoft BI - reporting
- Guru - knowledge management
- Workramp - learning management
- Gainsight - customer success

We have a really big internal tech stack. That was one of the things I was really focused on. Our tech stack gives us an advantage in getting in front of the market. For example, we have improved our win rates because we're only contacting accounts at the right point in their buying cycle. Obviously, the reverse of that investment is a need for people to run that technology – so we have quite a number of people in technical sales support.

Once you start scaling, you'll want to test everything. But you need to have the right data to be able to test something. If you don't get the systems and the fields in Salesforce right at the start, you spend so much time backwards dating. And then everyone eventually throws their hands up and says, "We're gonna have to start again." Or for an AB test that you can only roll back three months, you'll wonder, "How did this trend occur in Q4 last year?" and you won't know. So my advice is: own systems very early.

Our mid-market team utilizes more tools than the enterprise team, and more frequently. That's simply because they've got a much higher volume coming through that they need to disqualify out, as much as what they need to qualify in. So they're utilizing nurturing tools, and they're monitoring things that are bubbling up. It's a more reactive way of using tools, whereas we do more proactive sales in the enterprise segment.

— Neil Ryland, Chief Revenue Officer, Peakon

Stages of a typical sales process

In our 40 combined years as operators, we have seen countless sales processes at different companies.

In essence, all sales processes boil down to six prototypical stages through which your target company moves from being a prospect to becoming your customer.

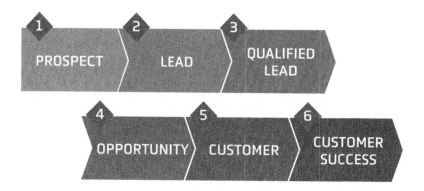

The names of the first five stages – Prospect, Lead, Qualified Lead, Opportunity, and Customer – describe how far the customer is advanced on the way to becoming your customer.

The final stage, Customer Success, describes selling to an existing customer. Although this effectively is a new sales process in itself, what happens after the initial sale is key for creating long-term, profitable customer relationships (which is why we include it here).

For each stage, there are four main variables: Input, Activities, Output, and Time box.

In addition, some stages have what we call "Entry points," where specific categories of contacts "skip the line" and enter directly into a more advanced process stage.

Stage variable	Content
Input	The information that needs to be found/activities that need to be completed before the prospective customer enters/advances into this stage.
Activities	The activities that you will typically perform at this stage to achieve the desired output.
Output	The defined goal of this stage (which will become the input for the next stage at the same time).
Time box	The expected time each potential customer will stay within this stage before moving to the next stage.
Entry point	Depending on where the potential customers come from, this stage (not Stage 1) is their entry point into the process.

Input, activities, and **output** are pretty straightforward: within those variables, you describe the milestones that you need to reach in order to complete each stage and move to the next one, and the activities you need to complete to reach these milestones.

You have to have clear "exit criteria" that have to be fulfilled before you can move your opportunity to the next stage in your sales process. For example: "We have shown how to solve the challenges and the prospect could sell it internally." Otherwise, especially beginners push opportunities through the pipeline in the CRM, when the prospect's status actually isn't that mature yet.

— Jörg G. Beyer, Co-Founder & former Co-CEO, LeanIX

Having defined the expected **time box** is important because it allows you to automatically highlight slow-moving prospects. By adding up all the time boxes in your process, you also get an expected overall lead time for your customers.

The **entry point** varies for customers depending on their connection to you. Customers that you research and contact (outbound lists) start the sales process at stage 1. If they contact you (inbound requests) or you approach them through a special process (like a tender), they can also enter the process directly at stages 2 or 4.

Taken together, a typical sales process with all six stages looks like this.

Example Process	1 Prospect	2 Lead	3 Qualified Lead	4 Opportunity	5 Customer	6 Customer Success
Input	Segmentation criteria and ICP defined	Individual contact data acquired	Interest validated, champion identified, etc	Budget available, decision-making unit identified etc.	Offer made, decision criteria, process and timeline defined	Solution successfully implemented
Activity	**Creating company lists, conducting desk research, attending events**	**Outbound: Emailing, calling, sending LinkedIn messages Inbound: Contacts through webform, calls, emails, received business cards**	**Emailing, calling Focused product demo**	**Demo & presentation**	**Conducting trial Negotiating contract**	**Retrieving references Evangelizing Resolving issues Negotiating expansion**
Output	Individual contact data acquired	Interest validated Champion identified	Budget available Decision-making unit identifi-d Pain points understood Decision-making timeline understood	Offer made Decision criteria, process and timeline defined	Contract signed	Upsell/expansion signed
Time box	1 day	1-2 weeks	1-2 week	4 weeks	3 weeks	
Entry points for	Outbound lists	Inbound requests		RFPs & Tenders		

What about the buyers' side?

Naturally, the sales process is laser-focused on the seller's perspective – *your* perspective – because these are the actions you can directly control.

However, put yourself in the shoes of your customers when designing your sales process. Understanding your customers' buying process as a mirror to your sales process will help you in many ways.

> Do not forget to also draw the buying journey – all the steps that a typical buyer has to go through until a final purchase decision – and map this journey against your sales process. Often, the process is a long hard slog on the buyer side as well: from first identifying the problem to exploring solutions and building requirements. And then the buyer still needs to select suppliers, validate the chosen solution and finally, get everyone on board. You will make your own job as a seller easier by asking yourself: How do we optimize this journey for the buyer?
>
> **— Tiffani Bova, Global Growth Evangelist, Salesforce and WSJ Bestselling Author, Growth IQ**

First, considering the buyer's perspective will prevent you from approaching the wrong people in your target company at the wrong time. For example, it doesn't make sense to try to impress an Economic Buyer with a demo of your solution when no one at the company is even aware that there is a problem yet!

Second, be aware of the customer's level of information at the different stages. This will help you to provide the kind of information and materials the customer needs. It's not helpful to launch into a detailed run-down of your product features if you haven't yet established your Champion's pain points.

And third, considering the sales process from the customer's side will give you a better understanding of the market and your proposition in comparison to the available alternatives. For example, your pitch will differ depending on whether your customers are just barely aware of their pain or whether they have already compared many competing solutions in detail.

Always consider the sales process from the prospect's point of view. Don't write down a process saying, "it would be convenient for us this way." Follow the buyer's journey and ask yourself: what's in for the prospect? Why would they join in?

— **Jörg G. Beyer, Co-Founder & former Co-CEO, LeanIX**

For our prototypical sales process, we have illustrated the mirrored process for the customers' side in the table below.

Example Process	1 Prospect	2 Lead	3 Qualified Lead	4 Opportunity	5 Customer	6 Customer Success
Seller Activity	Creating company lists, conducting desk research, attending events	Outbound: Emailing, calling, sending LinkedIn messages Inbound: Contacts through webform, calls, emails, received business cards	Emailing, calling Focused product demo	Demo & presentation	Conducting trial Negotiating operational contract	Retrieving references Evangelizing Resolving issues Negotiating expansion
Buyer Activity		Becoming aware of and understanding own pain/challenge	Researching options to address the pain Considering existing and new providers	Evaluating different options based on information given by the providers	Trialing product Generating buy-in across buying team Negotiating Receiving references Making decisions and complying with governance	Rolling out and using the product Escalating issues Negotiating
Buyer output		Feeling understood in own pain/challenge	Different options to relieve pain understood	Decision on best option to solve pain made	Contract signed	Upsell signed

Now let's zoom in closer and find out what is going on within the six stages of the sales process.

Stage 1: Prospect

If there is no previous connection to your potential customer, the sales process begins at the Prospect stage.

Output - Your desired output during this stage is to turn the abstract ICP or persona into individual contact data, or a "lead." Aside from the names of the company and person, there has to be some kind of personal contact data (email address, telephone, or LinkedIn profile) that you can use in the next stage. Some people refer to leads at this stage also as Marketing Qualified Leads (MQL).

Input - The input of the Prospect stage comes from the work you've done on segmentation and the ICP as well as the personas and Champions, as explained in Chapters 3 and 4.

Activities - Refer to the "How To" section in Chapter 3 on how to build a company list. Then start to identify Champions on LinkedIn through desk research. Depending on your target segment, attending industry conferences or similar events (or even just scanning the exhibitor list) can help you find specific companies and contacts. Document all company and individual data in your CRM to build a strong prospect database to serve as the foundation for your future sales activities.

Time box - In the Prospect stage, you need to find contacts for a large number (usually thousands for lower ACVs and hundreds for higher ACVs) of prospective customers each month. It is crucial that you balance the time and cost spent per lead and the number of prospects you handle. Usually, you will measure your time for each prospect in minutes rather than hours.

Our advice for the Prospect stage

There are two typical challenges founders struggle with at this stage:

1. You don't know where to start looking amongst the huge number of potential target companies out there.

If you struggle with an excessive number of companies to dig into, you have likely not defined your ICP well enough to be at a granular level. Because your search criteria are too broad, you find it difficult to identify a limited number of relevant customers to research in more depth.

Revisit Chapter 3 on segmentation and try to find another angle to narrow down your target segment. The goal is to go from millions of companies to thousands or hundreds that have a much higher likelihood of buying from you.

2. You gather the contacts of the headquarters' reception offices rather than specific individuals within the company.

While receptionists can help you find the right person within the company, you need to know who you're looking for if you don't want to waste a lot of time talking to the wrong people. (Needless to say, emails to an "info@company.com" address will never, ever be forwarded to any relevant decision-maker.)

First, find out which personas within the company are likely to have a need for your solution. Then decide on the amount of time you'll want to spend identifying the actual person filling this role within a specific company. Your list will grow more slowly this way, but the quality of your leads will be infinitely higher.

Stage 2: Lead

Output - The single purpose of the first (and short) interaction with your contact person in the Lead stage is to understand their level of pain and interest in your solution. The goal is not to sell anything yet, but to find out whether it makes sense to invest more time and cost into having further discussions with that customer. If your lead shows interest, follow up with them in the next stage.

Input - The input for the Lead stage are the contacts you researched in the previous stage: the email address, phone numbers, or LinkedIn profiles of one or more relevant individuals within the target company.

Entry point for inbound contacts - The Lead stage is also the point where inbound contacts enter your sales process.

Inbound contacts are people who have approached your startup in some way. This may have happened directly in person through emails, calls, or handing over business cards at events and trade fairs. Other contacts may approach you through referrals from other customers or your employees. A third possibility involves the individuals who left their contact data in a contact form on your website or engaged with your online content (downloading something from your website, commenting on your posts on LinkedIn, etc.).

By approaching you, inbound contacts have already demonstrated a higher interest in your company and proposition. This translates into a higher likelihood of buying – if you handle them well. Prioritize your responses to inbound messages, and answer within the same hour or day, at the exact time your potential customers express the most need. This is also a great opportunity to demonstrate your dedication to strong customer service early on.

Activities - Contact your leads using the data you gathered in the Prospect stage. Send emails, LinkedIn messages, or call them on the phone.

In the *Explore & Learn* phase, prioritize calls over written communication. A personal conversation, which is faster and allows for follow-up questions in both directions, will give you significantly more information about the customer. With each call, you will find out more about what kind of customers have a higher or lower interest in your solution. These short iteration cycles allow you to refine your ICP, which increases your efficiency in the Prospect stage. At the same time, you can test out how your contacts react to different arguments and messages and what approach gets the most attention.

Only in the *Standardize & Optimize* phase should you start optimizing your outbound channels based on their profitability and payback calculations (see Chapter 12 on Operational Sales Reporting).

Time box - You should be able to reach your contact via email or phone within one to two weeks. If no one opens or responds to your email or phone call, then deprioritize the contact and move on.

Our advice for the Lead stage

1. What not to talk about

It sounds counterintuitive if you eventually want to sell something, but if you talk to someone for the first time on the phone or at a trade fair, *don't* start by bombarding them with details about your awesome solution. Instead, ask high-level questions related to your field: What are their priorities? What are their current pain points?

Asking questions allows you to highlight the benefits of your solution in direct relation to the customer's real pain points, rather than showering them with abstract examples. This conversational style also gives the customer the feeling of being heard and understood, and it establishes you as a trusted consultant rather than an obnoxious salesperson.

> It's a mistake to begin by talking about features: "My product can do this and that." Because then it becomes a contest between your product versus the competition – what features are included in each and which are not. Instead, I ask: "What's your team's

daily workflow? Why is reporting important to you?" Base your conversation on your customer's use case. Talk about the user experience. This way, they feel that you identify with them and their problems instead of being just a vendor of your product.

— Arun Srinivasan, Co-Founder & CEO, Clarisights

If you choose to make the first contact via a written format, you'll have to make an educated guess regarding the customer's pain points based on your research. Include a concrete, ideally quantified benefit related to this pain point in your message.

Make sure that the benefit you are describing is relevant for the actual person you are contacting. For a senior executive, this would be cost savings, increased revenue, or a competitive advantage. For a mid-level employee you want to win over as your Champion, they would instead be interested in work-related benefits such as time savings, increased usability, or more fun at work (better to frame this as "innovative solutions").

2. Automate, but stay personal

The advantage of written communication is that you can automate your messages with tools such as Mailchimp (for email) or Dux-Soup (for LinkedIn invitations and messages). Use features like sequencing (automatic follow-ups after a certain time has passed) or open rate reports to optimize your approach at this stage.

However, automation does come with a caveat: nobody likes spammy, impersonal emails that look like a robot sent them to thousands of people at once. Therefore, we urge you to spend the extra time personalizing those messages based on your research. Depending on how many messages you are sending, you can also apply analytical methods to find out what subject lines and copy achieve the optimal open and response rates.

In recounting the early days of Celonis, Bastian Nominacher makes a case in point on automation and analyzing what works – applied to old-fashioned postal mail:

> You need to get to the decision-makers. But how do you get their attention when you are just starting? We soon learned that assistants would throw away letters before they even reached the decision-maker. So, what did we do to get past them? We hand-labeled envelopes. No assistants throw out something hand-labeled — it's probably from the manager's grandma! Of course, that was time-intensive, but it got us a 50x higher open rate.
>
> — **Bastian Nominacher, Co-Founder & Co-CEO, Celonis**

Stage 3: Qualified Lead

Output - In the Qualified Lead stage, your goal is to explore the demonstrated interest of your leads in more detail. Your output will be three kinds of information: who the decision-making unit is, how much budget there is for your proposition and the approximate timeline to reach a decision. These Qualified Leads are sometimes also referred to as Sales Qualified Leads (SQL).

In case you have a highly innovative or rather complex proposition, it is important to use this stage to better understand the pain points and existing solutions within your prospective customer's company. This allows you to validate if there is actually a substantial benefit of your solution over the status quo. In case there is, finding out how exactly your solution could help, and how it would be implemented, is the necessary basis for preparing an offer in the next stage.

Input - Qualified Leads are those leads who indicated an interest in the Lead stage. Other leads can be dropped (or relegated to a nurturing process).

Activities - Most B2B transactions involve more than a single person on the buyer's side. Refer to Chapter 4 to learn about the typical composition of a decision-making unit and how to identify the specific people in the unit within a company. But to sum it up: just ask them!

As hinted to in Chapter 6 on Pricing, most corporate organizations work with budgets. Budget size and authority are typically linked to the hierarchy levels within the company. It also makes a difference for your sales process if the customer already has a budget for an incumbent solution. This existing budget gives you a hint on the price sensitivity of the customer.

Ideally, at this point you'll also be able to gauge whether the prospective customer will be able to make a decision within a given period of time (for example 3-6 months). If you cannot get a clear answer on this question, or you learn that the decision may take longer, eliminate this prospect from the sales pipeline. Your resources will be better invested if you park this contact in a nurturing process instead.

If you offer a highly innovative product, the customer might not currently use any solution to address the underlying pain. In this case, your job in the Qualified Lead stage is to use the information from the discussions with the customer to quantify the monetary benefits of your solution, that way you establish a business case together, which the customer can then use to create a budget for the solution.

While asking questions and listening are the primary activities at the Qualified Lead stage, there's one exception: if you can, do an initial product demo at this stage. Focus on one or two features that address the central pain point of the customer – ideally by integrating the actual customer data or processes. As a result, the customer will have a concrete and visual idea of how the product will benefit them. This has proven to be an invaluable driver for them to move forward in the process.

We found that we could talk the prospective customer's ears off about the advantages of our product, but what excited them was a live demo. As soon as we showed what our software could do, we got them hooked.

— Bastian Nominacher, Co-Founder & Co-CEO, Celonis

We were able to give exceptional demos because we had brilliant demo accounts that we could use. We would put the business's logo on there, we tailored it exactly to their account.

At your demo, you don't need to show the customer the whole product. Our demos are probably quite annoying for customers, because of the half hour we booked, I ask them questions for the first 29 minutes. I'm trying to find your killer problem. And once I find it, that's the only feature I'm going to show you.

I know there's five or six killer problems that we can solve, because those are the reasons why other people use our solution. I use my question structure to find out if you have one of those problems. As soon as I find one problem, I keep going to see if there's another one. And once I know all of your problems, I do the demo. I've had demos where the person tells me, "Everything's great! It's just that each week, I have to manually upload 1,000 payments." I just show them the bulk import CSV and say: "Oh, you should look at this feature."

— Matt Robinson, Co-Founder & Board Member, GoCardless

Time box - Now that you already have at least one contact within the customer's organization, finding out the additional information you need should take about one to two weeks.

Our advice for the Qualified Lead stage

What goes for the entire process is particularly important for the Qualified Lead stage: make sure you hear enough "nos"!

At this stage, you need to probe hard to test how big the customer's interest *actually* is. Customers who are not all that interested often don't actually say so, unless you explicitly push them to make a statement on their interest. Instead, they let the process drag on, replying to your requests only slowly, and effectively wasting your (and their) time and energy.

Remember, your job is not to convince everybody and their grandma to buy your product. Make this stage about weeding out the customers who are not a good match or require more nurturing first, so you can focus on the more promising candidates.

> When we started out, we made the mistake of not pushing for "No" hard enough. Any sales call I asked about, I always heard, "Great! They're really interested!" I got sick of hearing that. In sales, you need to push for "No." There's such a thing as the right "No" percentage in the early days – if you're not hearing enough "No," you're not pushing hard enough!
>
> **— Ben Stephenson, Co-Founder & CEO, Impala**

Stage 4: Opportunity

Output - Your goal in the Opportunity stage is to make sure that the customer has all the relevant information to make their purchasing decision. The customer needs to know your specific offer and understand the benefits of your solution for their company. In turn, you should know the customer's criteria for decision-making. Both parties should have an understanding of how the following process and the related timeline will look like.

Input - To enter this stage, you need to have understood who the decision-making unit is and what the customer's budget looks like. This prevents you from wasting time by making offers to people or organizations that do not have the necessary authority or budget to meet your pricing expectations.

Entry point for RFPs (requests-for-proposal) or tenders - Companies that run a formal RFP process or invite tenders enter the sales process at the Opportunity stage, too.

Founders are often afraid of RFP projects. But for the large corporations, if you're not in the RFP process, you're in the innovation budget. RFPs are where the real world begins.

The big automotive manufacturers usually send out RFPs on certain topics to everyone who's registered in their portal, so it's important to sign up there.

— Stephan Rohr, Co-Founder & CEO, TWAICE

Activities - Once you have identified the decision-making unit and validated the available budget, your single mission in the Opportunity stage is to schedule a product demo and present your solution.

Make sure your audience includes all members of the decision-making unit, including the Economic Buyer. Hearing the different viewpoints will help you understand the objectives and trade-offs between the different members of the unit. Again: in the meeting, it's preferable to keep your demo short and reserve more time for answering questions or digging deeper into certain aspects the customer is interested in.

At the same occasion, propose a simple step-by-step process on how to come to a buying decision. This process should outline a time frame, name responsibilities on completing the steps on both sides and address additional information that needs to be shared before the deal can be signed. Discuss the process with the decision-makers, and include adjustments from their side. It's important that everyone is on the same page to not lose momentum toward the deal at this point.

One crucial piece of information to share is your formal offer. This document contains your proposition, your pricing and your terms. Because it builds the basis for the upcoming contract, do not just hand over your general price list. Base your offer on the specifics that you have gathered throughout the process: what the exact scope of your proposition is, including software, hardware, and professional services, which payments are recurring and which are one-off, and service level agreements. The offer itself should be comprehensive enough on all crucial points that, in theory, it could be signed and turned into the contract itself (see Chapter 7 on Contracts on how to format offers).

Time box - The Opportunity stage involves getting in touch with and coordinating a number of new stakeholders within the customers' organization. Each stakeholder has their own requirements and processes to run through. You might also need some time to gather specific information or coordinate meetings. On average, expect this stage to take around four weeks.

Our advice for the Opportunity stage

The meeting where you present your product demo is the lynchpin of your sales process. Here's the part where you can actually use some magic. But if you aren't a wizard, good preparation works as well:

1. Make your demo as customer-specific as possible

The more customer-specific and hands-on the product demo is, the better. If you have the chance, include actual customer data and demonstrate the results and benefits live in the meeting.

Our philosophy is that our potential customers should get value every step of the way in the sales cycle. That's why we only approach them once we see that they have an interest in it. And why we offer free insights on actual suppliers that matter to them.

— Tai Alegbe, Co-Founder & CEO, Contingent

This works even better if you have already established a trustful relationship with the people involved, as Arun Srinivasan of Clarisights elaborates:

You want people to lower their guard because then their real problems come out, and you get a chance to demonstrate how you are solving them. If the customer is a good fit, they will ask for a solution to their specific problem during the demo. If you can present the solution, they will immediately ask: "How much?" It's a very natural, easy process this way.

— Arun Srinivasan, Co-Founder & CEO, Clarisights

2. Make use of the Champion on your side

Let your Champion on the customer side help you prepare a customized demo that touches on the central pain points. Use his or her insider knowledge to better differentiate your proposal from the existing solutions.

Your Champion can also help you pass the requirements coming from the non-technical departments, as Stephan Rohr has experienced in RFP processes:

Once you send in your proposal, a two-stage process begins. First, the technical department evaluates your proposal. You need to build a good relationship with them, and with your Champion in them. Only once the technical experts have ticked the box, the deal goes to the purchasing department. By this time, if you have the technical department on your side, they will help you navigate the rest of the system.

— Stephan Rohr, Co-Founder & CEO, TWAICE

In the best case, your Champion can help you initiate a new RFP for the problem your solution solves. While the necessary coordination and communication around creating the RFP will add some time to your sales process, your head start from offering exactly what the customer is looking for will be worth the effort.

3. Create a "Wow!" effect

The best demos have a "Wow!" effect – where you surpass the expectations of the audience by far, and you can actually see and feel the excitement in the room. This is great feedback that you have found a message that is heads-on to the needs of your audience.

If you are in a meeting and the customers ask questions, or you see their eyes widen during your demo, these are cues that you're on to something.

— Arun Srinivasan, Co-Founder & CEO, Clarisights

If your product doesn't meet the customers' expectations, no amount of presentation talent will make up for that.

Stage 5: Customer

Output - The Customer stage is the last phase toward closing a sale. Your goal in this stage is to complete the sales process by signing the contract with the customers.

Input - The input for the Customer stage is your demo and offer in the previous stage. At this point, the customer should have all necessary information to make their purchasing decision.

Activities - With complex corporate organizations and the higher contract values involved in B2B deals, you will still have to jump over several more hurdles before you can sign the contract.

Because customers won't be able to fully understand and evaluate more complex products from just one demo session, they often will want to try out the new solution in a trial period before fully committing to the engagement and internal roll-out. In this case, offer a trial that is as short as possible but still long enough to demonstrate the benefit of your solution. Being able to prove your concept is especially important when you don't have many references from existing customers yet. However, be careful to frame the trial as the first phase of a long-term contract, not a separate period (see our detailed discussion of trials in Chapter 7).

The offer you made in the Opportunity stage is the baseline for the contract negotiations in this stage. Unless you have met the perfect customer with high demand and low price sensitivity, there will be a discussion on the terms of your offer. In theory, each part – the scope, the pricing, or your terms and conditions – can become subject of negotiation. Sometimes the customer even asks you to move toward their standard contractual template altogether. Refer to Chapter 10 on Negotiations to learn how to get the best deal in this stage.

The more complex the customer's organization is, the more important it is to align the different stakeholders involved (see the case on LeanIX in Chapter 4 for an example from the very high end). It's crucial that you actively work toward completing the steps you have outlined and agreed upon in the previous stage to successfully complete the Customer stage.

Time box - With a fairly smooth-running negotiation, expect this phase to last for three weeks.

Ideally, the Customer stage ends with a signed contract. And then, finally, the first payment will arrive in your account. Congratulations!

Our advice for the Customer stage

1. Make the trial period a part of your full contract

It's natural for a customer to want to try out your product first before making a long-term commitment. However, trials or proof of concept (PoC) phases entail the risk that you engage in a costly (long) pre-sales period only to learn at the end that your intended offer will never meet enough interest on the customer side.

To reduce this risk, we recommend integrating the trial period as part of the contract on the full operational roll-out rather than separating the trial contract from the full contract. This way, you can still give the customer the opportunity to cancel the contract after the trial phase. But there won't be any discussion at the end of the trial phase on whether and how the cooperation should continue – because all terms and prices are known and have been negotiated in advance.

2. Don't drop the ball once the contract is signed

If your solution is rather complex to implement, expand your sales process to include the first stages of the implementation. Make sure your allocation of internal resources to supporting the customer after the signing reflects your commitment to your customer's success (more on how to achieve this in Chapter 16).

By accompanying the go-live of your customer, or even guiding them to achieving their first results, you enable them to get the most value out of your solution. This prevents churn from a failed implementation and leaves you with a happy customer instead.

Keeping a close relationship beyond the initial signature pays off in the long run. A happy customer who loves your product and service will gladly open the door again to hear about your offers in the next stage.

3. Create a positive customer experience by the way you guide the customer through the process

The most successful founders pay the same attention to designing their sales process as to building their actual product.

This makes actual business sense. The way you handle the process is the customer's first impression on how you as a company work. Creating a rewarding experience for your customer throughout all of your interactions with them goes a long way toward the successful cooperation you're trying to close.

> We call our approach "product-assisted selling." This means that we let the product do the selling, and focus on facilitating the process to be as simple and frictionless as possible. We do this by actively helping them to get all stakeholders on board, making sure that there are no more questions on pricing and so on.
>
> **— Tai Alegbe, Co-Founder & CEO, Contingent**

Viewing the sales process as a key component of your business also helps you to see the opportunities to gain unexpected supporters along the way. Even potential veto players can become "fans" if you address them well. Erez Galonska's case on Infarm's sales process illustrates this perfectly – leveraging the delicious taste of the produce that the indoor farming startup offers.

HOW TO

Create powerful relationships with your customer through your sales process

By Erez Galonska, Co-Founder & CEO, Infarm

Sales is about emotions. The process is important, but it's not the sale. The sale is emotional, it's about relationships. People need to get excited in order to buy!

Our sales process has four stages:

1. **Tasting event** - We invite the people to taste our plants at an event we organize. At the event, all the different people from the company come together: buyers, software engineers, designers... we create an amazing and very unique experience for them. You could call it "event sales."

2. **Commercial stage** - This is a meeting where we present our offering and ask our customers what they want: Which plants from our catalogue? How many? When do they need them to be in the stores? With this information, we can configure our farms based on demand and coordinate the distribution of the plants. It's a straightforward step because we have everything ready, our unit economics, the logistics, and studies on quality of our produce, if the customer needs this information as well.

3. **Legal stage** - Other than the buyers, the lawyers haven't experienced our product and focus only on their mission. In order to pass this most difficult part of the process, we started to consider the lawyers our clients, too. We created an onboarding process specifically for them, where we present our contract model, but also our overarching vision. And it works – lawyers have become our fans!

4. **Implementation stage** - After the deal is signed, our operational team sets to work to get the plants ready at the agreed-upon harvest dates.

Stage 6: Customer Success

The Customer Success stage describes the sales process that happens with a customer who has already signed a first contract with you.

Output - In B2B sales, it is increasingly becoming a key success factor to not only keep, but *grow* each customer. This principle is also known as the "land and expand" strategy.

Expansion strategies work so well with B2B customers because companies rarely spend their full budget on a single provider they have never worked with before. It's just too risky. Instead, they start by purchasing a smaller package from you – maybe 20% of their total budget for the solution – and then evaluate your performance and the performance of your solution.

If you manage to fulfill or exceed their expectations, your chances are high that in the next step, you can increase the contract volume not by a few percent, but by multiple times the original amount!

Growing your existing customers' accounts requires that you reserve some portion of your solutions' value for the expansion – consider this when you design your revenue model (see Chapter 6). It also ties into your customer success efforts, which we will go deeper into in Chapter 16.

If you succeed with your strategy, expanding and upselling are significantly more profitable ways of increasing revenue compared to the acquisition of new customers, given the lower acquisition cost and the higher conversion rates.

Input - Most larger B2B solutions will take 3-6 months before they are implemented properly and have gathered a first following within the customer organization. Naturally, the faster the implementation works, the better. Only start your upsell or expansion activity once your customer is happy and eager for more. In practice, this is more realistic in the six to 18 months after the initial contract is signed.

Activities - Since you're already "inside" the customer's organization, the expanding and upselling process includes primarily the activities involved in the Opportunity and Customer stages – making an offer and working toward closing the upsell contract. However, depending on the complexity of your expansion strategy, you might want to run a separate sales process and even create a separate sales organization just for customer success.

How to manage your resources

To successfully run a sales process, you need to prioritize your own resources. There are only so many calls you and your sales team can make in your work day (even if it's a founder's work day!), and even fewer in-person meetings and business trips.

Example: Sales activities and time spent on selling a typical SaaS product

The example in the table below shows the activities and time required for selling a typical SaaS product:

- With a typical contract value of €10,000 to €100,000
- In a familiar product category (where the typical decision-making unit is known and there usually is an existing budget)
- Without a formal RFP process (which would require different activities and time allocation)

For highly innovative products, where the decision-making unit and the budget are unclear and the benefits need to be quantified and established first, the required amount and time spent on the activities can be a multiple of the numbers in the table below!

# of activities to win one customer	minutes / activity	1 Prospect	2 Lead	3 Qual. Lead	4 Opport.	5 Customer	6 Customer Success
Researching the prospect	10 min	1	1				
Sending emails/ LinkedIn messages to reach contact	1 min		3				
Call attempts to reach contact	1 min		3	2			
Intro calls with contact(s)	10 min		2	2			
Video calls to present solution	60 min				2	2	2
On-site meetings to negotiate	240 min					1	1
Total				15 h			

These 15 hours of work, however, are not the full story.

More importantly, you also need to account for the time spent on the other prospects that do *not* eventually convert into a customer.

Based on the durations of the sales activities as outlined above, the table below gives a calculation for the time spent on all sales activities, including disqualifying leads and pitching to customers who eventually don't buy.

Everything added together, the sample calculation results in 9,725 minutes (or roughly 162 hours) required for each successfully signed customer. That's an *entire month* of work for a salesperson (one Full-time Equivalent/FTE), and more than 10 times the time spent on the customer alone!

Effort to sign one customer	1 Prospect	2 Lead	3 Qual. Lead	4 Opport.	5 Customer	6 Customer Success	Total
Input contacts	200	160	16	5	2	1	
Conversion rate	80%	10%	30%	40%	50%	100%	
Progressing Leads/ opportunities	160	16	5	2	1	1	
Dropouts		144	11	3	1		
Total minutes required	2,000	5,760	352	576	691	346	**9,725**

Now assume that your salesperson gets a salary of €50,000. Broken down, that's €0.43 per minute (or €26.04 per hour, or €208.33 per day).

In the table below, we have used the previous calculation to find out how much signing one customer costs you in terms of personnel expenses:

Personnel expenses for signing one customer	1 Prospect	2 Lead	3 Qual. Lead	4 Opport.	5 Customer	6 Customer Success	Total
in €	€868	€2,500	€153	€250	€300	€150	€4,221
in %	21%	59%	4%	6%	7%	4%	**100%**

Based on your salesperson's salary, the calculation shows that signing a single customer costs you €4,221.

And this doesn't yet include the fully-loaded costs of your employee (tax, social security) as well as the overhead costs of rent, travel and software licenses.

Doing a bottom-up calculation like this is essential for developing, evaluating and improving your sales process and business model. To help you do the calculations for your own business, we provide you a sample calculation sheet on www.fastforwardbook.com.

In the following, we'll outline three ways to increase the efficiency of your sales process and reduce the associated costs.

Prioritize your leads by likelihood and time to buy

It's paramount to focus your attention on those customers who have a good chance of actually buying.

The guiding variable for prioritizing your resources is customer interest: the more interest a customer is showing, the more you should invest to move the customer quickly through the process.

Vice versa, quickly de-prioritize or eliminate customers who don't meet your qualification criteria or who don't demonstrate willingness to buy in the near future (the next 3-6 months).

Depending on the reasons for the mismatch, you don't necessarily need to eliminate them forever: for example, if a customer rejects your offer because they are busy with implementing another major project at the time, you can always keep them "in the loop" and approach them at a later, more suitable time (see Chapter 11 on Pipeline Management).

The key to allocating your resources appropriately across each customer is to define a set number of standard activities for each stage of the sales process.

The type and number of sales activities should reflect the typical effort necessary to have a high probability of signing a contract. Of course, this will depend on the size of your target company and the related number of people in the decision-making unit(s), as well as the price and complexity of your own product.

Having defined a benchmark for a reasonable number of activities to spend on a customer helps you to identify outliers – "high maintenance" customers – who require a lot more engagement relative to their contract value than other customers.

In general, knowing exactly what to do in each stage will keep you focused on results and prevents you from spending too much time on any individual prospect.

Focus on value-adding sales activities

Because your resources are limited, spend your time on activities that actually get you closer to signing a deal. That sounds logical: what else would you be doing?

In practice, it's surprisingly easy to work on activities that *look like* sales, but actually aren't, as Ognyan Vasilev from Salesforce explains.

Focus on the value-adding sales activities: Cold-calling potential customers. Identifying decision-makers. Following up. These are essentially activities to directly connect with your customers and learn more about how to add value to their business.

Actual sales	Could be sales	Not sales
• Prospecting • Identifying decision-makers	• Visiting conferences • Organizing events	• Trainings • Extensive customer research

Actual sales	Could be sales	Not sales
• Discovery • Negotiating • Follow-up • Cross-selling, upselling	• Client enablement • Resolving customer issues • Client dinners • Engaging in politics	• Discussions with colleagues • Engaging with others' clients • "Shaping presentations" • Checking emails

– Ognyan Vasilev, EMEA B2B Industries Advisory and GoToMarket, Salesforce

9 - SALES CONVERSATIONS

How to speak with your prospective customers

"Matthias, sorry to call you on such short notice. Good news, I have an important call with this big lead scheduled in two hours! But I just realized I have no idea what to actually say to them on that call. Can you help?!"

If you find yourself building a sales process for the first time and you're wondering how to actually talk to customers, you're in good company.

Defining *what* to do in your sales process – what you learned in the previous chapter – is not the same as knowing *how* to actually do these things when it's time to pick up the phone or send an email. That's something almost all founders struggle with at the beginning.

Fortunately, interacting with customers is something that can be learned.

In this chapter, we're going to get the rubber on the road and share with you a number of proven methods to effectively interact and communicate with your customers.

To put it plain and simple, you'll learn:

- what to ask your potential customers and
- what to tell (and show) them

in your sales conversations.

If you are looking to understand how to sell, my advice is to shadow someone who is selling professionally. Visit a call center and listen to the conversations the sales representatives have. Accompany a field sales rep for a week and see how they prepare and conduct their meetings.

— Bastian Nominacher, Co-Founder & Co-CEO, Celonis

How to structure your sales conversations

Intuitively, if you want to sell something, what you tell your potential customer about yourself and about your product might feel like the most important thing.

That's certainly one aspect. But experience shows that to get the process ahead successfully, it's much more important what you *ask* your potential customer and then actually spend most of the time listening.

We suggest using questions as a guideline for structuring your conversations with a potential customer.

In the following, we're going to introduce several frameworks that you can use to find out which questions to ask your potential customers, and when.

As you can guess from the frameworks' lengthy acronyms: they basically include a checklist of aspects you should talk about with your potential customer to get the information you need. Only if you cover all the questions on the checklist through your conversations with the customer, you'll have all the information you need to successfully close a sale.

Because frameworks help you to check if the customer is a good match, they are also called "qualification frameworks."

Some of the items on the checklists are pass/fail questions that help you determine whether a contact is likely to close a deal. For example, you should find out early on if the customer actually experiences the pain you're targeting, and if there is or likely will be a budget for your solution. If not, you can disqualify the contact and move on.

Frameworks for developing questions

The earliest qualification framework, BANT, was created by IBM in 1960. The acronym stands for "Budget, Authority, Need, Timeline" – a basic checklist for qualifying your potential customers.

Over time, a number of spinoffs of the original BANT framework were published, such as ANUM (Authority, Need, Urgency, Money), CHAMP (Challenges, Authority, Money, Priority) and SPIN (Situation, Problem, Implication, Need-Payoff).

Skipping ahead to the most modern evolutions of the original framework, we've based our personal sales approach on a combination of the following (increasingly hard to pronounce) frameworks.

Get ready for some impressive acronyms:

MEDDIC - Metrics, Economic buyer, Decision criteria, Decision process, Identify pain, Champion

MEDDIC, developed by PTC in 1990, treats qualification of a prospect as an ongoing task throughout the process, not only in the early stages.

While earlier frameworks included customer pain as a pass/fail criterion only, MEDDIC also aims to quantify pain and uses the amount of customer pain as a key metric in the sales process.

MEDDIC further emphasizes the importance of a granular understanding of the decision criteria and the buying process on the buyer side, and includes gathering information on the incumbent or competitive solutions.

PUCCKA - Pain, Unique Selling Proposition, Compelling Event, Champion, Key Players, Aligned Purchasing Process

PUCCKA, created by Mark Suster in 2013, is unique in that it compares the pain of a potential customer to your actual proposition in order to find the right product/customer fit.

PUCCKA is also powerful in its emphasis on getting over the finish line by focusing on the key players and how to align them in the purchasing process.

GPCTBA/C&I - Goals, Plans, Challenges, Timeline, Budget, Authority, Negative Consequences, Positive Implications

The GPCTBA/C&I framework was developed by Hubspot in 2018. It encourages an open discussion with the prospective customer around their goals, plans and challenges. Therefore, GPCTBA/C&I is particularly useful in situations where your solution is highly innovative, and the customer might not yet have a clear picture of how this solution might match their set of needs. Because GPCTBA/C&I helps you to identify opportunities in a broader sense, it's also a useful framework to structure broader outbound campaigns.

By asking about "Negative Consequences, Positive Implications (C&I)," the framework also helps to better flesh out the underlying motivations of the buying individual.

The great thing about the frameworks is that they are entirely compatible across each other – and with the sales process we have outlined in the previous Chapter.

If your solution fits in well with one of the frameworks, stick more closely to this one when developing your set of questions to ask. In this case, we recommend you read the respective book or blog in detail to learn more about the underlying checklists.

Generally, you are free to mix and match whatever components you feel are useful for operationalizing the questions you want to ask in your own sales process. By adapting the key elements to your market, customer and process, you can develop your own framework - and even give it your own awesome acronym if you feel like it :-).

How to time your questions along the process

Not all of the questions on the frameworks' checklists need to be answered in the first stage (and it would be an awkward conversation if you tried to do so).

The table below shows how the individual components of each framework align with the stages of our prototypical sales process – that is, in which stage you ask about which aspects of the framework's underlying checklist.

Note that your output in each stage will contain different kinds of information, depending on which framework you apply for generating your questions:

- For example, "Interest validated" in the Lead stage could mean that you identified the pain, its metric, and a Champion if you follow the MEDDIC framework.
- But it could also mean that you talked about the customer's goals, plans and challenges more broadly, if you follow the GPCTBA/C&I framework.

Example Process	1 Prospect	2 Lead	3 Qualified Lead	4 Opportunity	5 Customer	6 Customer Success
Output	Individual contact data acquired	Interest validated Champion identified	Budget available Decision-making unit identified Pain points understood Decision-making timeline understood	Offer made Decision criteria, process and timeline defined	Contract signed	Upsell/expansion signed
MEDDIC		Identify pain Metric Champion	Economic buyer Decision criteria	Decision process		
PUCCKA		Pain Unique Selling Proposition Champion	Compelling event	Key players Aligned Purchasing Process		
GPCTBA/C&I		Goals Plans Challenges	Budget Authority	Timeline	Consequences Implications	

What to talk about with your customer

In the following section, we're going to give you our own time-proven list of the most useful questions to ask in a sales process.

We've sorted the questions by stage of the sales process, leaving out the Prospect stage (because there's no interaction with the contact yet) and the Customer Success stage (because it's an entirely new sales process on its own).

You can use these questions as part of an actual call script: Print them out and put them right in front of you when you call your contact. This way, you won't forget to ask about crucial information. Also, build specific fields for them in your CRM, so you can fill the answers right in during or after the call.

Not least, having the list of questions in front of you will also give you something to hold on to when you're still a bit nervous about making those first calls!

Of course, if your customer is going to talk to you, they are doing so because they too want to achieve some output out of the sales interaction with you, too (see the discussion of buyer's activities in the previous chapter).

We have also gathered a number of time-tested recommendations on what to tell (and show) your customer by process stage.

To make the customer come to the right conclusion (from your point of view) in their own information-gathering process, you'll need to think about your own messaging and what materials can support your messages.

But before you start, one piece of advice...

Make it personal

Your conversation partners in your customer's organization are people. And people aren't decision-making machines. If they were, you could just send over a spreadsheet with the relevant data and rational arguments, and that would be your sale.

In our experience, customers never make important commitments without a strong personal relationship between the primary decision-makers on both sides.

> Sales is a little bit like a good novel. Some basic elements are always there: introduction, main part, closing, several plot lines, etc. You might be able to implement them. But to make the novel, or sales, truly great, it's essential to have this artistic, craft-like element that touches people on an emotional level.
>
> **— Michael Wax, Co-Founder & CEO, Forto**

People want to know who they are talking to. They need to build a relationship because they need to be able to trust you personally before they will hand over their money.

So what do we mean by saying you need to make your sales conversations personal? Definitely not that you should start sharing every detail of your family weekend, discuss your political opinions, or even your personal problems (please don't!).

What we recommend is that you actively go beyond the factual discussions to foster an emotional dimension in your relationship.

Apart from the official discussions on your topic, there are always a few minutes before and after the call or meeting that you can use to make a personal connection. Make small talk and ask about your conversation partner's day. Demonstrate personal attention by following up on personal topics your contact shared before. Ask about the dog they considered adopting, or how the weekend in the mountains went that they mentioned planning in the last meeting. And as similarities and shared interests are proven to help build trust faster, actively look for them: kids of similar age, a same region of origin or a shared university or field of study, for example.

In the later parts of the process, there may also be opportunities for an extended coffee break or a beer after a workshop. These personal gatherings are valuable opportunities to speak "off the record." This allows you to better understand the needs of the customer organization as a whole, as well as the personal motivations of the main stakeholders.

When do you know you've succeeded in your efforts to build a powerful relationship with your customer?

An anonymous founder shares one particularly bullet-proof sign:

> You know you've built an emotional relationship with your Champion when he calls you on the phone right before the meeting with Purchasing, gives you some key hints on how to answer their questions, and then says "... but this needs to stay between us, of course."
>
> **— Anonymous Founder**

With this piece of advice, let's get started with the "official" part of your sales conversations.

1. Lead stage

What to ask your customer

Output - As defined in the process outline, your desired output for the Lead stage is to validate the customer's interest in your solution. To do so, you also need to have identified a Champion for your solution within the organization. If not, you'll need to be asking around for the person a bit further before you can go deeper into the matter.

Conversation partners - In the Lead stage, you'll try to approach the person within the customer's organization who you think is most likely to become your Champion. Oftentimes, this is a person who's also an End User of your solution. You might need to talk to several people to identify your Champion.

In the following table, we have outlined below the key questions to ask in those conversations. But remember: it's really about having a conversation rather than an interrogation. A few prioritized open questions and a lot of listening will result in the best outcomes.

Key questions to ask in the Lead stage	
Questions to understand the customer's basic pain points	
Identifying pain	What we find is that many of our customers have faced the challenge of X, and hence reached out to us. Do you see a similar situation also on your end?
	How do you try and solve these challenges today? Do you use in-house resources or external providers to achieve that? Are you satisfied with the status quo?
	These key features usually work wonders with our customer and usually save them around X% of their associated cost. Would this be a solution you can also see work for yourself?
	What other challenges are you struggling with?
Identifying Champion	You mentioned that there is another team working on this type of challenge within your organization. Could you give me the contact details of the Head of this team, and perhaps even help with a short intro?
Quantifying pain	How do you calculate the cost of this process we discussed?

	Do you measure this lost revenue opportunity?
	How could you increase the speed of this process?
	How do you assess the delays/churn/penalties? What does it mean for you in monetary terms?
Questions to determine likelihood and time to reach a deal	
Determining internal priority	Where does this fall on your list of business priorities?
	Will this pay into your strategic goals on a company level?
	When do you need to solve this?
Determining internal resources	Do you think you have the expertise to deal with these challenges?
	Do you have the capacity to implement this product together with us right now?
Determining (Champion's) personal motivation	What would such a project mean to you personally?
	How can I help you personally to achieve this goal?
Questions to move the process forward	
Scheduling follow-up	Should we set-up a follow-up meeting to understand your situation in more detail and perhaps also bring on board relevant people from your organization?

Since conversations in the Lead stage are usually short, so you'll need to prioritize your questions. Choose questions that allow you to determine whether it makes sense for you to continue the discussion in follow-up conversations. If you're not sure which questions are essential: try them out and iterate until you've found your core questions!

What to tell (and show) your customer

Customer output - Through your activities in the Lead stage, you demonstrate an understanding of the specific pain points or challenges the target organization is currently facing. The Champion should feel that you are a credible conversation partner, and be interested in further engagement.

Key information the customer needs - The Champion needs to feel that you've well understood their need or pain, and will appreciate a quick overview of the solution. Describing 1-3 core features of the solution and their benefits for the customer is enough at this stage. The easiest way to create credibility is to name existing customers as references.

Materials - Useful materials for the Lead stage are:

- Concise email or messaging template (including the key information the customer needs, phrased in terms that signal your familiarity with the field)
- Easily accessible website (including easily recognizable key terms and references from previous customers)
- 1-5 page presentation

Messaging - The first contact in the Lead stage is especially challenging: your initial message needs to create enough interest for the contact to reply to you (in case of a written message) or be willing to spend time and answer your questions (on the phone). This also applies to all following "first contacts" within other people of the decision-making unit in the organization.

Whatever approach you choose: Keep it short!

For a call, keep the time you are speaking as short as possible. Introduce yourself, your company and your references briefly, then ask questions and listen to what your contact has to say.

Given the limited space and time for your first contact, it's all the more important that you prepare the messages you want to send in this first contact extremely well.

To grab your contact's attention among all the other things on their mind, the key is to stand out with relevance.

There are three ways to create relevance that work best if combined: personalization, references, and content.

Personalization - Personalize your message using the information you have on the contact's role, their history and their expected needs. With professional networks such as LinkedIn, there's a lot of personal information publicly available that you can use to personalize your message to the individual recipient.

In her free Sales Training course on FliptheScript.co, Becc Holland suggests a number of simple premises for personalization from LinkedIn, ranked from most to least personal:

1. Self-authored content: webinars, articles, posts
2. Engaged content: liked, shared, commented
3. Self-identified traits: profile line, headline, company line
4. Junk drawer: schools attended, personal interests, hobbies, recommendations, skill endorsements
5. Company: M&A, posts, blogs, hiring, website language

References - Because references and "logos" are so powerful, include them in your first contact, too:

> Nothing opens customers' doors faster than examples of other customers who are getting value out of your product.
>
> — **Avinoam Nowogrodski, Co-Founder & former CEO, Clarizen**

Ideally, your references come from companies in the same industry that are well-known to your prospective customer. The more specific, the higher the impact. For example, a quote from a senior decision-maker of a well-known company who praises your solution or even quantifies the benefit is more powerful than just a logo.

If you have the numbers, another way to achieve the same effect is to let statistics on customer experience do the job:

> We let our customers collectively speak for us by listing the benefits they experienced after starting to use our COVID-19 contact tracking solution:
>
> - 88% Reduction of founded quarantine cases
> - 88% Reduction of risk of a lockdown
> - 85% Reduction of time to react in case of infection
> - 82% Reduction of unfounded quarantine cases
> - 75% Share of employees with "very good" perception of digital safety
>
> **— Oliver Trinchera, Co-Founder & CEO, Kinexon**

If you're approaching your very first customers and don't have many impressive references yet, include other kinds of validations: articles in industry journals, speaking slots at industry events or awards or competitions you won.

Content - Your message will grab the attention of the recipient or conversation partner if you offer a very specific, even quantified, account of your perspective of the pain point before shortly describing your proposed solution. You'll want your contact to have the feeling that you are right on point with your description of their pain!

2. Qualified Lead stage

What to ask your customer

Output - The goal in the Qualified Lead stage is to fully understand the customer's pain points and to identify the budget, the decision-making unit and the rough timeline toward a possible decision.

Conversation partners - In this stage, you'll have conversations with each member of the core buying team – the Champion, other End Users, and the Economic Buyer. Use the Champion's insider knowledge of the organization to find the answers to your questions on the budget and the decision-making unit.

Key questions to ask in the Qualified Lead stage	
Questions to understand the customer's pain points in more detail	
Further quantifying pain and gain	These are the dimensions I have calculated in order to demonstrate the benefit of our solution, let's go through those and let me know if you recognize those.
	Does this solution represent a significant improvement regarding your existing solution?
	How would you measure the success of our joined project?
Questions to identify and validate the decision-making unit	
Identifying the decision-making unit	What other people do we need to bring on board?
Determining commitment	Would you sponsor this project?
Questions to identify and validate the budget	
Identifying budget	Will this purchase come out of your budget?
Determining commitment	Is this an important enough priority to allocate funds toward?

Questions to move the process forward	
Identifying decision-making process	How will you decide on this project? How long should this process be to reach a decision?
	How have you made purchasing decisions for products similar to ours in the past?
	Are you evaluating any other similar products or services?
Scheduling follow-up	Would you like to have a detailed demo of our product together with the rest of your team and flesh out how we could best work together?

What to tell (and show) your customer

Customer output - In the Qualified Lead stage, the customer should understand the option you are offering them to relieve the pain they're now aware of.

Key information the customer needs - If you have the chance at this stage, keep this one important lesson in mind: show, don't tell! A focused product demo often brings your point across better than just talking about your solution. Another way to create a better understanding of the specifics of your solution is to present a case study of one of your existing customers, ideally also with usage statistics that show the benefit.

In any case, make sure to include information on the two or three key differentiators of your solution versus your competitors' solution (without actively naming them) and the customer's current solution.

Materials - For the Qualified Lead stage, you should prepare:

- 15-minute product demo (to the Champion)
- 10-20 page presentation

Messaging - In this stage, the customer's door is already open and you have a Champion on the inside. Use this relationship and keep asking questions. The better you understand the customer's use case, the better you'll be able to sell your solution!

> Only if you understand the customer's use case, you are able to articulate the benefits of your solution in terms of improving what the customer is doing today, instead of what they will be doing with your product.
>
> **— Avinoam Nowogrodski, Co-Founder & former CEO, Clarizen**

If you share information with individual stakeholders in this or the next stage, make an effort to use terms that the customers are familiar with from their own field. Also remember, you're not negotiating a contract with lawyers yet, so focus on getting your message across instead of being 100% correct down to the last comma:

> When customers asked how much our product was, our salespeople used to explain to them: "Well, the API gives you two numbers: the VTP, vendor total payable, and the RRR, the recommended retail rate. The difference is yours in commission." The person on the other side could never follow that – I couldn't follow that! So now, when a customer asks about the price, our salespeople will say: "It's 3% of the transaction fee." To arrive at this number, you need to do the mentioned calculation – it's the same information. It's a question of learning to know how to talk about your product in terms that the customer can relate to. Our sales outcomes have become better and more consistent since we started to do this kind of product sales training.
>
> **— Ben Stephenson, Co-Founder & CEO, Impala**

3. Opportunity stage

What to ask your customer

Output - Your goal for the Opportunity stage is to make an offer that matches the customer's pain points closely. It should be clear to both parties what the decision-making criteria are and how the further process and the timeline look like.

Conversation partners - In the Opportunity stage, you need to address everyone who is involved in the customer's purchasing decision: the Champion, the End User, and the Economic Buyer. This is also the time to get in touch with the decision-makers from Purchasing/Sourcing, Legal, and IT/Security.

Ideally, all parties are participating in your demo meeting and can fully experience the product, hear the discussion and ask questions. However, if this is not feasible, make sure you approach the individual decision-makers separately to get answers to all your questions. In this case, ask your Champion to introduce you to all key players to warm up the contacts and increase trust.

Key questions to ask in the Opportunity stage	
Questions to understand the decision-making criteria	
Defining and ensuring success	How would the success of this project look like for you?
	What are the next steps if we fulfill the success criteria?
	In your perspective, where does our solution stand out against our competition and where do you see room for improvement?
Identifying decision-making criteria	Do you have particular criteria for this purchase decision?
	How would you evaluate different providers against each other?
	Which metrics around cost, efficiency or additional revenue do you need to achieve?

	How do you calculate the ROI for this project to justify the investment?
	What are the technical criteria to make a decision?
Questions to understand the process and timeline	
Agreeing process	What is the legal set-up? What is your process to sign documentation?
	What objections to this purchase do you anticipate encountering? How do you think we can best handle them?
	What does the approval process look like? How long does it usually take?
Questions to move the process forward	
	Would you like us to provide you with a detailed offer for our product/partnership?

What to tell (and show) your customer

Customer output - In the Opportunity stage, the customer's goal is to decide on the best option to relieve their pain.

Key information the customer needs - To make their decision, the customer needs to know the price of your solution and be able to compare it to a detailed quantification of the cost savings or revenue increases they can expect from using your solution. Because you don't want the deal to be stopped by organizational hurdles, it's also necessary that you demonstrate how your product meets the customer's functional, technical and legal purchasing criteria.

Materials - For the Opportunity stage, you need:

- 30-minute product demo (to the broader buying team)
- Your offer (including pricing, terms and conditions)
- Cost-benefit analysis using the customer's actual data
- Comparison data vs. your competition or the customer's current solution
- Project plan on how to get to signing the contract

HOW TO

Do a powerful demo

By Veronika Riederle, Co-Founder & CEO, Demodesk

1. **Intro (5 min)** - Your initial goal is to reconnect with the customer and continue to build trust following up on the conversations so far in the Lead and Qualified Lead stages.

2. **Set the stage (5 min)** - Then you clarify the expectations for the demo and make sure you understood the pain points from the previous calls correctly. Give your customer the chance to say, "You got problems A and B right, but C is actually not a big deal. On the other hand, I'd like to improve D." Based on this, share your agenda: what are we doing today?

3. **Solution mapping (15 min)** - Now you move into the demo and show the customer the three most important features that solve their main three pain points.

4. **Next steps (5 min)** - In the end, reserve enough time to clarify the next steps. When will you speak again? What needs to happen until then on both sides? If this meeting already is the closing meeting, ask about open issues: "What hinders you from closing tomorrow?" That's how you get the next call, or hopefully just sign the deal.

Messaging - As the discussion broadens and deepens across the organization, it is important to adjust your messages and depth of detail based on your audience. The Champion or End User of your product is typically interested in understanding particular features of your product. In contrast, the Economic Buyer may just assume that your product is doing its job, and drill deeper into the P&L impact of your product instead.

As the breadth and depth of topics increases, make sure you (and later your sales team) are up to speed on all the questions the customer might ask. Bastian Nominacher from Celonis has solved this by creating an "FAQ" on their product:

> After two or three years, we realized that customers always asked the same questions. We used these insights to create a sales package that answered all those frequently asked questions. That kind of standardization was necessary to scale the business.
>
> **— Bastian Nominacher, Co-Founder & Co-CEO, Celonis**

4. Customer stage

What to ask your customer

Output - Your goal in the Customer stage is simple: get your contract signed.

Conversation partners - Again, in this stage, involve everyone who has some say in the customer's purchasing decision. Beyond the core decision-making unit (Champion, End User, and Economic Buyer), in this stage you'll also need to talk to the decision-makers from Purchasing/Sourcing, Legal, and IT/Security.

Key questions to ask in the Customer stage	
Questions to move the process forward	
Driving toward signature	From your perspective, did the result we have from the trial meet our agreed success criteria?
	From our perspective, we have agreed on the main terms. Should we finalize the documentation now, or are there any open points?
	Now that we have a clean contract, what are the steps to get a signature on your end?
	I just wanted to follow up regarding the signature of our contract. Is there anything else that we can help with? When can we expect to receive the signed contract?

What to tell (and show) your customer

Customer output - The customer's goal mirrors your own goal for the Customer stage: signing a contract.

Key information the customer needs - Since you have handed over all your information in the previous stage, this final stage is heavily driven by the customer and their organizational needs. Your role is to provide any information that the customer organization requests, and to convincingly respond to possible objections.

Materials - Preparing information proactively addressing the individual departments' concerns (e.g. from Purchasing/Sourcing, Technical or Legal) in dedicated formats will not only speed up the process greatly, but also show your dedication and professionalism.

These can include:

- Contract draft including Terms and Conditions (T&Cs) (if these documents were not yet included in your offer in the Opportunity stage)
- Filled-in questionnaires (if you are participating in a standardized RFP purchasing process)

- IT/security certifications
- References

Messaging - In this stage, many different stakeholders in the customer's organization will address you. Similarly as in the previous stage, it's important to understand the responsibilities and motivations behind each of these key players. The following table lists some of the typical concerns (some of which they won't discuss with you, of course) of each department that your messaging should address.

Key concerns of your customer in the Customer stage
Purchasing/Sourcing
• By how much has the price decreased between first offer and final contract? Were we able to negotiate the 10-20% reduction in price we need to be able to sign this (and achieve our bonuses)? • Have we been able to enforce our own buying T&Cs? Or have we at least been able to shift the balance of the T&Cs toward us, so that we are able to sign it?
IT/Security
• Does the provider meet our security requirements? • Is the provider certified, e.g. through ISO certifications? • What are the Service Level Agreements regarding downtime, bug fixing etc.?
Legal
• Who retains intellectual property for the standard product and dedicated developments for us as a customer? • Who carries liabilities and up to what amount?

Don't be confused if you encounter competing interests within one and the same organization – for example between different business units, or between a group organization and a country organization, or between a business unit and a research unit. In most cases, the Champion will be able to help you understand these "company politics" and find a way to navigate the supporters and the opponents in your organization.

Teaching your team how to speak with customers

By now you know that a sales conversation is not primarily based on conversational talent, but on a clearly structured process and its operationalization into specific questions and messages.

This means that you can learn how to sell – and also teach others in your team how to sell!

At the beginning of the *Explore & Learn* phase, sales training starts with yourself calling up or writing to your first contacts. In this stage, there's a steep learning curve, since there's no sales playbook to run by yet. Ben Stephenson from Impala has good advice for this stage that is both helpful in developing a process and alleviating your initial anxiety:

> As a founder doing early sales calls, it is extremely beneficial not to care about closing this specific customer you're on a call with. Instead, tell yourself "I'm just going to answer this person's questions." If you do this four or five times, you realize what all the questions are, and can script a successful sales call for your organization to scale.
>
> **— Ben Stephenson, Co-Founder & CEO, Impala**

Ben's approach works best if you don't call your most interesting lead in your first attempt. It's likely that you'll still stumble a bit in your conversation when you do it for the first time. Instead, do a couple of practice calls with lower-priority contacts until you feel more secure about your messages and overall approach.

Scripting and developing a sales playbook is the key to scaling your sales activities.

To do so, document everything about your sales process. At a minimum, all your sales professionals should have access to a Frequently Asked Questions (FAQ) list. It's even better to structure your documentation in knowledge or learning management systems.

In the beginning, the training materials will be based on your own sales insights as a founder. Later on, your Product, Marketing and Sales leaders will develop relevant information and messaging and distribute it into the sales organization.

> In the first place, there are big variations in the quality of the salespeople that you get. It's my job to educate them so they are qualified to sell a complex multi-faceted product like ours. We use specific software for internal education and certify them.
>
> **— Kai Leppanen, former SVP, Global Accounts, Opera**

As long as your organization and product are not too diversified and complex yet, it can also make sense to foster bottom-up information sharing and training as well, as Firmin Zocchetto from PayFit explains:

> We believe that everything these days has to be a game, especially in the sales team. So we used TeamDrill to create a training game called Sales Training. It builds on a huge database of questions a prospect could potentially ask during a meeting. For each game session, it generates ten random questions coming from that database. After answering them, the salesperson can self-evaluate how well they've done and check their overall advancement on a dashboard. No one else will check their results – but they all understand that knowing the answers well does have a direct impact on their closing rates.

The most amazing part of the tool, though, is that it's a collaborative project: the database is enriched only by actual prospect questions and the answers the sales team members suggest. This makes our training tool as dynamic as we need it to be: we have to continuously adapt and learn, as both labor laws and our product are always on the move.

— Firmin Zocchetto, Co-Founder & CEO, PayFit

No learning system, however, can replace actual sales experience on the job with real customers.

Keep training your sales professionals with new learning objectives and challenge them to specialize and get better.

I make sure that our salespeople specialize in a certain customer segment. So for 12 months, I send them to Germany where they only sell to automotive companies, or only sell to media companies. It's important that they learn to speak their customers' language.

— Kai Leppanen, former SVP, Global Accounts, Opera

Our philosophy is to constantly improve yourself by training on the job. I would estimate that our salespeople spend 70% of the time training, simply because they constantly test out new arguments and approaches on the phone. We further scaled our training through onboarding, buddying, and a clear career path. We hired a sales enablement manager to provide the team with the most relevant content about product, competitors and industries.

— Firmin Zocchetto, Co-Founder & CEO, PayFit

10 - NEGOTIATIONS

How to get the best deal possible

As you know by now, successful B2B sales involves much more than a single sales meeting with a customer where you skillfully convince them of your solution. However, there is a stage in your sales process where the cliché of the all-deciding meeting comes closer to reality (just a little bit, though!).

This crucial stage is the negotiation: the final step before your lead signs a contract and becomes a customer.

Most founders intuitively think of negotiation as an intense live interaction of two or more people bargaining hard to reach an agreement. Negotiation in a B2B sales context differs from this mental model in two important ways:

- **Both sides are typically looking to enter into a long-term business relationship.** You and your customer are aware that this first deal will likely be only the starting point for this relationship, and that many small and large negotiations will follow. Making sure that both sides gain value from the transaction is therefore more important in the negotiations than getting the absolute maximum out of this single deal, which significantly smoothens the process.

- **The final negotiation is only the end point of a longer process.** Many important questions are addressed long before the final negotiation at different stages of the sales pipeline. This reduces the potential for tactical maneuvers during the negotiation stage.

There are three steps in each negotiation. Each one involves different stakeholders:

Solution. What does the customer want? What's in our portfolio that we could sell to them? What do they need right now, what can be rolled out later? We typically discuss these questions with the End User and the Digital Champion.

Scope. How many licenses do they need? How do you package them, in which price tiers? Are there discounts? This negotiation usually involves the Digital Champion and the Primary Economic Buyer.

Price. This is the very last step. These pricing negotiations happen outside the standard organization. Usually a professional negotiation team from Procurement comes in to try and get the price down by some additional 5-7% percentage points.

– Gregor Stühler, Co-Founder & CEO, Scoutbee

This is not to say that negotiations are not important, or – even worse – that you should neglect careful preparation.

Understanding and mastering the basic concepts of negotiation is a crucial way to ensure that the deals you close are valuable in the long term.

Bargaining styles and the Negotiator's Dilemma

Imagine how you would feel and act in two different negotiation situations:

- Negotiating with a seller at a flea market on the price of an antique tea pot you want to buy.
- Negotiating with your partner on who does your common tax declaration (a task you both hate).

When Martin asks the participants of his negotiation workshops to describe their strategy, most entrepreneurs choose to fight hard on maximizing their own profit in the first case. They do so by bargaining on the price and the scope of the offer: Go down 20% and throw in the set of tea cups and you have a deal!

In the negotiation with their partner, most entrepreneurs suggest an agreement where both sides make concessions that cost them little but are highly valuable to the other side. If you do the dishes for a month (which you find relaxing anyway) and your partner does the hated tax work (which takes just one evening), you both gain more than you give.

The previous examples illustrate the two extreme styles that negotiation theory describes as "distributive bargaining" and "integrative bargaining."

Think of the styles as ways to share a pie: You can gain a bigger share by claiming a larger piece (distributive). But you can also work on making the entire pie bigger, so that the same percentage of the pie results in a bigger piece (integrative).

Integrative bargaining

In integrative bargaining, the goal is to increase the value gained for both parties.

In the integrative bargaining mindset, the other party is not your opponent, but your partner.

This mindset applies well to the B2B sales context. There is typically ample room for a long-term relationship. The ideal outcome is a win-win situation: as long as your customer is highly satisfied with the value gained for their company, your startup profits from a reliable monthly income.

Integrative bargaining is built on two bases:

- **Shared interests.** Mutual gains are based on shared interests. Some of these interests concern the process: both parties will value an efficient deal-making process with respectful interactions and as little involvement of lawyers as possible. Another example for a shared interest could be the joint publicity from publishing a success story.

- **Trade-offs with asymmetrical gains and losses.** Often one party can create lots of value for the other one with a concession that is rather small for themselves. If there's another topic on which the trade-off works in the opposite direction, you can combine both, and both sides will be better off.

Distributive bargaining

In distributive bargaining, you claim value by obtaining something that implies a cost to the other side.

Every business negotiation inevitably includes one of more those topics where the mechanics of the translations just require distributive bargaining. The most obvious issue for distributive bargaining is the price of your product and service. Beyond this, the scope (how many licenses, which set of functionalities) and the level of services you provide can fall in this category, too.

Your relative strength in any distributive negotiation is determined by the alternatives available to you and your opponent.

If you *have* to sign the customer in front of you because they are the only one who you currently have in your pipeline, you'll be hard-pressed to make concessions and not risk the deal. That is one reason why you'll always want to have a full sales pipeline: so you aren't pressured to give in to customers demanding terms that are inconsistent with your overall pricing. Your remuneration system (see Chapter 15) should also ensure that your sales reps are never too desperate for any single deal.

Vice versa, your chances to negotiate a good deal are much better if you generate a large value increase above the potential customer's incumbent solution (or competitive products they are considering). In this case, the customer has a lot to lose by *not* signing a deal with you. Prioritizing leads in your pipeline according to how much they need your solution is key when preparing for negotiations.

Beware: because of its confrontational style, distributive bargaining can easily become intense and attention-consuming if you don't watch your involvement.

Jörg G. Beyer gives good advice in terms of staying focused on the big picture before you're letting yourself be sucked too deep into the distributive mindset:

> Avoid management distraction from trying to squeeze the optimal revenue from every single customer. Focus on a fair closing, then move on to the next customer.

> **— Jörg G. Beyer, Co-Founder & former Co-CEO, LeanIX**

You'll soon see that many negotiations in B2B sales follow a standardized model, especially when you're dealing with procurement professionals in a large organization.

It is essential to understand your counterpart's role in the game in order to play it well yourself.

Negotiations with the procurement department are a dance. Don't be afraid of the dance. Procurement people often come off as super tough. For example, you have a €25,000 deal, and they say they can't go higher than €20,000. When you offer €23,500, they say, "Sorry, this won't work out," and hang up. But the next day, they'll call you and say, "It's fine, can you please send over the order?" They have to do this. I've talked to procurement people who said they're even trained to lie, to say they have two more offers for 40% less. It's simply their job, so don't be afraid.

In negotiations, you need to push until you hear a "No." Most founders are afraid of hearing "No" because they're afraid of losing the deal. If the customer really wants you, they'll come back with a better offer after their initial "No." And if not, what happens if you call them back two hours later to say, "Okay, we'll do it your way"? Nothing. Absolutely nothing.

— **Stephan Rohr, Co-Founder & CEO, TWAICE**

The Negotiator's Dilemma

A negotiation in a B2B sales context is somewhere in between the extremes illustrated by the previous examples: the terms of the current deal matter a lot, but there is also a lot of value in building a long-term relationship.

For this reason, a typical B2B sales negotiation will contain both distributive and integrative elements. This creates a dilemma for founders

– because the basic methods of distributive and integrative negotiation are fundamentally opposed, as the following table illustrates.

Integrative negotiation (increasing value)	Distributive negotiation (claiming value)
Optimize value for both sides	Optimizing value only for oneself
Exchange a lot of information	Use information tactically
Open, truthful exchange	Bluffing
Flexibility	No unnecessary concessions
No pressure	Pressure and power games
Focus is on mutually acceptable options	Gain strength from strong alternatives on your side or poor alternatives on the other side

In practice, you might discover that the methods of one negotiation style feel more natural to you.

However, you will need to be able to apply both integrative and distributive methods to achieve the best results for your startup.

In the following part of this chapter, we will help you to understand and apply both bargaining methods to navigate the Negotiator's Dilemma effectively in your own negotiations.

How to apply bargaining methods

How to jointly make a bigger pie

Understanding the interests of both sides is essential to reaching a good integrative result for both parties.

Begin by defining what exactly *you* want out of the deal with your prospective customer.

For example, as a founder, you need to be clear on whether you prefer a one-time payment (to optimize cash flow) or recurring revenue stretched out over a longer period (to optimize company valuation) – and to what degree trade-offs between those two parameters are acceptable.

Everyone representing you in negotiations needs to be aware of those priorities. Include the guidelines in your training and briefings for negotiations, so that the negotiation mandate is clear. Your remuneration system (see Chapter 15) also needs to be consistent with these priorities.

You might even think about sharing your preferences directly with your negotiation partners to open the discussion for joint optimizations. For example, you might say: "We are currently optimizing our recurring revenue. That's why we would rather reduce our one-time payment than the monthly fee."

In principle, finding out the other side's interests is simple: just listen actively and ask lots of questions.

In the context of B2B sales, bear in mind that there are two levels of interests: the interests of the organization and the interests of the individual in front of you. These can, but don't necessarily have to overlap.

You might find, for example, that the Head of Marketing of your target company is hesitant about recommending your solution to the Economic Buyer. You probe around for a while until she eventually explains that she thinks your product will greatly help the company, but she is worried about losing functionality from the previous system that she personally liked. Only after you have learned about this concern, you have the chance to mitigate it by demonstrating your product's solution for the functionality. (This is called "objection handling" in operational sales training.)

Often, the true interest of the individual or the organization is hidden behind what sounds like a hard position. Maybe your counterpart rejects your pricing by saying "We won't pay that much for your solution." Instead of trying to convince the "stubborn" negotiation partner to accept your pricing, ask questions to find out where the position comes from. You might find that the actual interest is not primarily to pay less, but the manager's need to stay within this year's budget. In this case, you can start searching for a solution to work around this organizational constraint together.

Understanding the interests of the other party does not necessarily mean that you have to accept them at your expense.

As the previous examples illustrate, understanding your counterpart's interests is key to making progress toward finding a solution that helps both sides. In this joint process, you'll sometimes find creative solutions that neither side would have thought of beforehand.

The head of marketing was very excited about the product, but it was multiple times more expensive than the current solution (which wasn't solving the problem). He just couldn't see a way to get the budget for it, and was heartbroken. So I said: "If you like the product, and it solves your problem, I will not let the price be the breaking point here. I give you my word as the founder of the company." So instead of canceling the deal here and then, we worked out a way to convince his procurement department together – and he signed up!

— Arun Srinivasan, Co-Founder & CEO, Clarisights

If nothing else, your effort to come to a mutually beneficial result and the joint solution-finding process itself will leave good memories with your customer. This will also contribute to the quality of your business relationship with your counterpart going forward.

HOW TO

Listen actively

Many people are poor listeners, but this isn't out of malice or bad character. Often, we do not listen properly as we are already thinking about our own next steps. Whether we're excited or feeling pressured to chime in, we sometimes may even interrupt our counterpart the first time they take a breath. And even if we listen patiently, we often don't demonstrate our attention clearly enough: Are we looking at the speaker silently because we are paying full attention, or because we are already thinking about our plans for the weekend?

Luckily, listening is a skill that can be learned. In business, it can be a useful tool for building a human connection to your counterparts in business. A useful starting point are three techniques that are often collectively referred to as "Active Listening:"

- PARAPHRASE – Repeat and summarize what you have heard
- INQUIRE – Ask open-ended questions that show your interest
- ACKNOWLEDGE – Search for the underlying emotion of your counterpart and name it.

In Martin's negotiation workshops, participants practice these techniques in a simple exercise that you can also practice yourself with a friend. In this exercise, one person, the speaker, is advancing an extreme view on a controversial topic (such as climate change, death penalty, liberalization of drugs, etc.), while the other person, the listener, is only allowed to use the three "active listening" techniques above while listening to a speaker advancing the opposite view of a polarizing topic (such as climate change, death penalty, liberalization of drugs, etc.). Afterwards, the two people switch roles.

Most participants learn two things: The listeners learn how much discipline it takes to listen without starting to argue. And as speakers, they really enjoy being on the receiving end. One participant actually called the ten minutes of being actively listened to "wellness for the soul."

When it comes to negotiating deal terms, exchanging "packages" is the high art of integrative bargaining.

Fighting over each minute point of a complex contract turns any negotiation into a battle of argument and willpower. This is exhausting and unproductive. It's much more constructive to exchange "packages," where you make concessions or offer contributions in certain areas while asking for cooperation on other topics in exchange.

Many entrepreneurs use package deals where they offer discounts or other benefits in exchange for non-monetary contributions from their customers that are equally or more valuable to them. For example, LeanIX's Jörg Beyer lists a number of non-monetary benefits that he is willing to give discounts for:

Never give discounts without asking for anything in return. It can be anything of value for you:

- Permission to use their logo on your website and brochures
- Joint success story/case study
- Joint speaking on conferences
- Availability for reference calls by other prospective customers
- Signing of multi-year contracts

If you have to give monetary concessions, only give discounts that don't hurt your growth. If you offer a customer free onboarding worth €20,000 in the beginning and it helps to get the deal signed, it doesn't hurt your long-term revenue – and you can move on to the next deal. Examples for revenue-compatible discounts are:

- Professional services (like free onboarding)
- Lower automatic increases in pricing
- Longer payment terms
- Free additional product features

— **Jörg G. Beyer, Co-Founder & former Co-CEO, LeanIX**

Include a list of possible trade-offs in your sales manual and update them once you have learned what combination works well in this regard. Veronika Riederle from Demodesk illustrates this systematic approach to bargaining:

Currently, our negotiation mode is to start with the list price and prepare to give certain discounts, depending on what objections the customer raises and how important the specific company is to us. For example, you get a discount if you pay for a yearly contract in advance. Or we drop the setup fee as an argument in the negotiations.

— **Veronika Riederle, Co-Founder & CEO, Demodesk**

How to claim a bigger piece of the pie for yourself

There are entire shelves of books written on the psychology of distributive bargaining, but the most important methods are summarized in the following figure:

Anchor and defend against anchors	Use psychological biases	Manage concessions consciously
• Consciously set first offer • Identify opponents' anchors and consciously defend against them	• Frame the situation • Watch your own vulnerabilities	• Consider the message each step sends • Demand corresponding concessions
Use criteria tactically	Strengthen own alternatives, weaken alternatives of the opponent	Assume self-affirmative stance
• Use data and facts that support your position	• Prepare good alternatives to safeguard against closing bad deals • Understand opponents' alternatives and weaken them	• Convince yourself that it is legitimate to claim value • Don't lie!

We'll just focus on the essentials here: anchoring/defending against anchoring, and managing concessions strategically. No matter which method you use, all of them, first and foremost, require good preparation.

The most common tactic for distributive bargaining is "anchoring" – setting a mental orientation for the right price point with an aggressive first offer.

In an enterprise sales context, often you'll be the one to set an anchor when you share your price list for the first time. In this context, be aware of the psychological effects of "price anchoring": for example, your customer may perceive €25,000 as a high price when presented on its own, but not if it's presented as the "basic" option of a three-tiered offering with "professional" for €50,000 and "enterprise" for €75,000.

From a negotiation perspective, the list price should always be a certain percentage higher than your target pricing. That's on top of our experts' recommendations to "aim high" (see Chapter 6 on Pricing)! It's not uncommon to discount your software by up to 50% if you aim to break into a large account, depending on your market and competitive context.

The key to successful anchoring is to make the price high enough to reserve some room for negotiation, but not so high that your potential customers are scared away upon hearing it for the first time.

Keeping some room for negotiation is even more relevant in B2B sales, where your initial offer will likely be negotiated more than once: first by your Champion, then by the Economic Buyer and the company's Purchasing Team, and finally by the other corporate stakeholders who approve the deal.

Because anchoring is such a well-known and proven method, be prepared to encounter it on the customer's side as well.

The procurement department, for example, may state: "We were expecting a price around …," or: "We just cannot go higher than …" Don't be too impressed if you hear this in the beginning of the negotiations. Instead, challenge the statement by referring to the monetary value that you deliver (see Chapter 5 on Pain).

Once both initial positions are announced, the parties typically start to move toward each other by giving small concessions.

During this stage, watch out for signs the other party is sending, and be aware of the messages you are conveying at the same time.

For example, it's a sign of weakness and/or eagerness to close the deal to move twice in a row without waiting for a concession from the other side. The same applies if one party suddenly makes a giant concession after initially starting out with baby steps.

If you observe those signs in your counterpart, raise your ambitions for this deal – your customer apparently really wants to make this happen! If you, on the other hand, feel like you're too eager or are under pressure to close the deal, the customer is likely to sense this and demand further discounts or other concessions from you.

How to optimize your negotiation outcomes

The basis for a good negotiation outcome is always in the preparation stage. This is encouraging especially for founders who feel intimidated by the thought of tough negotiations. Like sales, it's not about talent – good preparation is a lever that is available for everyone.

To help you prepare for the three stages of a negotiation, we have prepared a downloadable version of the checklists in this chapter on www.fastforwardbook.com.

Before the negotiation

Before you enter any negotiation, gather the basic information you need. This includes data and facts on your own situation and the situation of your counterpart, but also an analysis of the negotiation situation itself.

Take particular note of who will take part in the negotiation session, and what implications this has from your side and the other side.

If there are multiple participants on your side, what are your roles (talker, data cruncher, observer, etc.) and how will you coordinate during the meeting? Also, consider who will take part in the meeting from the other side. Are you familiar with everyone and have you mapped them in the decision-making unit?

We also recommend to prepare by roleplaying the situation. Especially if you take turns at representing the other side, you'll become more aware of how the negotiation may feel from the other side.

Finally, clarify your mandate for the negotiation with your co-founders if they won't be present in the meeting.

And right before walking into the negotiation room, activate both your assertiveness (to fight for all your interests) and your empathy (to be open to listen and learn about the other side and their interests).

Checklist: Preparation of sales negotiation	
Facts and data	• Gather facts and resolve open questions • Verify the status of the previously exchanged information and contract drafts
Interests	• Identify and prioritize your interests
Alternatives	• Identify and prioritize your alternatives

Perception	• Identify your perceptions and possible biases
Tactics	• Determine your ideal outcome and limit (based on alternatives) • Prepare arguments and messages
Other party	• Identify decision-making unit on the other side (Champion, End User, Economic Buyer, Influencer, Veto Power) • Identify interests, alternatives, perceptions for each role in the decision-making unit
Criteria	• Determine possible criteria and benchmarks for your own position and identify the most beneficial ones

During the negotiation

Once you are in the room (or the video conference call) and ready to close the deal, start by checking whether both parties are on the same page regarding the purpose and the agenda of the meeting: is it to close a deal or to explore options only?

Along the same lines, clarify whether the other party has a mandate to close a deal live in the meeting, or whether the participants will only collect a proposal for a decision-making process to follow.

After clarifying those questions, you can proceed into the main body of negotiation. We have summarized our key recommendations for this phase in the following table.

Checklist: During the sales negotiation	
Exchange information	• Exchange information following the idea of "give and take"
Defend against counterattacks	• Stay in control when you encounter difficult counterparts
Bargain	• Use differences in values and priorities to find the optimal solution
Gauge possibilities	• Try out extreme combinations of wins and concessions
Create options	• Be creative in creating new options
Assemble packages	• Assemble packages to determine preferences and priorities
Find solutions	• Resolve distributive questions, ideally based on criteria and benchmarks

HOW TO

Deal with difficult negotiation counterparts

In some sales negotiations you will encounter particularly obnoxious counterparts that try to beat you using pure tactics instead of substantial negotiation strategies. Especially common and unpleasant tactics are extreme anchoring, nibbling (salami slicing), variations of "bad cop/good cop," or displaying exaggerated arrogance and time pressure.

Here are four steps you can take to deal with such situations:

1. **Notice the disruption.** In these situations, it is important first and foremost to simply *notice* that something odd is going on that may require a counter-reaction before you can go back to the substance of the negotiation. If you are negotiating as a team, a quick break might be in order to decide about your reaction.

2. **Consider ending the negotiations.** One standard response to unacceptable behavior is always to stop the negotiation – but this would, of course, take away the sales opportunity for your startup. Still, consider canceling the negotiations strongly if this behavior comes from a person who would play a key role in your business relationship in the future (like the Economic Buyer or the key End User). It's easier to be more flexible if the obnoxious behavior comes from a person that you will likely not meet regularly again (like an over-eager procurement person).

3. **Change the persons involved.** A softer, but often efficient approach can be to change the involved person. For the other side, you can propose: "Why don't we reschedule and meet again, but include Mr. X and Ms. Y to represent the department in charge?" You may also consider changing the delegation on your side by adding or subtracting people. This is also helpful if the number and the hierarchical levels of the people in the room don't match.

4. **Name the disruption to reset the process.** Just mirroring the behavior of your counterpart, for example countering an aggressive anchoring with an equally aggressive counter-anchor and then only moving in baby steps toward a goal, can sometimes help to point out the problem of that

behavior. Often, however, it is more constructive to name the activity that is disturbing you and reset the process: "It feels that we have a good cop and a bad cop in the room. I don't find this particularly helpful. Why don't we take a step back. It would be helpful for me to better understand your interests regarding…"

Closing the negotiation

After all arguments are exchanged, it's time to make the final decision. This is a critical moment in the negotiations. Moving slowly and deliberately in this phase is essential to avoid making last-minute mistakes. Use our checklist to make sure you have resolved all open issues and questions before closing the deal.

Checklist: Quality of the negotiation outcome
☐ Are all questions resolved?
☐ Are your own interests reflected?
☐ Is the outcome better than your best available alternative?
☐ Can the outcome actually be implemented?
☐ Is there no more room to improve the outcome with more creative solutions?
☐ Is the outcome contributing to the long-term relationship?
☐ Is the outcome fair? Can it be explained to others?
☐ Are the interests of the other party (parties) reflected?
☐ Is the outcome clearly documented?
☐ Does your mandate cover all aspects of the outcome?
☐ Are the next steps for the implementation clear and aligned?

If you can tick all boxes, clearly commit to the agreed-upon outcome. Also, make sure to collect an equally clear commitment from your counterpart before you proceed to clarify the next steps. In B2B sales, translating this commitment into a formally binding form typically means that you will sign a written contract – completing the final step of your sales process.

Getting a signature

First-time founders of B2B startups are often surprised to learn how long it can take to get the actual signature after everyone has agreed on all the terms of the deal.

To receive a "Yes" from your customer, we recommend to proceed in three stages:

1. Ask the Economic Buyer for a reply to your email confirming that they would like to go ahead and sign based on the attached contract and your terms and conditions (T&Cs).
2. Ask for a purchase order number that includes the budget allocated toward your agreed-upon offer.
3. Ask for the signed contract including the T&Cs.

Although the End Users are usually keen on starting right after the initial informal confirmation email, we recommend at least asking for a binding purchase order number first, if you can't wait for the signed contract. Once you start delivering your first milestones, it's hard to create the required urgency within the customer's purchase organization to actually move forward with these bureaucratic steps.

On a final note, even if you trust your counterpart completely – remember that investors love to see signed contracts as proof of your traction, and much prefer these over confirmation emails or product orders.

Debriefing: Closing the learning loop

Don't forget to use the negotiation as a learning opportunity for yourself and for your sales team. Many founders and sales teams give away valuable business potential by negotiating poorly. Make sure to integrate structured information-sharing on lessons, challenges, and best practices into your sales operations.

Checklist: Debriefing	
Reflection	• What went well? What didn't?
	• Were there surprises? Insights?
Debriefing	• Inform the team and other involved people and feed the insights back into your company
Lessons learned	• Analyze potential improvements and work on them with your team

Negotiation across your sales process

As you have seen, the negotiation process in B2B sales is not just about a single meeting where all the action happens. In fact, a lot of what you do within the sales process already contributes to your negotiations.

The Qualified Lead and Opportunity stages are where you prepare for the final negotiations: you collect lots of information about the other side, especially about the interests on all levels. Make this a qualification criterion in your sales process, too: if your research indicates a great fit with the customer's interests, prioritize them; in turn, drop them if the interests are less aligned.

With presenting your offer and price list in the Opportunity stage, you'll throw in the first anchor for your negotiations. Ideally, at this time, you should also find out the relative importance of issues on their side. Even if the deal is not going to be closed in this first presentation, make sure that you or your salespeople are crystal-clear about your own interests and their mandate: which deal parameters can you accept on the spot, and which should you reject outright?

The final negotiation, where the deal is closed, marks the transition from the Opportunity stage to the Customer stage. This is the most important step in the sales process – even if it's not the last. Until the contract is signed in the Customer stage, and for each upsell you make in the Customer Success stage, there are likely to be more (smaller) negotiations to follow as part of your long-term business relationship.

11 - PIPELINE MANAGEMENT

How to keep your sales flow going

In the previous chapters, you have learned how to convert an individual prospect into a customer with a signed contract through a structured process, effective conversations and negotiations.

Once you get started with your sales activities, you will be in touch with a lot of contacts. Because you contacted them at different times, and they respond differently to your sales activities, they will not advance simultaneously, but soon be distributed all across the different stages of the process.

The most common way to describe the distribution of your contacts across the different stages is the "sales pipeline" (or "sales funnel").

Why the name? Just look at it visually: every sales process starts with a larger number of prospective customers who are channeled through your sales process before a smaller number of them eventually becomes signed customers.

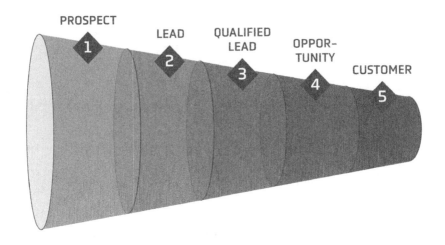

What your sales pipeline tells you

Looking at all the contacts across the entire pipeline instead of just individual contacts is essential in order to manage your overall sales activities.

For example, you'll learn a lot about the strengths and weaknesses of your sales process and organization by analyzing how the pipeline looks like at any given moment (snapshot view) and over time (evolutionary view):

- Is it full at the inlet, but very little comes out at the end?
- Does it look like the pipeline is clogged somewhere?
- Do some contacts take much longer to move through the pipeline than others?

Diagnosing the status of your pipeline is key to improving your overall sales processes and organization.

In the following part of this chapter, we'll be looking at the most important characteristics of the pipeline for you to watch and work on:

- **Conversion rates:** the percentage of contacts that move to the respective next stage (for example from Prospect to Lead, from Lead to Qualified Lead, and so on) within a certain time frame.
- **Shape and length:** the overall number of contacts entering and moving through the pipeline (pipeline volume) and the overall time it takes them to move from the beginning to the end of the pipeline (pipeline velocity).

Knowing these basic indicators for the status of your pipeline, you can start to focus your attention and resources on optimizing its flow.

Example: Your monthly pipeline

For the purposes of this chapter, let's look at a concrete example for a pipeline. To simplify, we will only analyze a single monthly cohort: contacts that newly enter your sales pipeline in the Prospect stage during this month.

You start entering contacts into the **Prospect** stage of the pipeline. This month, you have identified 200 companies that match your ICP. With some experience and a good database to pull contact data from, you are able to retrieve the contact information for a relevant person within 160 of those companies. Those 160 contacts move forward into the Lead stage.

In the **Lead** stage, you contact these 160 persons via email. 16 persons respond and express an initial level of interest in your solution. Those 16 contacts move up to the Qualified Leads stage. The other 144 leads that never reply or say they're not interested drop out from your sales pipeline for now.

In the next stage, you follow up with your 16 **Qualified Leads** to find out in more detail whether their needs actually match your proposition. At the same time, you try to identify the respective company's decision-making unit and validate whether there's an actual budget for your solution. You succeed with five contacts. The other 11 contacts drop out for different reasons: because you don't get access to the relevant stakeholders at the company at this time, because the company doesn't prioritize the topic right now despite a general need, or because the company turns out to be a bad match after all.

With the five contacts left in the **Opportunity** stage, you arrange meetings to do a detailed demo of your solution and discuss it with the people in the relevant decision-making unit. Two of those companies say that your solution looks useful and accept an offer for your proposition. Three companies tell you they're not interested in your solution at this point. They prefer keeping their current solution or decide to go for a competitor's product.

Of the two contacts that enter the **Customer** stage, you manage to successfully negotiate and sign a contract with one of them.

Funnel to win one customer	1 Prospect	2 Lead	3 Qualified Lead	4 Opportunity	5 Customer
Input contacts	200	160	16	5	2
Conversion rate	80%	10%	30%	40%	50%
Contacts moving to the next stage	160	16	5	2	1
Dropouts		144	11	3	1

Conversion rates

Only a portion of the contacts in each stage fulfils the criteria to move to the next stage.

We refer to the portion of contacts advancing to the respective next stage as the conversion rate.

For example, if 16 of your 160 contacts move from the Lead to the Qualified Lead stage, the conversion rate between those stages is 10%.

Generally speaking, conversion rates are lower at the beginning of the pipeline (starting with the first interaction with the customer in the Lead stage) than the conversion rates at the end of the pipeline. That's because in the early stages you have precious little information on the contacts. You will need to weed out a lot of contacts as not interested or not qualified after learning more about them. If you target a very broad market segment, the conversion rate from Lead to Qualified Lead can easily be less than one percent.

In contrast, once you reach the Customer stage, the conversion rate is quite high, even in the first run. At this stage, you have already established a detailed need, identified an interested decision maker and sufficient budget, run through several demos, and have been asked to submit an offer – there are simply few reasons left for the company to *not* sign this deal.

Some startups also calculate conversion rates over several stages, for example from the Qualified Lead to the Customer stage (12% in our example). Doing this might give you a better picture of the overall sales process's efficiency.

Generally, you may find it helpful to compare your conversion rates with those of other startups to identify possible weak points of your process and work on them.

This is not to say that a conversion rate of 10% versus 12% of your peer group should worry you – but if the difference is 20% versus 80%, you should take a closer look! To avoid comparing apples to oranges, focus on metrics that are rather independent of industry and market. For example, compare process-dependent variables such as the number of contact attempts per month, or the conversion rate from offers to signed contracts.

How to use conversion rates to evaluate and improve your sales process

The conversion rates from one stage to the next tell you a lot about the strengths and weaknesses of your sales process.

In the table below, we have gathered some key factors that contribute to a good conversion rate in your sales process.

Process stage	How to achieve a good conversion rate to the next stage
Prospect	• Excellent segmentation and ICPs (this has the highest impact on lowering sales cost!)
Lead	• Excellent methods for the identification of the interested entry point • On-point marketing message addressing a relevant pain point
Qualified Lead	• Excellent methods for identifying the budget, the decision-making unit • Deep customer understanding
Opportunity	• High competitiveness of your proposition against existing solutions and competitors
Customer	• Excellent objection handling Excellent skills in driving for closing
Customer Success	• Excellent alignment of product development • Deep customer understanding

In the *Explore & Learn* phase, measuring conversion rates within the pipeline doesn't make too much sense yet. You'll have just a few contacts in your funnel anyway, so calculating percentages will deliver moot results. Also, the process will change all the time, so that the rates are hardly comparable.

Only after you have had hundreds of contacts pass through the pipeline and have closed your first 10 or 20 customers, conversion rates become an important metric for improving and fine-tuning your sales process.

To identify effects from actual changes in your sales process (instead of random variations over time), the analyzed time intervals have to be long enough. We recommend looking at monthly or quarterly cohorts. Once your company has matured even more, compare your conversion rates year by year to avoid seasonality effects (like lower rates in the vacation month August versus the back-to-school month September).

Over time, your conversion rates for each stage will stabilize within a certain range. For example, about 50% of your contacts will typically sign a deal within one month of entering the Customer stage. At this point, you can start to forecast your future revenues for the next month, quarter or half year, using the number of contacts and the conversion rate in the respective stage. Don't forget to compare the forecast to your actual achievements in order to continuously increase the forecast quality and the data quality in your CRM.

How to handle dropouts

As you can see in the example, a large portion of those contacts that initially enter the pipeline in the Prospect stage eventually drop out of your sales pipeline. In fact, in our example, 199 of your 200 prospects drop out somewhere between the Prospect and the Customer stage in their first run through the pipeline!

The emphasis here, however, is on "first run."

While a certain dropout rate is absolutely normal, don't forget to analyze the reasons for dropping out and to qualify the dropouts for possible follow-up actions.

The metric I'm most interested in is "Lost Reason." What was the reason why the prospect did not choose to go with us? What can we improve or change about the product to make it more relevant to the client?

**— Charles Delingpole, Founder & CEO,
ComplyAdvantage**

If you make the mistake of indiscriminately eliminating the dropouts from your sales activities, it means that you have wasted the time to gather information on them in the first place, and that you will have to multiply your efforts to generate an entirely new set of leads.

What you need to do with the dropouts depends on the reasons for them dropping out, and the stage at which they drop out. Document and categorize those "Lost" reasons in your CRM system to be able to systematically act on them.

The following table lists typical "Lost" reasons. For each of these reasons, you can take a number of remediation actions to convert the customer at a later time.

Reason		Typical stage	Remediation action
Contact	Contacted the wrong Champion and/or Economic Buyer	Lead, Qualified Lead	Ask for introduction to right contact or conduct further desk research
Interest	No pain identified	Lead, Qualified Lead	Nurture and contact again in x years

Timing	No priority right now	Lead, Qualified Lead	Nurture and contact again in x months
Budget	No budget available	Qualified Lead, Opportunity	Help customer to create budget Nurture prior to new budget cycle
Competition	Customer closed a contract with a competitor's solution	Opportunity, Customer	Identify competitor and difference in pricing and features Nurture after competitor implementation/prior to end of contract term
In-house solution	Customer opted for building own solution	Opportunity, Customer	Identify difference in features and cost Nurture after in-house implementation

For dropouts at all stages, it is worth to "park" them for a while – usually three to 6 months – and just contact them again to see if their situation has changed: maybe there is more budget available now, or a relevant stakeholder has changed, or the contact person has made a bad experience with another solution in the meantime and is ready to give yours a try now.

Especially for dropouts in the Lead or Qualified Lead stage, it often makes sense to revisit these stages and identify another contact person within the company who might be more open to your proposition.

If contacts pass the first qualification, but drop out in the later stages (Opportunity or Customer), they have already demonstrated significant interest in your field and solution. Chances are high that they will reconsider their rejection after having tried out another unsatisfactory solution, or because a new window of opportunity has opened internally.

Naturally, as we continue to emphasize, not every company will have a need for your offering or be a good match for you. You can reduce dropouts by a certain rate and convert more prospects into customers, but if there is simply no need or no budget for your solution, it would be a waste of time and resources to pursue this contact any further.

Overall, it's worth setting up a "nurturing" process for parked companies separately from your immediate sales activities.

Through nurturing, you can keep in touch with them and work on relationships that you can convert into customers at a more fitting time.

For less close relationships, nurturing can mean general marketing activities like a newsletter or regular mailings to inform those contacts of your company's progress or of new product developments. For those contacts that were farther along in the pipeline, design specific reactivation activities based on the time that has passed and the last interactions with them. Some criteria for reactivation could be:

- A new relevant contact joins the company
- The company shows a new activity in your field
- The cancellation period for their incumbent solution has passed

Ognyan Vasilev from Salesforce suggests a tiered system for qualifying leads and deciding which process to apply to them:

I recommend splitting sales activities according to customer tiers: Tier-1 are customers with whom the founders are already in touch and are highly interested and likely to buy – for example, companies that are quite aware of their needs and have pressing pain-points. Tier-2 customers will likely have an interest, but there is no connection yet or they are not fully aware of the needs for a solution – keep in touch with them regularly through events or tailored emails. Tier-3 customers are those that require the most nurturing before they will open up to your sales proposition, but will fill the pipeline in the future.

– Ognyan Vasilev, EMEA B2B Industries Advisory and GoToMarket, Salesforce

Shape and length of your pipeline

How many contacts should you enter into your sales process each month? And how much time should your contacts spend in the process?

That depends on how much revenue you want to come out at the end – and how fast you can realize this revenue through your sales process.

How to size the inlet of the funnel

How many contacts do you need to enter the Prospect stage of your sales pipeline during a given time? Speaking visually: how much input do you need to put into the top of the sales funnel?

The kind of "animal" you are hunting for is key to determining the number of prospects you need to take in at the inlet of the funnel.

If you are hunting Deer (customers with an ARR of €10,000) you will need to close more deals to arrive at your monthly revenue goal. Consequently, your funnel inlet will be much wider to take in thousands of prospects. Conversely, because of the complexity and higher effort required to hunt Elephants or Whales (customers with an ARR of €100,000 or €1 million), you'll focus on much fewer prospects and instead spend more effort on converting these few to achieve your revenue goals.

Deer (€10,000 ARR/customer)

	1 Prospect	2 Lead	3 Qualified Lead	4 Opportunity	5 Customer
Input contacts per year	24,000	19,200	1,920	384	115
Conversion rate	80%	10%	20%	30%	100%
Deal value per year	€240,000,000	€192,000,000	€19,200,000	€3,840,000	€1,150,000
	Pipeline volume				**Yearly revenue**

Elephant (€100,000 ARR/customer)

	1 Prospect	2 Lead	3 Qualified Lead	4 Opportunity	5 Customer
Input contacts per year	2,400	1,920	192	38	12
Conversion rate	80%	10%	20%	30%	100%
Deal value per year	€240,000,000	€192,000,000	€19,200,000	€3,840,000	€1,150,000
	Pipeline volume				**Yearly revenue**

Whale (€1,000,000 ARR/customer)

	1 Prospect	2 Lead	3 Qualified Lead	4 Opportunity	5 Customer
Input contacts per year	240	192	19	4	1
Conversion rate	80%	10%	20%	30%	100%
Deal value per year	€240,000,000	€192,000,000	€19,200,000	€3,840,000	€1,150,000
	Pipeline volume				**Yearly revenue**

To size the inlet of your startup's funnel, we recommend to enter your average revenue per customer and your conversion rate into a spreadsheet, then play around with the input numbers to determine how many contacts you need to achieve your desired outcome at the end of the funnel.

How to define the length of your pipeline

How long will it take contacts to pass through your pipeline – to move from first contact to signed deal?

To find out how long your pipeline is, add up the time boxes you defined for each stage of the sales process.

The result gives you a rough indication of the length of your pipeline, or how long your entire sales process is going to last. In the process we describe in Chapter 8, for example, the time boxes for all stages add up to almost four months.

Whether your sales cycle is longer or shorter again depends largely on your customers' ARR. Typically, the lead time from first contact to signed contract stays within four weeks to three months for Rabbits or Deer (€1,000 to €10,000 ARR). At the other end of the continuum, for Elephant or Whale deals with a volume of €100,000 to €1 million ARR, the sales cycle can last from 6 to 12 months or even longer.

Another good rule is: the more innovative and complex your proposition is, the more time you can expect to spend with contacts in your sales process (especially in the Opportunity and Customer stages).

Thinking about the length of your pipeline adds other strategic dimensions to managing your sales process.

The length of the process for one customer is strongly related to the level of pain the customer experiences. Even large enterprise customers can be surprisingly agile if the pain is strong enough and senior management is prioritizing the issue. To accelerate your pipeline's flow and close deals faster, filter the market constantly for those customers who experience the highest pain and allocate the highest priority toward closing a contract fast.

When you set the time boxes for each step of your process, use the fastest possible processes you have experienced as the benchmark in order to keep your qualification standards high.

Having a shorter pipeline means that you need to refill your funnel faster and more continuously to keep the deals flowing and prevent your pipeline from drying up. If your pipeline is very long, it's even worse to forget about filling it up: you will have to endure a long dry phase until new contacts have passed the process and will generate new revenue.

How to manage the pipeline

Now that you have identified the basic characteristics of your pipeline (conversion rates, shape and length), the real art begins: using this information to continuously improve your overall sales processes and organization. The way you focus your attention and resources on different stages of the pipeline has a huge impact on your outcomes.

In the following, we will show you how to diagnose five mistakes we often see founders make in managing their pipeline – and how to fix them.

Mistake 1: Pipeline leaks at the inlet (low early-stage conversion rates)

We often see founders dump long lists of companies into the funnel, of which the vast majority soon drop out again in the Lead or Qualified Lead stages. This may be acceptable if you only run automated email campaigns on large databases in the early stage, where you can work even with one-digit conversion rates. But if you actually put time and effort into calling your prospects, making ten calls to qualify one lead isn't feasible in the long run.

If your pipeline suffers from an extremely low conversion rate in the initial stages of your process, you haven't spent enough time on segmentation and defining your ICP yet.

Given that the majority of the total cost of sales occurs in the early stages of the pipeline, being more selective in defining who your customers are will release valuable resources that you can focus on converting those matches.

Mistake 2: Pipeline is clogging up (conversion rates too low/slow)

Some startups boast good initial conversion rates because their product generates a lot of interest, but suffer from a relatively high dropout rate in the later stages (Opportunity or Customer). Or those customers who are currently in these stages frequently exceed their allotted time boxes, so that the sales reps end up holding a lot of balls in the air without scoring any goals. The pipeline gets clogged up.

If your sales pipeline seems to leak or clog up in the later stages, you haven't qualified your leads rigorously enough throughout the early stages of the process.

When qualifying your contacts, make sure that you not only know the decision-making unit and validate the budget, but also get a sense of how long the customer will realistically take to close the deal.

If you feel that there is no commitment to closing within a certain predefined period (e.g. within 3 months), disqualify the prospect for now. Either eliminate them entirely or park them for later take-up. This way your sales team can focus on the deals that they can close soon. It's a good rule to spend 70% of your resources in the later stages on deals that you can close within 3 months.

> We achieved a high conversion rate among those who passed the qualification and entered the sales process. The leads who just wanted to learn more are filtered into the nurturing process in the qualification stage.
>
> — **Jörg G. Beyer, Co-Founder & former Co-CEO, LeanIX**

On the other hand, we see some founders excel in building up a long and detailed list of prospects and leads, but these contacts never move on to the later stages. This often happens with founders who feel insecure about actively approaching their customers to start working with them toward a deal.

If the pipeline is clogging up at the top of the funnel, you are not putting enough effort into the later stages in order to drive the customer through the decision process and "close the sale."

The key to successful management of the pipeline is to balance the resource allocation across the pipeline. In total, the value of customers within the pipeline should always be growing.

Mistake 3: Pipeline is drying up

> Startup founders often focus all their energy in completing the deals that are right in front of them. But that leaves the pipeline empty in a few weeks' or months' time.
>
> – **Ognyan Vasilev, EMEA B2B Industries Advisory and GoToMarket, Salesforce**

We often see founders laser-focused on closing their first customers by guiding them closely through all steps of their sales process. However, while they're busy working on these customers, they neglect to build up a new set of leads in parallel. The pipeline dries up.

Rather than this being a matter of resource allocation, Christoph Janz hints to a possible underlying psychological cause:

> Many founders make the mistake of not being honest with themselves when qualifying their leads. It's easy to become completely consumed by working on the 10 or 20 leads you have, even if these obviously aren't the right ones. In part, that's just human because you do want to sell – especially when a big logo is dangling like a carrot in front of you.
>
> The catch is that to be able to qualify rigorously, you have to have other leads to focus on. And if you want your sales team to always focus on the best leads only, you have to be excellent at lead generation.
>
> **— Christoph Janz, Co-Founder &
> Managing Partner, Point Nine Capital**

The beginning of the pipeline (the Prospect and Lead stages) needs to produce a steady stream of Qualified Leads.

Letting the pipeline dry up is a typical mistake of early-stage founders who are just finding their way into sales. We realize it's a lot to do at once, but don't neglect to regularly fill up your pipeline even at this stage to ensure a steady deal flow and – just as importantly – keep the motivation up:

Many startups neglect pipeline coverage as a metric to watch. As a consequence, they focus too little on top-of-funnel lead generation. Your goal should be to stuff your expensive top salespeople with opportunities, so they have the luxury of choosing the most profitable customer instead of giving discounts to get the only one they have.

**— Moritz Zimmermann, Co-Founder &
former CTO, Hybris**

A good strategy to prevent the pipeline from drying up is to fill it with Prospect groups whose profiles vary slightly – for example by their size, geography, or the role of the included contacts. Experimenting with different subsets of your market segment will also help you refine your ICP by discovering which companies move through the pipeline faster or more slowly.

Mistake 4: Neglecting reporting and evaluation

As every plumber knows, missing out on early indicators of flow problems usually leads to a big mess later. These pipeline failures are preventable – but only if you closely watch your key indicators.

Without careful evaluation of sales data, there's a high risk that you'll miss imbalances in your pipeline.

If you just start with the key metrics described in this chapter – watching the number of deals and their value in the pipeline, the average deal size as well as the average time deals take – you should already be safe from any major surprises.

To always be on top of what's happening in your pipeline, the first requirement is that the data exists at all. Therefore, make it a habit for yourself and your sales team to diligently fill up your CRM with up-to-date data on each contact you're dealing with.

In the following chapters on reporting, we'll cover in more detail how you can use regular and granular reporting to understand the status of the pipeline, its evolution and areas to focus on for improvement.

12 - OPERATIONAL SALES REPORTING

How to use data to get better and manage your team

When I joined Liana as Chief Global Sales Officer, I first tried to find out how the five regional sales offices were doing. It felt like I was looking through fog. The regions had no standardized metrics to measure their progress in their CRM, so it ended up being a "garbage in, garbage out" system. It was unmanageable.

— Kai Leppanen, Chief Global Sales Officer, Liana

It keeps surprising us in our daily work with startups how far you can come without having proper sales reporting. If you're scaling fast with a good product, growth just happens: you learn on the go and keep selling.

So why is neglecting sales reporting a problem?

- **You are wasting resources.** If you don't know who is doing what with whom in your pipeline, you can't tell what the factors for failure and success are. You risk yourself or your team wasting time doing things that don't generate as much revenue as you would have had you prioritized your resources differently.

- **You are flying blind.** Without a clear idea of what goes into your pipeline and what will happen on the way, you have no control over what comes out at the other end. Not knowing what your revenue is going to be in 3, 6 or 12 months' time is a big business risk.

Granted, these are risks that don't make your startup crash immediately. But in the mid-term, neglecting proper sales reporting will severely hamper your growth and let you fall behind against your competition.

Fortunately, getting operational sales reporting in place is possible at any stage – if you know how, as Kai Leppanen's story shows:

> I called a meeting with the top 10 out of 60 salespeople and asked them basic questions: "Who do you sell to? What stages are there in your sales process?" It turned out that their approach was based on a freeware CRM system that did not tell you anything about where you were in the pipeline from the buyers' perspective.
>
> After seeing this, we invested in a professional CRM system after testing it with the teams. It sure costs a lot of money per seat, but now, when I wake up in the morning, I can have a look and immediately see where the elephant deals are, where our challenges lie, and how I can effectively work on bringing these customers in.
>
> **— Kai Leppanen, Chief Global Sales Officer, Liana**

In this chapter, we're going to show you how to get started and how to use reporting to constantly improve your sales activities. The earlier you start, the better!

Going into management, one thing you learn very quickly is the importance of being analytical. When you're doing math at school, you think, "When am I ever going to use this?" When you get into SaaS, you do actually use it. Taking the time to understand the inputs is what makes you successful, what has made some of the top reps I see brilliant. I call it KYB – Know Your Business, the inputs of what you're doing. If you don't understand your inputs, chances are that it might work once, but it's not repeatable. And everything in SaaS is about this: how to make it repeatable and more efficient.

— **Neil Ryland, Chief Revenue Officer, Peakon**

Metrics to evaluate and improve your sales process

When you first set up your sales reporting, start simple. The point is not to generate heaps of data for its own sake, but to decide on the smallest possible set of metrics that you need to evaluate and then improve your sales process.

There are three levels that you can gather data on and analyze:

1. Pipeline health
2. Process performance
3. Outcomes

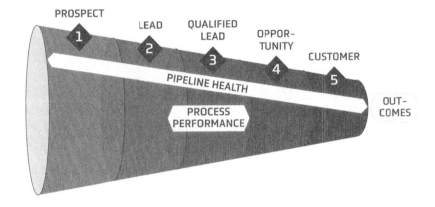

1. Pipeline health

First, you need to gain a comprehensive picture of what's going on in your pipeline: which and how many contacts are at which stage in the process, and what you are doing to convert them.

As discussed in the previous chapter, the bird's perspective on the pipeline allows you to determine the pipeline's overall health – whether there are any clogged up or leaking segments, or whether the pipeline is running dry.

Don't forget to track your own daily activities as well to find out how much time and effort is needed to win one customer. This is mandatory for benchmarking your sales team, too, as described in the second half of this chapter.

Metric	Definition	Relevance
Expected ARR in €	The expected deal size of the contacts within the pipeline	• Tells you what "animal" your contacts in the pipeline are • Tells you whether your sales process catches the animals you're hunting for

# of contacts per stage	The number of contacts in each stage of the sales pipeline	• Is the basis for all analyses around process performance • Tells you whether your pipeline is leaking, clogged or drying up
# of activities per contact per stage	The kind and frequency of activities you do to convert a single contact into a customer in each stage of the sales pipeline	• Is the basis for all analyses around resource management

2. Process performance

To find out where your process is working well and where you need to refocus your attention and resources, track the performance of your sales process using the following basic metrics.

Metric	Definition	Relevance
Conversion rate	The portion of contacts advancing to the respective next stage	• Tells you how effective your sales process is in getting to a deal • Tells you if there are problems with a certain stage
Average time per stage/per sales cycle	The average time a contact stays in each stage before moving on to the next one/in the entire pipeline	• Tells you if there are problems with a certain contact (e.g. if it remains in that stage too long) • Allows you to forecast revenue (e.g. 3, 6 or 12 months into the future)

3. Outcomes

By analyzing the outcomes of your sales process, you can determine where the bulk of your revenue actually comes from. Taking a more long-term perspective, you can also discover where and how you are losing revenue again from customers who churn (cancel or downgrade their contracts).

This will partially reflect your business model: the metrics will look different for an upsell-heavy land-consume-expand model than for a regular subscription model. But it also gives you an indicator on where you need to invest additional resources to realize additional potential or prevent negative consequences such as customer churn.

Metric	Definition	Relevance
ARR growth in period	Annual recurring revenue added in a certain period (e.g. per month)	Best measurement of total sales success. If you compare it with previous periods and the underlying budget, you get a clear picture of your sales performance.
ARR growth from new customers	Annual recurring revenue added in a certain period (e.g. per month) from new customers	Your ability to add new customers to your customer base is the basis for sustained growth.
ARR growth from existing customers	Annual recurring revenue added in a certain period (e.g. per month) from existing customers	Your ability to grow your revenue from existing customers is a key lever for further growth.

ARR lost through churn	The annual recurring revenue lost from all customers canceling their contracts in a certain period (e.g. per month) or reducing their contact volume	Tells you if there are problems after the deal is signed, e.g. because of overselling, failures in onboarding or lacking focus/resources for customer success.
Churn rate in %	The rate of customers who cancel their contracts in a certain period	Related, but more comparable metric than the absolute loss in revenue through churn.
Net retention (ARR minus churned ARR)	The annual recurring revenue across all existing customers minus the ARR from lost customers	Positive net retention (more upselling/expansion than churn) shows that your company is healthy and growing. This is also a strong selling point to investors.

Many operational sales dashboards also contain data on customer acquisition costs (CAC) and the payback period (the time until break even for an individual customer). Because these metrics are strongly tied to your overall business model and strategy, we will discuss them in more detail in Chapter 13 on Strategic Sales Analytics.

Example: Metrics along your sales pipeline

To illustrate what the different metrics might look like along your sales pipeline, the following table gives you an overview of metrics that we have found useful to start with.

We recommend analyzing these metrics for your entire pipeline. It may also be insightful to run separate analyses for individual members of your sales team, or for different market segments, in order to recognize differences and patterns.

Reports	1 Prospect	2 Lead	3 Qualified Lead	4 Opportunity	5 Customer	6 Customer Success
Activity	# contacts researched	# emails, calls	# emails, calls	# demos & presentations	# pilots	
	# data points entered in CRM (contact details etc.)	# data points entered in CRM (situation, needs, responsibilities etc.)	# data points entered in CRM (budget, decision-maker etc.)	# data points entered in CRM (process, timing etc.)	# data points entered in CRM (decline reason, competitors etc.)	# data points entered in CRM (decline reason, competitors etc.)
Contracts				# offers	# contracts	
# trials	# contracts					
Performance		Conversion rate	Conversion rate	Conversion rate	Conversion rate	Conversion rate
Revenue					€ ARR	€ ARR

Metrics to manage your sales team

Once you have a team of sales professionals to manage (see Chapter 14 on Sales Organization), you also need metrics to evaluate, benchmark, and compensate them (see also Chapter 15 on Remuneration).

By operationalizing value-adding activities and their results into metrics that your team is evaluated by, you keep your sales professionals focused and motivated.

However, not all metrics make sense for each role in your sales organization, which is why it's important to differentiate.

Account Executives (AEs)

Your Account Executives (AEs) are your main salespeople: the team members who are responsible for converting a lead into a signed customer.

The basic metrics to measure the performance of your Account Executives (AEs) are relatively straightforward. In essence, you want to know how successful your AEs are in closing deals, and how big their contribution is (in terms of revenue) to the entire organization's success.

Metrics to measure AE performance	
Middle of the funnel	• Quantity and quality of data points in CRM
	• Quantity of emails/calls/meetings
	• Opportunities created
	• Forecast/Pipeline coverage
	• Conversion rate
	• Sales velocity
	• Ratios per won customer

Bottom of the funnel	• Quota achievement
	• Won deals and won value
	• Pricing and payment terms

From capturing those metrics, you'll also find out what the number and value of leads is that an AE can realistically convert in a given time period.

Use this information to synchronize your staffing with your goals for revenue and growth. For example, if your average AE signs €400,000 in deals in 12 months, you need at least five sales persons to achieve a revenue goal of €2 million that year.

Sales Development Representatives (SDRs)

The role of Sales Development Representatives (SDRs) is to identify new contacts and turn them into leads that your AEs can then convert into customers.

Because SDRs hand over the responsibility for closing the deal to other members of the team at a certain point in the process (usually the Qualified Lead stage), measuring them only by that other person's success in closing or not closing the deal wouldn't make sense.

Therefore, you need to develop a distinct set of metrics to measure their contribution by. Beyond their contribution to achieving your sales objectives, you can add metrics that capture their focus on value-adding activities.

Metrics to measure sales development representative (SDR) performance	
Top of the funnel	• Quantity and quality of data points in CRM • Quantity of calls and emails
Middle of the funnel	• Quality of lead scoring • Quantity of demos scheduled • Ratios per Opportunity • Ratios per Won customer

Because it's complicated to fairly capture the SDR's contribution, feel free to adapt your metrics to your own organization and business model if this helps to make your system more transparent to your team.

We have defined our own KPIs to measure SDR performance. In effect, we look at the ratio between what we call PMRR (PayFit Monthly Recurring Revenue) and Growth PMRR. The resulting number is the value of the SDR's contribution.

- **Growth PMRR** refers to the total value of a deal that is created by the SDRs and added to our sales pipeline.

  - For example, if the basic plan is €99/month + €14/user, the total deal value/Growth PMRR of a company with 25 users is = €449.

- **PMRR** is a derivation of Growth PMRR. It factors in a coefficient for lead source (inbound vs. outbound), and a coefficient for how close the lead is to our ICP (measured by number of users).

- For the above mentioned example, the PMRR would be €449 (deal value) x 20% (coefficient for inbound leads) x 100% (for a target that's within our ICP) = €89.8.

– Firmin Zocchetto, Co-Founder & CEO, PayFit

Sales teams (and team leaders)

At some point, your organization will have grown to the point where you can no longer manage all the individual salespeople yourself. You'll have to hire more people, and also group them into teams. When your perspective moves up one level to managing and evaluating teams, your metrics to watch also become more high-level.

Metrics to measure sales teams' performance	
Contribution to sales goals	• Revenue generated (absolute and in %) • Churn (absolute and in %)

While you can still measure your teams' contributions to your overall sales goals by straightforward contribution metrics, it's important to also look behind the numbers. There are several factors that influence team efficiency. Consider them when deciding if and how to act on the performance metrics you'll see between the teams.

Team growth/turnover. If you're building a new team or growing your organization fast, the ramp-up time and costs for onboarding and training your new team members will necessarily detract from your primary sales goals. By benchmarking the teams against each other, you can find out how much growing pains slow down a team or even cause permanent problems, e.g. from high turnover because of failed onboarding.

If team growth is permanently impacting your sales performance, it might be helpful to establish a more standardized, efficient hiring and training process to reduce ramp-up time, costs, and turnover.

Geography/market specifics vs. individual contributions. By benchmarking the members of the individual teams against each other within the team, you can identify whether each team's performance is impacted by the specifics of the geography or market they are operating in.

For example, if you find an underperforming team where two salespersons are doing great and two are not signing anything, it's likely that there's a difference in skills and training that you need to work on. But if the entire team is underperforming in comparison to others, the specific region or industry they're working on might just be harder to crack.

Tools: CRM and dashboards

As you can see, even a minimalist reporting system for measuring and evaluating your sales process already contains a significant number of data points that you need to gather.

Without proper tools to gather, aggregate and analyze the data, you'll quickly lose track of the important inputs.

Fortunately, there are a number of great tools available that can help you in gathering, aggregating, and analyzing your sales data.

The prerequisite for using them is that you introduce a professional CRM tool early on (see the "How To" in Chapter 8 for our take on which CRM tool is suitable in which phase of your company).

Set up your CRM properly to reflect your process. Then make sure that your team knows how and when to enter data. Acceptance and the actual usage of the tool is crucial – otherwise, you end up with the "garbage in, garbage out" system Kai Leppanen describes.

Once your CRM is filling up with actual data, you can start to generate and analyze insights by aggregating metrics and automatically calculating important ratios.

We recommend visualizing your sales insights in a pre-configured dashboard that aggregates all key data in one spot.

This way you can identify problems early on and act on them. You can also share selected parts of the dashboard with your team or the entire sales organization. Again, this helps to keep your team focused and motivated on the metrics that contribute most to your individual and common success.

Based on the metrics we've discussed in this chapter, here's an example of a simple dashboard that integrates the key metrics on pipeline health, process performance and outcomes.

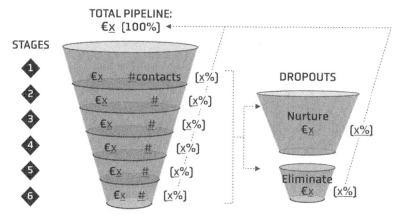

Forecast this month [quarter]

	Actual	Exp. Value	Weighted Pipeline
Pipeline	€x	€x	€x
Best Case	€x	€x	€x
Committed (Stage 4 ✅)	€x	€x	€x
Signed (Stage 5 ✅)	€x	€x	€x

New business + Upsell this month

Customer	ARR added
Company A	€x
Company B	€x
...	...

Open pipeline by quarter

Q4   Q1   Q2   Q3

Win rate by quarter

\#

€

Av. time to close

This month: ...

Last quarter: ...

Av. deal size

This month: ...

Last quarter: ...

Notes:

- *On Forecast Value: "Actual Value" = signed contracts; "Expected Value" = forecast on contracts to be signed; "Weighted Value" = forecast weighted by probability*
- *On Pipeline Value: "Best Case" = total pipeline value ; "Committed" = contacts past the Opportunity Stage; "Signed" = contacts past the Contract stage*

There are many free resources available online to inspire your own analytics and dashboard design. Check out our website www.fastforwardbook.com for a comprehensive list of up-to-date links.

HOW TO

Use operational sales reporting in practice

By Neil Ryland, Chief Revenue Officer, Peakon

It's important to be selective about what you include when you do the board reporting. I wouldn't want them to see certain things monthly. For example, if there's a swing deal, they could panic, although especially on enterprise deals, these things happen. That's just how the sales cycle works.

Just because I report something to the board on a quarterly basis doesn't mean I don't monitor the activity monthly. I proactively look at the data and go, "Okay, this is different than last month, is it because it's summer or did something change?" Europe pretty much switches off in the summer – the Swedes literally disappear. They're off. Another example is RFPs: the monthly data shows me when companies typically run RFPs, so I can bat this back into the quotas at the right time.

When you work in SaaS, there's so many things you can measure. We generate loads of data and I've got it all. But you need to know what questions you need to ask. You need to interrogate the data versus having the data flow overwhelm you.

- The questions I ask the regional VPs of Sales in my weekly forecast calls are:
- How many reps are going to hit their quota? How many teams?
- What is the pipeline coverage for the following quarter? We know from experience where we need to be at in order to be successful.

- Where is that pipeline coming from? Only if I know where it's coming from, I can start to work on efficiency.
- What is the forecast for the big deals in that region? How many are committed? What's the best case?
- Are there swing deals among the larger deals I can dig into and offer a discount or make something happen?

Every quarter, I dive a little deeper into the regional performance:

- Are we on track with our hiring plans?
- What's the pipeline spend per dollar that we make on each of our channels? In this calculation, we separate out the different channels, e.g. PPC [pay per click], or hosting physical events. Our model also factors in the salary of the SDRs and the demand generation team.
- What's the average deal size being created at the first stage of our pipeline?

At the board level, we discuss across all regions:

- What's the status of our big swing deals (>€100,000)?
- How are we doing with our key accounts?
- What is our sales efficiency?
  - What's our SaaS Magic Number?
  - What's the ROI of each region?

13 - STRATEGIC SALES ANALYTICS

How to diagnose your business's health

In the previous chapter, you learned which metrics you need to tune your sales process and team into an ever more efficient sales engine.

As a startup founder, however, your job doesn't end at the door of the sales department. You want your business on the whole to be healthy, grow, and thrive. Toward this goal, we will leave the operational level and assume a more strategic perspective on sales.

Instead of asking about the efficiency of the operational process, the question becomes: Taken together, are my sales activities bringing in more value for the business than they cost?

If you can answer this question with a solid "Yes, multiple times!" then we guarantee you that investors are going to love your startup.

Before diving deep into the calculation of the key metrics for business health, let's first have a closer look at the general idea of a "healthy business."

Understanding business health

On his blog, serial entrepreneur, VC, and startup guru David Skok summarizes the three key tasks for creating and growing a successful B2B business as simply as follows:

1. Acquire customers
2. Retain customers
3. Monetize customers

To determine how well your business is doing regarding these three tasks, you need to ask three questions:

1. Are your customers worth the investment?
2. How long do your customers stay?
3. When do your customers start generating profits for you?

1. Are your customers worth the investment?

Your startup will prosper if the cost of acquiring a customer is significantly smaller than the profit you will generate with this customer during the length of the business relationship (i.e. the time the customer will remain a customer of your company).

This means that you need to watch and compare two basic metrics:

Customer Acquisition Cost (CAC)		**Lifetime Value (LTV)**
The cost to acquire a typical customer.	⟷	The retention (time) and monetization (profit) for a typical customer.

GoCardless founder Matt Robinson describes the right ratio between CAC and LTV as a clear acceleration signal for your business:

As long as you've got good CAC versus LTV and a sensible payback period, then you've got a scalable engine. Sure, CAC's not Total Cost of Sales. But the reality is: when the margins are good, and the lifetime is long, that stuff just disappears. For SaaS, when your margins are 70, 80, 90%, it makes sense just to pour money into the machine and just acquire growth at all costs. Cost of sales is not a big priority. Because time in the market is your friend.

**— Matt Robinson, Co-Founder &
Board Member, GoCardless**

An often-quoted rule – also referred to as "Skok's Law" – is that CAC should be (at least) three times smaller than LTV.

Don't worry too much if your CAC-to-LTV ratio doesn't comply with Skok's Law when you're still in the *Explore & Learn* stage. CAC can also be temporarily higher when you have to address new segments, new geographies or competition intensifies. However, if you have reached the *Standardize & Optimize* stage and still don't see yourself anywhere near this ratio, your business model likely needs revising.

In this case, you have two options:

1. You treat your CAC as given and work on increasing LTV to at least three times CAC. You can do so by raising your price or retaining customers longer.
2. You consider your LTV as given and work on reducing your CAC to at least one-third of LTV.

Deriving your maximum CAC from your customers' LTV gives you a clear indication of the level of sales effort you can afford per customer. If your customers' LTV is low, you can only operate a highly automated, low touch sales process. Only high customer LTVs justify a high touch, human sales effort.

A field sales model only works if you have 6-figure deals because of the inherent cost for the sales person and their expenses.

— **Moritz Zimmermann, Co-Founder &
former CTO, Hybris**

2. How long do your customers stay?

A great indicator for retention as a key part of your business's health is the churn rate.

The churn rate describes the percentage of all your customers who cancel their contract with you ("churn") in a given month.

This is one of the most powerful, yet often overlooked metrics for startups with a recurring revenue model.

The table below demonstrates the disastrous effect of churn on your overall customer base.

Recurring revenue from existing customers					
Start	**Monthly change**	Revenue after 6 months	Revenue after 12 months	Revenue after 24 months	Revenue after 36 months
100	+2%	115	129	164	208
100	0%	100	100	100	100
100	-2%	87	77	60	47
100	-5%	70	51	28	15

Due to compound effects, with only 2% monthly churn, you will have lost 23% of your revenue within a year. If churn continues at the same rate, you're left with less than half of the revenue you originally earned after just three years.

Reducing your churn rate is a very powerful lever to improving the health of your business (see Chapter 16 on Customer Success on how to achieve this). If you keep your customers or – even better – grow your revenue from existing customers to offset losses from churning customers, you'll be doing extremely well. The "+2%" line in the table gives you a clear indication how powerful such a growth driver can be.

3. When do your customers start generating profits for you?

The idea that the profits generated by a customer throughout their average contract duration ("lifetime") should outweigh the cost of acquiring the customer makes intuitive sense.

The catch in this calculation is that the "average duration" of your customers' contracts is still unknown if your startup itself isn't already a few years old. If you don't know the lifetime, looking at the CAC-LTV ratio doesn't make too much sense.

Until you have a good grasp on the realistic lifetime duration of an average customer, focus on another metric: the time to breakeven for an individual customer.

In essence, you can imagine this as making an investment into one customer that is slowly paying off. The breakeven point is the point where the profit generated from the customer outweighs the investment you initially made.

Calculating the time to breakeven – also described as "Months to recover CAC" or "Payback period" – has the advantage that you don't need to know how long the customer will eventually remain a paying customer. The only information you need is already available: your CAC and the monthly revenue (and profit margin within that revenue) you will generate from this customer.

$$Time\ to\ breakeven\ (months) = \frac{CAC}{MRR * Gross\ Margin}$$

Assuming that your CAC investment is €6,000 and your monthly profit (calculated as MRR multiplied with your gross margin as percentage) from a customer is €500, the resulting cumulative cashflow for that customer will look like this:

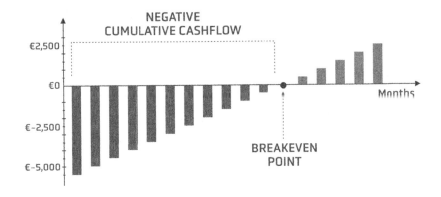

This graph shows both the beauty and the challenges of a business model based on recurring revenue:

- Your customers are immensely profitable in the long run, especially if the churn rate (the rate at which they drop out and cancel their contracts) is low. This is what investors love about recurring revenue models!
- However, you'll have to find a way to cover the negative cumulative cashflow until you reach the breakeven point. In our example, you need to survive 12 months before you begin to make a profit on your customer. This challenge multiplies (the cashflow hole gets deeper) if you invest in acquiring more customers at the same time.

The sooner you recover your CAC and reach breakeven with each customer, the less you need to worry about the negative cashflow – and the burden to pre-finance your growth will be much lighter.

A CAC recovery rate of three to six months is ideal. The general recommendation is to try to stay below 12 months.

A longer payback period can be fine too, if you have good reasons to expect to build a long-term relationship with your client. Balderton Capital's Sales Playbook cites the average payback period for small and medium businesses as six to 18 months, for enterprise clients even 24 to 36 months.

How to calculate your business health metrics

The figure below summarizes the most important business health metrics and their relationship among each other. Many investors, including us, look very carefully and critically at these strategic sales metrics when reviewing an investment candidate.

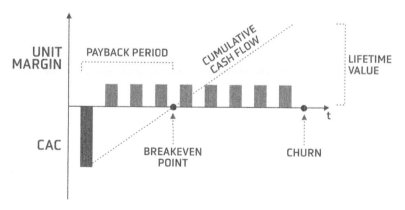

Because these metrics are such crucial indicators for determining your business's health, your underlying definitions and calculations need to be absolutely solid.

In the following section, we explain how we, as investors, expect you to calculate the most important business health metrics for your startup. If you want to dive deeper into this topic, check out our website www.fastforwardbook.com for free templates on additional sales metrics.

Customer Acquisition Cost (CAC)

CAC describes the total cost you have to sign a new customer. Like the other sales metrics, CAC is calculated for a certain period (usually a month or a quarter).

On his blog, David Skok introduces the following simple formula:

$$CAC = \frac{sum\ of\ all\ sales\ and\ marketing\ expenses\ (per\ month)}{number\ of\ new\ customers\ (per\ month)}$$

The number of new customers added is a pretty straightforward metric, as you typically know how many contracts were signed or purchases were made in any month.

In our experience, the sum of all sales and marketing expenses tends to be more of a conundrum. Including only direct sales or advertising costs in this calculation, as many founders mistakenly do, falls short of accounting for the wider cost of the entire sales organization.

For the CAC figure to make sense as an indicator for your business's health, it's essential that you factor in all the costs that contribute to this:

- Salaries of your employees in sales and marketing (incl. ancillary cost)
- Overhead cost per sales and marketing employee (e.g. for office space and equipment)
- Sales-related travel and entertainment expenses
- Marketing expenses (e.g. for advertising, PR agencies)

Magic Number

A concept related to CAC is the Magic Number. This describes how much revenue you generate in a certain period for every euro (or dollar) you spent on sales and marketing.

The Magic Number is a metric for your sales efficiency: The higher the number, the more efficient are your sales activities.

$$Magic\ Number = \frac{revenue\ generated\ from\ new\ customers\ (per\ quarter)}{sum\ of\ all\ sales\ and\ marketing\ expenses\ (previous\ quarter)}$$

More than the absolute CAC, this metric helps you to evaluate and improve your sales process from period to period, which is why it becomes especially important in the *Standardize & Optimize* phase.

For example, if you increase your recurring revenue from €12 million to €16 million during Q4 2021, after having spent €3 million on sales and marketing in the previous Q3 2021, your Magic Number is 1.33 (you spent €3 million to generate €4 million in recurring revenue). In this case, you should keep doing what you're doing, because you're getting back more than you invested!

For one-time revenue, the Magic Number should be greater than 1.0 – you need to recover more than your investment for the deal to be profitable. Because recurring revenue grows over time, the Magic Number can initially be a little lower. Balderton Capital sets the lower limit for the Magic Number at 0.75: if you reach this number, start increasing your spending on sales and marketing to grow!

Lifetime Value (LTV)

The average lifetime value (LTV) of your customers is the total amount you will earn from a customer before they cancel their contract.

Rephrased as a formula, this looks as follows:

$$LTV = \frac{average\ revenue\ per\ customer\ (per\ month)\ *\ gross\ margin\ (\%)}{average\ retention\ time\ per\ customer\ (months)}$$

Taking our example from before and assuming that the average retention time per customer is 36 months, this means that the LTV goes up to €12,000 before the customer churns.

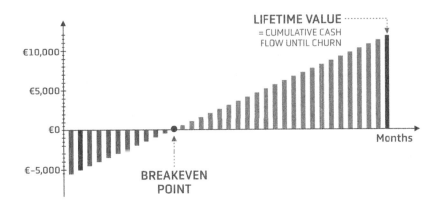

Looking at this formula, you'll see that LTV is driven by three factors:

1. Average revenue per customer

Your average revenue per customer per month is a direct result of your pricing. If you want to change this, you'll need to adapt your pricing strategy (see Chapter 6).

2. Gross margin

Your gross margin is largely determined by your cost structure, as the following simplified formula illustrates:

Gross margin = Revenue - Cost of Goods Sold

B2B software businesses typically strive for a high gross margin (80% of revenue or more). This becomes possible due to the high scalability of software, as the costs for serving 100, 1,000, or 100,000 customers increase only marginally.

By improving your processes and increasing your efficiency, you automatically bump up your margin and generate more profit from each customer.

3. Average retention time per customer

Retention time, the average time before customers "churn," is a crucial but often overlooked metric in recurring revenue business models.

Especially given the high impact of your CAC in the initial months of the customer relationship until the recurring revenue makes up your investment, a low retention time is fatal for your overall business health.

Going back to the earlier example, an early churn (e.g. because of neglected focus on customer success in onboarding) causes you to lose much of your initial investment. Even if the customer churns after 12 months, you'll still have made zero profits from them! After that, each month that the customer remains a customer, they generate predictable value for you – it's worth working hard to keep them on!

Veronika Riederle describes the effort Demodesk puts in to stay close to the startup's customers:

We're still at a stage where we focus a lot on product-related customer success KPIs in order to improve our value proposition. Like, how many demos do customers do with our product? What's the quality score the customers assign to every meeting? We also ask for the overall NPS regularly to get a general picture of customer happiness. For our larger customers, we call them personally and ask if they have everything they need. All of this helps us achieve "negative MRR churn," an indicator that is very important to our investors.

— **Veronika Riederle, Co-Founder & CEO, Demodesk**

How to uncover the stories behind your metrics

Up to now, we have looked at *aggregated* KPIs only: the churn rate of *all* customers in April 2021, or the ARR across *all* customers in 2021. This is perfectly fine if you want to evaluate your business's overall health or performance.

However, if you're trying to find out more about why things develop the way they do, this aggregate view doesn't tell the whole story.

Your aggregate data may show, for example, that your annual churn rate is 20%. This rate may go up or down in the next year, but the data doesn't give you any clue as to why. Also, you don't know if all your customers are experiencing equal churn rates, or whether a specific subgroup is more or less affected.

These unanswered questions are a problem. If you don't know what is happening when and to whom, you can't do anything to prevent the churn before it happens.

If you want to get better insights on why certain metrics change, you need to disaggregate your data by splitting your customers into cohorts.

A cohort is a group of customers who share a certain characteristic – like the date of their first signing. If you sort your data based on cohorts, you gain a perspective that is very different from the aggregate picture. The cohort data also shows you whether KPIs are worsening or improving with your most recent customers.

Take the example above, where you saw 20% average annual churn. If you analyze the churn rate separately for each cohort of customers who started their contract at the same time (or in the same month), you may find that the annual churn rate for each cohort is only 10% in the first year, but 30% and more in the second and third year. Alternatively, you might also build cohorts around customer segments and discover that your churn rate differs significantly based on the customer segment.

These new insights don't automatically tell you why things are happening. However, by making them visible in the first place, they allow you to investigate what is going on.

In the example, you could have your customer success team investigate what is changing for customers after the first year. You could then follow up with strategic measures to prevent the dropoff at this point.

Analyzing customer retention and churn is a typical use case for cohort analysis.

Turning the focus around, cohort analysis can also give you a clearer picture on increases in customer value through upselling and expansion.

In the example below, you see a positive trend, where churn rates improve for each successive cohort. Using a monthly view, this trend becomes visible much earlier than in the aggregate view.

Cohort Churn Analysis (1st year churn)							
% of customers retained/starting date of cohort	1st month	2nd month	3rd month	4th month	5th month	6th month	7th month
from Jan 2021	100%	94%	90%	88%	88%	86%	84%
from Feb 2021	100%	97%	94%	91%	90%	88%	
from Mar 2021	100%	98%	96%	94%	92%		
from Apr 2021	100%	98%	97%	95%			
from May 2021	100%	98%	97%				
from Jun 2021	100%	98%					
from Jul 2021	100%						

Matt Robinson, Co-Founder of GoGardless, views cohort analysis as the most insightful tool to evaluate your sales strategy:

> The metric I look at the board level the most, and I think is most useful, is the cohort chart. The guys refer to it as "Matt's chart." Every annual cohort is lined up, and it shows what they were worth after n months. It shows you if there's a mismatch in what you pour in and what you get out, with a certain delay because of the sales cycle.
>
> We had a couple of years where I was convinced we didn't have the right sales leader in place. And I could see it in that chart. We had increased our spend on sales and marketing by six times, and our cohort value only went up about 60%. That was clearly not working.
>
> **— Matt Robinson, Co-Founder &**
> **Board Member, GoCardless**

14 - SALES ORGANIZATION

How to grow your sales team step by step

Now that you know what's done in each step of the sales process and how to measure and improve your sales activities, let's look at who is actually doing all this stuff: the people in your sales organization.

From a leadership perspective, it's best if a single person holds responsibility and accountability for the entire sales process, from selecting leads to retaining and expanding customers.

This is pretty easy to organize if there are only one or two people doing sales – you and your co-founders.

But as soon as your startup grows in size and complexity, it's time to hire more people and start thinking about how to organize them.

The goal is to assign roles in a way that the different responsibilities and skill sets complement each other and tie into each other seamlessly.

How to build up your sales organization

Like your startup on the whole, your sales organization grows in different stages. It's important to realize that this is not a linear development, where you just keep adding more people to the same structure.

The evolution of your sales organization follows a threshold pattern, where the entire structure changes once you reach a certain stage of size and complexity.

For logistics startup Forto, the evolution of the sales organization transitioned through four stages, each one marked by the entry of a new sales leadership:

Our revenue engine includes everything from outreach to implementation. Our sales organization of 75-80 people is split in two core teams: Growth (with about 25 people) and Sales (about 50). Growth includes marketing and SDRs. Sales includes the key account management team and the implementation team for each of our sales regions or market segments.

Our first Head of Sales was Markus. He joined us 9-12 months after our founding, when we were about 10-20 people in sales, 50% of whom were interns. He had a lot of experience in selling, also internationally, and helped us set up our first professional sales organization. This included coaching and training of our employees, development conversations, and, very importantly, setting up a compensation system.

We entered our second evolutionary level when Fabian became our VP Growth, 12-15 months later. At the time, we were about 20 people in sales, including 25% interns. He helped us to unlock the next customer bracket and grow from single-stakeholder sales to multi-stakeholder sales, and to solve our churn problem. Fabian has a unique talent to identify the problems with the 50 tiny control levers in the sales process and then optimize them one by one – across the entire journey. Like, what is the right ratio of industry experts versus hungry graduates? What are the right messages for our target groups? Are there persona-specific management objections? Where is the handover from SDRs to AEs, how is it mirrored in the CRM? Once we are in the meeting: what sales deck do we show? Who's in the meeting? Do we present ourselves as a startup, an SMB? And so on.

Our third evolutionary level began when we implemented a second line of sales leadership under the existing VP of Sales. We had noticed that we had reached a breaking point when our VP of Sales had about 15 direct reports. The employees became unhappy. Some left because they didn't feel appreciated anymore. It's simply unsustainable to have more than 8-10 direct reports under a leader. That's why we introduced 2-3 Heads of Sales responsible for different regions or customer segments under our VP of Sales.

To head our current growing organization, and to get us from €10 million to €100 million ARR, we hired Kenneth, a leader with yet another profile. We needed someone who had lived through the process of growth and international expansion, who can explain the fine details of sales and sales training to me. In addition to knowing the sales business and representing our company to external stakeholders, leadership skills and internal communication had also become more important, both upward to the board and downward to our team. Our sales leader needed to be able to articulate a vision, develop a strategy, stand in front of 200 people or a round of accomplished investors and convince and inspire them.

— Michael Wax, Co-Founder & CEO, Forto

A typical B2B sales organization goes through four successive phases:

1. Founder sales
2. Sales Team phase
3. Sales Management phase
4. Specialization phase

In the following, let's look at the four phases one by one.

1. Founder sales

As we've emphasized in our discussion on product/market fit in Chapter 3, doing founder sales is simply mandatory in the *Explore & Learn* phase.

The sales organization in this stage couldn't be more straightforward: you do everything sales. Period.

Founder Sales

Founder

In our experience, you and your co-founders need to run the complete process and pipeline until you have a minimum of 10 customers before you have sufficient insight into the key dynamics of the market.

> In the early days of Northvolt, both me and my co-founder Paolo were out there meeting our key customers. We continue to put a lot of effort in maintaining those relationships.
>
> **— Peter Carlsson, Co-Founder & CEO, Northvolt**

To put it another way, don't proceed into the next stage before you know

- the most promising entry points into your target companies (especially the typical roles Champions hold),
- the most effective communication channels,
- the positioning and messaging that drives the highest interest with your Champions,

- your customers' typical price sensitivity and key competitors,
- the key triggers and ways to handle objections in order to close contracts.

2. Sales Team phase

The second phase of differentiating your sales organization starts when you hire specialized sales professionals for the first time: Analysts, Sales Development Representatives (SDRs) and Account Executives (AEs).

The role of Sales Development Representatives (SDRs) is to identify new contacts and turn them into leads that your Account Executives (AEs) can then convert into customers. Analysts are a supportive role, specialized on researching new prospects in line with your ICP criteria.

Sales Team

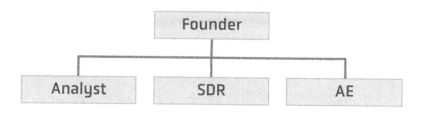

AE Account Executive   **SDR** Sales Development Representative

Again, you don't hire these people to do your groundwork for you or to take over the entire sales process immediately.

The objective of hiring these professionals is to gain support with key parts of the process, so that you have more time for personal discussions with your customers.

Priorities for your first team hires

Which experience and skill set you prioritize for your very first hires depends largely on the deal sizes that you are after.

If you are hunting Deers with smaller deal sizes, you will have to process hundreds or thousands of new leads per month. Because the sales cycles for Deers are short (typically 1-3 months), you need team members who contribute to fast lead generation and qualification to prevent your pipeline from drying up.

Hunting larger animals like Elephants and Whales (6 or 7-digit deals) means that you have a lower deal volume in your pipeline (only dozens or a few hundreds of new leads per month). To unlock revenue from selected large enterprise customers in longer sales cycles (3-12 months or longer), you need senior salespeople with strong experience and existing networks in the industry.

Looking at the stages of the sales pipeline, the new team members add value in different parts of the sales process.

- More junior analysts and sales development representatives (SDRs) free up your time by doing many of the repetitive steps in the beginning of the process.
- More senior account executives (AEs) help you with closing opportunities toward the middle and end of the process.

Startups with high-volume pipelines often choose to first hire a junior SDR to help them with lead generation and qualification.

These hires are relatively low-cost (€30,000 to €50,000 for a SDR with one or two years of experience). The big advantage of hiring such a junior: if the person works closely with you, the position is great for learning sales from the bottom up. That's why junior SDRs often move toward a more senior AE role after one to three years.

In one case, I first hired a junior guy whose job was to qualify the inbound leads by deal size. He then took over the small deals and sent the larger ones to me – so he was a SDR and a sales rep at the same time. After a while, we had figured out what companies spend how much on this kind of deal, and we had established a standardized sales process.

— **Paul Salazar, Head of Sales Central Europe, Couchbase**

The more leads you need to generate to fill your pipeline, the more helpful it is to hire an Analyst.

The responsibility of the Analyst role is to use the very first Prospect stage of the pipeline to generate a steady stream of new leads for the SDRs to qualify.

With a growing number of more advanced deals, or to convert a slower-moving pipeline with larger customers, it makes sense to directly hire an AE.

AEs are more senior sales roles. They help you by taking over the middle of the sales process. Often, you as a founder will hand over inbound leads to them to manage, and then jump in again at the very end to close the deal. Eventually, as the role title "Account Executive" indicates, the goal should be that the AE is the single primary contact for the customer over its entire lifetime. Owning the customer relationship is crucial to minimize handover friction between the different sales roles.

In our experience, for AEs to hit the road running, this person needs three to five years of experience, and will be a little more costly (expect to pay around €50,000 to €70,000).

The following table summarizes the transition from founder sales to a professional sales organization with each initial threshold.

	Prospect	Lead	Qualified Lead	Opport.	Customer	Customer Success
0-5 customers <€100K ARR	Founder	Founder	Founder	Founder	Founder	Founder
6-10 customers <€300K ARR	Analyst	SDR	Founder	Founder	Founder	Founder
11-15 customers <€500K ARR	Analyst	SDR	AE	AE	Founder	Founder

3. Sales Management phase

The threshold to the third phase is crossed when you delegate the management of the sales process entirely to a professional sales manager (and later management team). Along with growing team size, this entails introducing a rigorous people and performance management.

The job of these professional sales managers is to further professionalize the sales process and pipeline management.

In addition to your SDRs, AEs, and Analysts, a new role often enters the sales organization in the Sales Management phase: the Customer Success Manager (CSM). This role focuses on retention and customer growth after the customer is first closed.

At the same time, you might want to hire external support in addition to your Analysts to generate more prospects for your growing sales pipeline.

Taken together, you'll see the following specialization of roles along your sales process:

	Prospect	Lead	Qualified Lead	Opport.	Customer	Customer Success
16+ customers €1+ million ARR	Analyst/ Out- sourced	SDR	AE	AE	AE	Customer Success Manager (CSM)

Your organization chart at this point might look something like this:

Sales Management

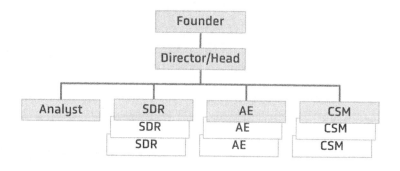

AE Account Executive   SDR Sales Development Representative   CSM Customer Success Manager

It makes sense to separate out CSMs as soon as there is a relevant pool of existing customers with opportunities to expand and upsell.

Role	Activity	KPIs	Experience & Skillset
Customer Success Manager (CSM)	Retaining and expanding customers	Lost revenue, expansion revenue	Senior – Service/ Sales

Hiring a CSM is a great way to focus on retention and customer growth early on. When introducing this role, carefully align the timing and the stage in the process where your AEs hand your customers over to your CSMs. Along those same lines, make sure to adjust your AEs' remuneration system for building long-term customer relationships.

For complex products with extensive onboarding processes, it's best practice to make AEs responsible for the customer relationship for the first 12 months after signing. For simpler products, this period can be reduced until the customer starts using this product, usually after one week to one month after signing.

If you fail to hold your AEs accountable for the time after closing the deal, there's a risk that they will "dump" the customer to your customer success team to build a long-term relationship. In practice, this often leads to a bad customer experience in the crucial first stage of the customer relationship. The key is to introduce a well-defined handover between sales and customer success, as Jonas Rieke explains:

Within Personio's teams, there is a clear cut between lead and customer. Once a lead is converted, Sales hands over the customer to Implementation and later Customer Service. The idea behind this is to create focus, to separate "hunters" (the Account Executives in Sales) from "farmers" (our Growth team). This clear cut between "hunting" and "farming" works well for us for two reasons:

- We take great care to get the incentives right, and we measure precisely which team and person is responsible for which contribution. For example, there is a clawback for customers who churn within 12 months to prevent Sales from closing unsustainable deals.
- In our industry, the HR sector, hunter and farmer characters aren't actually that far apart as they might be in other sectors. Our average hunter is less of a bloodhound and more of a relationship-builder.

— **Jonas Rieke, COO, Personio**

People management and organizational culture are paramount for the long-term success of your sales organization.

Starting from the *Explore & Learn* phase, make sure to set the right tone from the get-go by managing your first sales employees closely in a supporting and motivating way. The positive culture you will build in the sales team will directly transfer into your team's conversations with customers and hence into the broader market. Don't forget: your salespeople are your ambassadors. The public image of your company depends on them.

This also means that you start easy on your sales system and the goals that you set. As you well know from your own time selling as a founder, in the early stage there is no clear idea of right and wrong yet. A lot of information about the market is still missing, and it is very difficult to set targets. Aim to lead, motivate and manage by setting a positive example rather than strictly implementing a particular system and rigid quotas.

Moving into the *Standardize & Optimize* phase with a growing sales team, your management style will need to evolve. To achieve results, you now need to base your decisions and leadership on a clear set of KPIs, uphold tighter management, and exercise control through processes, meetings and systems.

In this field, modern US software sales systems are pushing the boundaries by following a granularly defined process, a detailed sales script design, pipeline and forecast management, and a single-minded focus on numbers and results. In our experience, having these systems in place is indeed a prerequisite for getting the best sales results, but they need to be balanced by a strong and positive-minded people management to avoid losing your top talents. Balancing both aspects will become an ongoing and never-ending challenge for you and your sales management talents.

Priorities for your first management hire

Your first sales management hire needs to be strong in all the areas that were your responsibility before: closing deals, accompanying, training and coaching the sales team, and generally leading by example.

"Hands-on" is the one attribute that came up over and over again in the interviews with successful founders:

> For the first sales management hire, the first attribute that comes to mind is "hands-on." The person needs to be a hunter, keen on closing deals. He or she needs the energy to push sales to a different level, to get things done.
>
> **— Avinoam Nowogrodski, Co-Founder & former CEO, Clarizen**

Paul Salazar, Head of Sales at Couchbase and himself a serial "first sales management hire," offers a detailed list of boxes to tick for this position:

> As a founder interviewing my first sales hire, I have five questions to ask:
>
> 1. **Can he or she sell?** Ask for proof of past sales success. Be aware that in a tech startup, the person needs to be sufficiently technically versed to engage in a meaningful conversation with a CTO or a CIO to be able to sell, and have the skill to actually close on his terms
> 2. **Can he or she manage other people?** Make it clear that you're looking for someone with experience in managing people, not projects, not channels, not partners. Managing people requires raw experiential knowledge of

how to hire a team, how to set up quotas, how to devise a compensation plan, how to hit targets. Challenge your candidate to give details about their past experience: "I set an €3.4million ACV target with a €6.8million multi-year target, divided on x people…" They should be able to rattle this off from the top of their head – otherwise, forget about them!

3. **Does he or she have some operational sophistication?** One of the first things they need to do on the job is to set up a CRM system, a structured compensation process, a clear pricing and discount strategy, and rules of engagement for reps to manage their territories. Without a proper operational process, you can't scale!

4. **What's his or her sales strategy?** Which customers do they plan to target, in which geography? How will they do forecasts? How will they generate and manage the lead flow coming in? They don't need to know it all, but should be able to state specific ideas, ideally based on hands-on experience, for these questions.

5. **Bonus question: Is he or she comfortable with legal processes?** It's a practical matter: For big contracts, you need serious contracts, real paper. So you've got to have a lawyer who is going to work with sales. The candidate's role is to understand the contracts at a sufficient level of depth, so that they can manage customer expectations, communicate the content of your contracts, and also stand up to unacceptable terms in customers' contracts. Every sales contract outlines the risks assumed by the customer and those by the vendor; knowing how much each side can bear is an experiential trait, something that is a huge bonus if you plan to have global enterprise companies.

— Paul Salazar, Head of Sales Central Europe, Couchbase

4. Specialization phase

In the Specialization phase, you start multiplying your sales organization from the Sales Management phase.

Instead of having one sales team composed of the roles described above, you now have two or more.

This also means that you will need a new level of leadership – like a Vice President of Sales (VP Sales) or a Chief Sales Officer (CSO) – to manage the different sales teams and their leaders. Assuming that your new sales teams focus on small and medium enterprises (SME) and enterprise sales, respectively, your organization chart might now look like this:

Sales Specialization

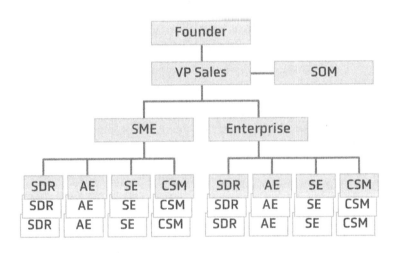

SDR Sales Development Representative   AE Account Executive   SOM Sales Operations Manager
CSM Customer Success Manager   SE Sales Engineer

In the organization chart, you'll notice some new roles supplementing your team: the Sales Operations Manager (SOM) and the Sales Engineer (SE). By providing cross-organizational support, these roles greatly add to the overall effectiveness of your teams.

SOMs (also called Sales Enablement Managers) help your VP Sales to further professionalize the sales team by continuously improving all aspects of the sales process. Ideally, SOMs gather and analyze actual sales data to leverage unused potential.

For example, they work on:

- Defining KPIs/metric reporting
- Developing sales materials
- Training and career planning of the team
- Designing compensation and commission systems
- Implementing and managing the tool environment (e.g. your CRM and sales support tools)
- Developing learning and knowledge management

SEs are very helpful when your product is so complex that AEs cannot necessarily answer all of your customers' questions regarding the technology anymore. Having SEs accompany your AEs to meetings and answer technical questions helps to keep discussions at eye-level, even in conversations with very specialized partners on the customer's side. Because this isn't relevant for every single customer, it's usually sufficient to have one SE support several AEs within a sales team.

Role	Activity	KPIs	Experience & Skillset
Sales Operations Manager (SOM)	Process optimization, tool enablement, commissioning	Lead times, Pipeline Velocity, Sales profitability	Senior - Analytical
Sales Engineers (SE)	Technical consulting	New revenue generated	Senior - Technical

In regard to your process, you'll find the following roles in each stage (or crossing several stages), respectively:

	Prospect	Lead	Qualified Lead	Opport.	Customer	Customer Success
€10+ million ARR	Analyst/ Out- sourced	SDR	AE	AE SE	AE	CSM
	SOM					

For entering the Specialization phase, the growing size of your organization alone can be a trigger:

> From 1-15 people, it's all about building structures, setting up operations and strategies, building the culture and style of the team. I am comfortable working this way: your work is very close to the customers, to the street.
>
> At 15-20 quota-carrying sales reps, you need to create a new organizational level. You need to break your team into segments because sales is so hands-on, you can't manage more than 4-5 people at once. I myself have been a manager of sales teams, but not a manager of managers of sales teams – that requires a new skill set.
>
> **— Paul Salazar, Head of Sales Central Europe, Couchbase**

Besides growing team size, other reasons for specializing can be the expansion into a new industry or a new geographical market.

The idea is that specialized teams have higher knowledge in a specific target industry or country, and thus achieve better conversion rates.

When you specialize your teams, it makes sense to pool your SDRs and AEs into dedicated teams or "pods" and specialize them on a particular segment, industry, or country.

Our sales teams are organized around small pods that are specialized in talking about a specific customer problem. Some pods focus on hotels in a certain country. Others specialize in small customers, or big customers.

The pods are a great structure for us because those small units of people work together very well. It also works well because for us, there is no single access to the customer – if there were, we would just need a big sales team focused on one particular task. Instead, once we develop a new focus, the small pods can quickly move to the new customer segment.

— Ben Stephenson, Co-Founder & CEO, Impala

In contrast, because of their more generally applicable skillsets, your Analyst and CSM team members can still be utilized across pods. This may change if your specialization narrows even further.

Overall, the decision on how to specialize or segment your sales teams depends entirely on your sales organization's goals. Sometimes, with very different business models, you might even need to create separate organizations within your own company:

We have two very different sales organizations:

Our laser scanning device business unit is pretty straightforward – we sell hardware and software to surveying and engineering offices. We do this through localized sales pods. These are functionally separate units that include technical support, customer success and SDR resources in addition to the sales representatives. Localization turned out to be crucial: if we send a German speaker to France, they won't sell anything.

Our enterprise sales business sells solutions for specific use cases. It's also localized, but focused on mega-accounts, with long sales cycles and ticket sizes of 6-7 figures per year. It's crucial to approach these customers at the right strategic level – in the past, I have used some of my old McKinsey contacts to get a foot into the door. We developed our own workshop formats to help customers find the greatest value levers for them. Our overall sales approach here is very solution-oriented and requires a lot of consulting and custom engineering resources. We also need to include external partners for system integration and have to deal with issues like IT compliance and certification processes.

— **Felix Reinshagen, Co-Founder & CEO, NavVis**

Despite all advantages of specialization: take care not to specialize too early.

In their overall drive for specialization, we often see startups who organize lead generation away from sales into a separate marketing department. However, prior to generating €10 million in revenue in a proven sales process, instead of generating additional efficiency, this risks breaking the necessary iteration cycles to find the ideal customer.

Another typical risk is to separate customer success responsibilities too early. As explained above, maintaining the AEs focus on successful onboarding and customer satisfaction for as long as possible mitigates the risk of a devil-may-care signing attitude.

How to manage your sales team

As soon as you move into the Sales Team phase, and even more after you have entered the Sales Management phase, it is important to structure your team's week in a regular manner.

We have seen three types of meetings that founders and sales managers institutionalize on a weekly basis: forecasting meetings, one-on-one meetings, and customer meetings.

1. Forecasting meetings

In forecasting meetings, the entire sales team comes together to share their respective forecasts for the month or quarter (depending on the primary period you have chosen for managing your sales).

Based on the inputs into the CRM and the resulting forecasting report, these meetings will give your team a good sense on the most important question: whether or not the team and therefore the company will reach the target revenue in the current period.

Use this meeting not only to reflect the status quo, but to discuss what hurdles need to be crossed to convert each opportunity, and how you, your sales leadership or other parts of your organization can help to overcome them. Focus on deriving concrete actions that will drive your team to hit its target.

2. One-on-one meetings

The second category of meetings are one-on-one meetings between you or your sales leaders and the respective SDRs and AEs. The purpose of these personal meetings is to review and evaluate your team members' individual performance in the period and beyond, both in comparison with the targets set and relative to the performance of their peers.

Use these meetings to have a transparent and direct discussion about the personal strengths and weaknesses that drive your team member's performance. Be constructive, but don't beat around the bush if your team member is not meeting their targets while others do. Granted, these conversations are not exactly pleasant, you are neither doing them nor you a favor by sugarcoating (ongoing) failure.

Again, for the success of these meetings, it is essential to focus on deriving specific follow-up actions: for example, to offer additional training and coaching to low performers, or to ask your high performers to mentor other team members.

3. Customer meetings

The third category is customer meetings. There are two kinds of meetings that you or your sales leadership are primarily involved in: meetings at your customer's initiative (inbound contacts) and meetings based on your initiative (outbound sales).

Meetings at the customer's initiative happen when a large or otherwise important potential customer approaches you or one of your AEs. In this situation, it's advisable to show the appropriate attention and commitment from your side by participating in the first meeting personally, together with your team member. After the meeting, you can decide if it makes sense to hand over the follow-up process to your AE.

Meetings at your initiative, in turn, happen when your AE invites you or your sales leaders to come along to their customer meetings. Again, this serves to demonstrate strong commitment toward that particular potential customer. In the Customer stage of the sales process, you might also need to come along to the negotiation meetings to contribute the necessary seniority.

Sales versus non-sales activities

Forecasting meetings usually last for around one or two hours. Assuming that you or your sales leaders each manage a team of five to 10 people, completing all your one-on-one meetings should not take longer than half a day to a day.

If you want to drive your business forward, prioritize customer meetings over all other meetings in terms of time spent. In the Sales Team phase, we recommend that you and your sales leaders allocate at least 80% or four days of your time toward customer meetings. In the Sales Management phase, customer meetings should still take up at least 60% or three days of your time.

Operational sales team members, such as AEs and SDRs, should spend maximum half a day a week on non-sales activities, such as forecasting and one-on-one meetings. The rest of their week should be productive time with customers. And just in case someone asks: data entry into the CRM is considered productive time ...

How to hire and fire

We received many applications from big IT corporations – none of these people were any good for us. They were more or less used to doing a different kind of sales. In our startup, they didn't have a team, they didn't have sales engineers, they had to do everything themselves.

In fact, we tried hiring a VP of Sales more than once, but it never really worked out in the early years. One focused exclusively on creating structures and processes that everyone had to follow. Another one hired a bunch of people and then withdrew entirely from active sales, only to intervene (unsuccessfully) in important negotiations.

Maybe this explains why I'm an advocate for sticking with founder sales for a long time.

— Jörg G. Beyer, Co-Founder & Co-CEO, LeanIX

Hiring the right people may be the greatest challenge in building a successful sales organization.

Most founders struggle more with recruiting people for sales roles than with recruiting for other roles (for example in marketing or product development). In our view, there are two reasons for this:

- Many founders don't have a clear image of what a sales person actually does. Therefore, they can't define a clear profile of who they're looking for (by reading this book, you've excluded that reason).
- Salespeople are black boxes: before you actually see their results on the job, it's extremely hard to evaluate whether a candidate is a good salesperson or not.

Both factors result in a very high percentage of hiring misses and turnover in sales teams. A rate of failed hires and turnover of 30%, respectively, is not at all unusual in sales. This is extremely costly – especially in case of leadership roles.

One of the things I wouldn't do again is hire very late-stage people who know exactly where we should be 10 years from now – but don't know how to get there from here. I would only hire people who have seen what our current stage looked like.

— Nicolas Dessaigne, Co-Founder & Board Member, Algolia

That's why we advocate for clearly defining what you actually want very early in the process of building your sales organization.

Pro-actively seek the help of experienced sales managers – for example among your business angels or investors – in order to interview and select candidates. The earlier you know what you want, the more you can focus on scouting for the right people.

In the following part of this chapter, we've gathered some of our own advice and collective founder wisdom on finding (and winning) the right people for your sales team.

Who to hire for your sales team

Although SDRs and AEs together constitute the core of your sales team, their roles have a different focus:

- **For SDRs,** it's crucial to have high energy and be self-motivated. They need to be able to take a lot of "nos" while learning about and adapting to different personas.
- **For AEs,** the core competence is to be able to create trust and strong customer relationships while immersing themselves into the needs and detailed context of your customers (in addition to their technical skills, this is also required of SEs, who you'll need for selling a technologically complex product).

Translated into selection criteria for each role, this results in the following typical profiles for SDRs and AEs.

Note that these requirements are not meant to be spelled out literally in a job description. Instead, look for tangible proof, either in numbers, in references from their former employers, or through case studies or roleplay during your recruiting process.

	Sales Development Representative	Account Executive
Qualification	1-2 years of experience Bachelor's degree	3-5 years of experience Bachelor's/Master's degree
On target earnings (OTE)	€30,000-€50,000	€50,000-€70,000 for a Junior AE €90,000-€200,000 for a Senior AE

	Sales Development Representative	Account Executive
Personality	High energy and self-motivated	High energy and results-focused
	Very strong communication skills (phone, email, social media)	Very strong communication and presentation skills
	Strong desire to win	Strong desire to win
	High level of integrity	Understands and optimizes sales methodologies
	Amicable and engaging with customers	Able to develop trust and lasting customer relationships
	Learns fast and has innovative ideas	Willing to dive deep into product and technology with customers
		Open to mentorship and coaching
Teamwork skills	Collaborates with distributed internal sales and marketing teams	Collaborates with internal teams including product and technology
	Effectively uses core sales tools (Salesforce, LinkedIn Sales Navigator etc.) and processes	Effectively uses and optimizes core sales tools (Salesforce, LinkedIn Sales Navigator etc.) and processes
Proven experience	Not mandatory	Worked in market segment with similar target ARR, product complexity and target buyer level
		Demonstrated success in qualifying, pursuing and closing sales opportunities
		Exceeded monthly, quarterly and annual quotas

Beyond experience and skills, there's another line of thought worth following: How well do your new hires fit into your startup's culture?

Peter Carlsson, co-founder and CEO of Northvolt, takes a holistic perspective on recruiting and framed the right attitude as a matter of personal culture and background:

> When building a new company, focus on recruiting and on building culture. Your culture and the speed of your operation are the single most important competitive advantages you have versus bigger and more established companies.
>
> In refining our recruitment strategy, we also reviewed very critically which people integrated best into our culture. It turned out that hands-on people from fast-growing companies – those who knew how to build the rails in front of the train – integrated the best: they had done the journey before and were not afraid of taking ownership. On the other hand, we had huge integration problems with people from established companies: they were just not used to defining their own processes, and were totally lost.
>
> **— Peter Carlsson, Co-Founder & CEO, Northvolt**

Moritz Zimmermann of Hybris cites another reason for a cultural mismatch. He suggests building your team up from the ground up as a possible solution – a solution that many startups have successfully used to build their own sales teams.

> Many corporate salespeople are spoiled by large commissions for easy-to-hit quotas. They are used to earning a lot and spending a lot, so they aren't likely to join a startup. That's why it's so

important for a startup to use fresh talent, and to invest heavily in training.

— **Moritz Zimmermann, Co-Founder &**
former CTO, Hybris

How to get experienced salespersons to join your startup

Especially if your startup focuses on Elephants or Whales with large deal sizes, you might feel that you need experienced salespeople with figurative (or actual) "grey hair" to appear credible in front of your big clients.

In this case, you wouldn't be the first founder to find yourself in a bind:

How to convince salespersons at such a senior level to join your young, potentially unproven startup and (let's face it) take the inevitable pay cut?

This is exactly the situation NavVis was in at the beginning. As Felix Reinshagen tells their story, sometimes you are able to catch the right people at the right time:

> To make sure our sales was top-notch from the start, we decided to hire two old sales hands. Normally, a startup wouldn't have been able to afford this caliber. But we caught them in a sweet spot: at 50+ years, they had already reached the top in their career, making billions of revenue for big corporations.
>
> However, these guys weren't just executive sales managers who were most comfortable looking at dashboards in their corner office – keep away from those people!

Instead, looking back at their long career in sales, our guys had found that the field work – getting to know people, creating value for the customers and their company – was what they had enjoyed most. Selling is their life. And for us, seeing how well they read people, watching them navigate any environment comfortably, is incredibly inspiring.

— **Felix Reinshagen, Co-Founder & CEO, NavVis**

Depending on your market niche, you might not even have a choice. This is often the case if you're dealing with traditionally conservative, established industries. You might need to simply need to bite the bullet and consider the expenses for these sales veterans as an investment in your success like any other.

To fill our first sales roles, we brought in highly skilled, senior technical salespeople with strong project management credentials. Of course, those people come at a high price, and most startups would shy away from executive pay at this early stage. But for us, this was a crucial part of our success. Consider that at this time, we had just four or five critical relationships. You don't need many salespeople to maintain those relationships.

— **Peter Carlsson, Co-Founder & CEO, Northvolt**

In the face of the challenges in hiring for leadership positions in your organization, Peter Carlsson has further advice on investing in people:

The mindset I brought back from Tesla was: if you want to build a world-class company, you can't just look at the local labor market.

It was very costly for us as a startup to help world-class people transition to our local setting, but this investment was worth every cent.

— **Peter Carlsson, Co-Founder & CEO, Northvolt**

Who to hire for your sales leadership

Hiring leadership roles for your sales team is even harder than hiring team members – and the chance to fail in your investment is higher, too.

More than for any other sales role, we recommend getting expert help to interview and select candidates for your sales leadership.

The key to minimizing the risk of a mishire is to understand exactly which phase of organizational buildup you're currently in and what requirements your leader must to fulfill.

For our purposes, we have boiled down Jason Lemkin's classic "48 Types of VP Sales" into the leadership archetypes for three different phases:

Leadership types / Organizational phase	Key activities	Key responsibilities
The Founder Founder sales and SDR & AE phase (€100,000 to €1 million ARR)	80% Doing 20% Building	• Creation of process, pipeline and frameworks

The Builder Sales Management phase (€1-10 million ARR)	50% Doing 50% Building	• Professionalization of process, pipeline and frameworks • Hiring talent and firing underperformers • Coaching and training
The Optimizer Specialization phase (€10+ million ARR)	20% Doing 80% Managing	• Professionalization of metrics, reporting and compensation • Creation of career plan and sales academy

In our experience, the transition from Founder to Builder is the most challenging task in growing your sales organization.

The single most important requirement of the Builder is that he or she has a strong understanding of how to build a sales system and team from the ground up within a fast-changing and ambiguous context. In this way, the Builder is an entrepreneur himself/herself.

One mistake we often see is that founders attempt to hire or promote successful salespeople into a management role.

However, the best sales person isn't necessarily the best leader:

Once I was hired as the first sales person in the company, my job was to both close deals *and* build a team. That means management responsibility! Founders should be aware that not all salespeople want to assume a management role, and that not all managers want to run deals hands-on for the first six or twelve months. But you need both for your first sales professional.

— Paul Salazar, Head of Sales Central Europe, Couchbase

The same is true for hiring senior sales leaders from "big logos" into the role of the Builder.

Most of the time, sales professionals from big corporations are Optimizers rather than Builders.

They almost always lack the ability to lead the sales process by example and create a working system from scratch. More than one of our founder experts used the label of "dashboard builder" to warn about sales professionals too far removed from the hands-on business:

It's impossible to bring someone from SAP's or Oracle's management into the job. These people are great at building dashboards – but in a startup, there's nothing yet to show!

— Avinoam Nowogrodski, Co-Founder &
former CEO, Clarizen

There's nothing wrong with being an Optimizer rather than a Builder. But for the first person you hire to lead your sales activities in your startup, the willingness and desire to get their hands dirty and lead by example is a cornerstone of their profile.

You'll want someone like Paul Salazar, who has long years of experience taking over at the point where the founder hands over sales leadership. Paul has made it a habit to jump right into the thick of it:

The first thing I do in a new job is to immediately step into the existing pipeline and work on owning the ongoing deals as soon as possible. Briefings are important, but the quickest and most effective way to learn is to get on calls, on a plane, on the road, as soon as possible. I need to look into the customers' eyes, take the temperature of the room, see the reactions.

— Paul Salazar, Head of Sales Central Europe, Couchbase

In the following table, we have summarized the key requirements for hiring a Builder (any role from Director to VP and CSO/CRO).

	Area of experience	Detail
Qualification level	Minimum 5 years of experience	2-3 years doing and 2-3 years managing doers in competitive markets, with software deal sizes in the sought-for range, both outbound and inbound sales
Compensation	€100,000-€200,000	
Personality	Leadership	Likes and knows how to recruit, inspire and lead a high-performing sales team Brings both strong interpersonal skills and a structured approach to people development
Personality	Leadership	Leads by example: knows you can't manage a team if she/he doesn't do the groundwork and closes deals her/himself Optional: attracts further exceptional team members through strong positive aura
	Sales	Likes and knows how to negotiate with and win business and enterprise customers Is eager to overperform and to enable the team to overperform Has a highly energetic, outgoing sales character and more hunter than farmer experience

	Area of experience	Detail
Professional skills	Sales	Handles setbacks well and shows stamina
		Has a confident and experienced appearance in front of C-level decision-makers
		Is ambitious, eager to travel and manage key accounts
		Is happy and curious to dive deep into the technical aspects of a product
		Has worked in a successful sales culture
	Marketing	Is able to take responsibility for continuous lead generation (e.g. outbound sales lead generation and performance marketing)
		Has marketing capabilities in terms of selling and steering product positioning
	Specialized experience (also depending on your market)	Has experience in your target geography
		Is fluent in your company language and English
		Has excellent organizational and project management skills
		Has effective verbal and written communication skills
		Optional: has experience in your industry
		Optional: understands modern product architectures
Track record	Leadership	Has recruited, developed and coached 5-10 people
		May have led new customer acquisition as Head of/Director instead of leading the entire sales team (as VP Sales/CSO)
	Sales	Had a similar revenue target level per year in the past (e.g. €10 million or €50 million of new ARR)
		Has sold complex software products to enterprise customers in the sought-for revenue range in your industry
		Has sold to functional, product and IT teams, including pitching to Head/Director and C-level

	Area of experience	Detail
	Building	Has worked in high-growth environments (e.g. a successful Series B startup or a smaller SME with strong revenue growth) rather than in an established large organization
	Building	Has structured sales organizations (process, system, documentation, etc.) so that winning customers became repeatable Can communicate well in accurate reporting and forecasts
Culture fit		Understands that she/he works for a startup (is able to deal with uncertainty) Truly believes in the product and vision
Other assets		Can contribute her/his own network (for potential customers and key hires)

When to let underperformers go

> Only every fifth person we hired in sales worked out well. These people stayed and took on more responsibility over the years, while the others left or were let go.
>
> However, all things considered, the high churn rate in sales was our own fault. We could have prevented two thirds of churn by just training people better. And the last third, those cases where the people were just not cut out for it, were our fault too: we should have had better selection processes in recruiting!
>
> **— Alex Meyer, Co-Founder & Partner, 42CAP**

While Alex Meyer is right (and very humble) in pointing out possible avenues to mitigate a high turnover in sales, the fact remains across all stages of your sales organization: it is extremely hard to hire the right salespeople.

The only thing that helps you under these circumstances is again to have a clear definition of what you want in your sales professionals – because this also helps you to determine quickly when a sales hire has *not* been successful.

Identifying underperformers as early as possible and then letting them go is often easier than trying to recruit the right people from the start.

If you are just starting to build the team, in fact, we recommend to hire two candidates for the same role. By pitting them up against each other, you are able to identify the better-performing person, who you will then keep at the end of the notice period.

If that sounds hard – it is. And it often goes against the naturally strong team spirit in a startup. But being tough on underperformers is simply necessary.

It's extremely important to let go of employees who don't sell. This is one of the hardest things I've had to learn as a founder. They will always find good reasons why they haven't been successful! That's why you need to find a way to measure their performance objectively.

> In our device business, where sales cycles are 2-3 months and you see results fast, this is easier. In the enterprise business where sales cycles can last up to 18 months, measuring success is an art rather than a science. But we benchmark against other successful colleagues and trust our intuition: do they follow up fast after meetings? How many points of contact are there, do they enter into dialogues? If these indicators don't look good, we let them go. This applies to about one-third of all new hires in the 6-months probation period.
>
> **— Felix Reinshagen, Co-Founder & CEO, NavVis**

15 - REMUNERATION

How to motivate your sales team

How much do your team members contribute to the success of the company? That's hard to quantify for each individual in the product or technology department. Here the whole is more than the sum of its parts, and simply counting hours at work or lines of code written doesn't mean anything.

For your sales team, you can actually quantify each individual's impact to the success of your company.

You can count how many sales activities each member of your sales team completed, and more importantly, how much revenue they brought in for your startup. That's why it makes sense particularly for your sales team to reward them (partially) based on their contribution to your company's success.

Introducing variable pay for your sales team isn't just good practice simply because it's feasible. It's actually great because it feeds directly into the motivation of your team. It also helps to align the individual targets with your company targets.

In fact, the best sales talents are the ones who are the most competitive.

They are as eager to beat their peers as they are to beat their own past performance. Because they like to have numbers to prove that they are the best, they take pride in the measurement of their performance and results.

How to set the basic parameters of your remuneration system

Building a compensation plan is an art – but it's at the base of every sales organization.

— **Avinoam Nowogrodski, Co-Founder & former CEO, Clarizen**

Fixed and variable remuneration

The power of a good remuneration system for your sales team lies in the combination of fixed and variable compensation parts for each member of the sales team.

The fixed part of the remuneration reflects your team member's basic salary. It is usually oriented toward the lower end of a similarly qualified role in marketing or product teams.

The variable component of your team member's remuneration varies in relation to their contribution to your company's goals. Sales team members who perform strongly should earn significantly more than their peers in other functions. That's how it becomes the key motivation driver for your salespeople.

In fact, because commissions are such a powerful motivational driver, we strongly recommend that all team members who contribute to the success of the sales process receive a variable salary component. Beyond your immediate sales team, this specifically includes team members in marketing focused on prospect or lead generation.

Every sales role in our organization has variable compensation. Our sales reps are measured by closed deals that are assigned to this individual. The directors are measured by their respective team's performance. SDRs are measured by demos scheduled. And our demand managers are measured by the entire ARR.

— **Jörg Beyer, Co-Founder & former Co-CEO, LeanIX**

The following table shows a typical remuneration package that combines fixed parts (the basic salary) and variable parts (the commission).1 Both remuneration components combined are called on-target earnings (OTE) because they're only paid out if the team member hits his or her sales target.

	Basic salary	Commission	On-target earnings (OTE)
SDR remuneration package	€40,000	€10,000	€50,000
% based on basic salary	100%	25%	125%
% based on OTE	80%	20%	100%

When you talk about your remuneration system, be clear about what you base your percentages on: basic salary or OTE. We will refer to the basic salary as 100%, which implies that commissions are a bonus to be earned.

---

i   Note that there are other variable components of remuneration that have a more long-term view and can therefore be applied more widely across all your team members, such as employee stock option programs (ESOPs). This is another highly relevant topic, but we won't focus on this as part of this book.

Ratio of fixed vs. variable remuneration

The ratio of fixed vs. variable pay varies widely across different countries. Companies in the USA and the United Kingdom allocate a higher part of their salaries as variable pay than companies in Continental Europe. Consider this when you set up your pay system to make sure you attract the top talents in your market.

> In the early days, nobody got variable compensation. It just wasn't necessary because all our salespeople were intrinsically motivated. But when we expanded to the US, where salespeople are used to variable compensation, we had to transition to a variable system globally to treat everyone fairly.
>
> **— Jörg G. Beyer, Co-Founder & former Co-CEO, LeanIX**

The variable part of the remuneration generally increases by the level of seniority. The idea behind this is to align the incentives of your team members and leaders with the goals of the company: the more responsibility your team members have for your revenue growth, the higher will their personal reward be if they are successful.

To begin with, we recommend setting the variable part to 20-40% of the basic salary, based on the level of seniority.

A variable part of less than 20% is too small to have much of an impact on your team members' motivation at all. In contrast, with variable parts above 40%, you run the risk that your salespeople focus more on closing the deal at all cost instead of starting a long-term relationship with your customer. The resulting race for closing deals also endangers the team spirit within the sales team.

Of course, with time you'll learn what ratios work best for your team and product. Once you move into the *Standardize & Optimize* phase, you might also try to experiment with larger variable allocations.

The following table shows examples for different ratios and on-target earnings for different roles and seniority levels in your sales organization.

	Basic salary	Commission/ bonus	On-target earnings (OTE)
Account Executive	€50,000	€20,000	€70,000
	100%	40%	140%
Head/Director	€100,000	€50,000	€150,000
	100%	50%	150%
VP/CSO/CRO	€150,000	€150,000	€300,000
	100%	100%	200%

Level of on-target earnings

In the beginning, try to adjust your team's on-target earnings to about 20-25% of this team's target revenue contribution.

Or to turn the calculation around: an AE with an OTE of €50,000 should generate 4-5 times her annual remuneration, or €200,000 to 250,000 in ARR.

Orienting the OTE toward the revenue you expect to make can be difficult if you are just starting out and don't know what realistic results look like, both in terms of the actual performance of your team and what your market can support.

Generally speaking, the efficiency of AEs is lower in more competitive markets (USA or United Kingdom) than in Europe. The efficiency of your AEs also depends on the maturity of the product domain and geographic market: more established markets allow for shorter lead times, which makes the job of your AEs easier.

Once you have more experience with setting realistic overall revenue targets, you can (carefully!) adjust the OTEs for new hires accordingly.

Whenever you adjust the system: take care to keep the ratios fair across your entire sales organization. Any change toward the advantage of one group only will seriously demotivate the other members of the team. In particular, don't neglect the supporting sales roles over the focus on AEs as your immediate deal closers.

As you plan and implement changes to the system, always keep a close eye on the (possible) effects on your top performers to make sure your new system works well for them. To make sure you don't accidentally demotivate them, it's best practice to play through the results of previous periods in a spreadsheet simulation to see how individual payouts would be changed under the new system.

Timing of variable remuneration payments

To determine the variable remuneration payments for each team member, naturally you need to define a certain time period for which you measure their success against your targets.

If you're just starting out, it's good practice to organize both target setting and commission payouts on a quarterly basis.

Because targets will necessarily be more guesswork the less data you initially have, a quarterly target gives you enough time to observe and evaluate the work of your sales team. Then you can set more precise targets next time. This helps you to avoid overly high or low sales targets (and the according overpayment or underpayment of your sales team).

Setting a quarterly target and organizing commission payouts on this schedule also is a good rhythm if your business model depends on a smaller number of larger deals that take longer to close. In contrast, if your startup focuses on smaller deals that your sales team can close faster, you don't have to wait three months to evaluate each member's success. Instead, start setting monthly targets as soon as possible to keep motivation high.

I want us to run like we have 12 year ends. I want that energy running through us all the time. If we have that level of rigor and focus, we're proactive on the data, and don't wait two and a half months each quarter to do something with it. We're in a fast-growth market, which means we're probably not alone in it. It's a race, and we have to run faster than everyone else.

— **Neil Ryland, Chief Revenue Officer, Peakon**

Like any tight deadlines, the motivational effect of shorter timelines for your sales targets can be huge.

If it's feasible for your business model at all, try setting shorter target timeframes as soon as you have enough data to substantiate these targets. This will create a more regular "closing rush" for your team members and keep the adrenaline flowing.

Set your quotas and pay out commissions quarterly, or even better, monthly, to keep everyone busy all the time. You'll see that in the final two weeks of the quarter, all the deals will be closed. If your dealflow allows for doing it monthly, that's a big advantage for your startup!

— **Avinoam Nowogrodski, Co-Founder &**
former CEO, Clarizen

Setting a tighter schedule for targets and payouts also prevents your AEs from a particular way of "gaming the system": pushing deals to the next quarter if they have already fulfilled their target for the current one, in order to have a better chance to reach their bonus in the next quarter.

Additional rules

Part of the art of setting up a successful remuneration system is to implement additional rules that maintain fairness and motivation in specific situations.

One typical question concerns customer cancellations and whether you should implement clawback rules as part of your remuneration system.

On the one hand, you want to avoid a devil-may-care attitude among your salespeople, where they work toward signing customers indifferently of whether they actually want or need your solution. On the other hand, implementing clawbacks – the reduction of commission payouts if the customer cancels in a certain period after signing the deal – can be highly demotivating for your team.

In our experience, it's favorable to make full commission payments only once the customer is onboarded and live, perhaps even to wait until the revenue is in the bank. Particularly if you have long onboarding and payment cycles, this is not always what your sales team wants or feels is fair – but the strong impact of this policy on your team's efforts for high customer retention should override those concerns, and pushes your organization on the whole toward minimizing onboarding and payment cycles.

If you see a disproportionately high rate of customer cancellations, it could be your incentives – but it could also be your product or your sales process. Rather than just implementing clawback rules, we strongly advise getting to the bottom of this and fixing the underlying reason for your cancellations (for example a single AE who tends to overpromise when closing deals). That's much better than permanently frustrating your entire sales team.

Another question that founders face is how to deal with variable remuneration in the ramp-up period for new hires.

In the first time after joining your startup, new team members naturally won't be as productive as established members of your sales team. They need to ramp up knowledge and experience within the new context first before they start generating results for your organization. This can take anywhere between one and three months.

To be fair, make sure to manage their expectations and let them know they will be earning the fixed part of the remuneration only during this period. Alternatively, you might also want to initially incentivize your new hires based on activities rather than their contribution to revenue generation. This will help them to generate at least part of their commission and support their ramp-up process. Their line manager should define which goals specifically they need to fulfill in this case.

How to implement your remuneration system

Calculating the variable remuneration

There are two basic ways of calculating the variable part of your sales team's remuneration:

- **Fixed commission** - In this system, you pay out a fixed amount for each completed activity (e.g. €10 for each demo scheduled by a SDR) or a fixed percentage of the revenue signed (e.g. 3% of the MRR generated by an AE).
- **Percentage of target** - Following this approach, the variable payment is based on the percentage of the revenue and/or other targets that your sales team member has achieved.

The fixed commission system has the advantage of simplicity in setting it up initially. There are few questions about how to measure and pay out the variable remuneration. However, this advantage disappears when you consider the numerous changes your metrics and targets will go through during your journey from €100,000 to €1 million, €10 million, and €100 million in revenue. Maintaining and adjusting these parameters over time frequently turns out to be a major hassle, with lots of potential for discontent in your team.

For this reason, we recommend implementing a system where the variable remuneration is calculated based on the percentage of the target your sales team member has achieved. Most systems of this kind are measured and communicated on the basis of a traffic-light system:

- Green: Target achievement of 100% and more
- Amber: Target achievement of 80-99%
- Red: Target achievement of below 80%

This three-tiered system makes it easy for everyone to understand and compare the overall performance of the company, the teams and the individual team members. While everybody will still have their individual targets, your team members have a clear mission of which bracket they want to be in at the end of the month or quarter. This directly drives the energy within your sales team.

For you as founder and for your managers, the target-based system has the added advantage that it can easily accommodate changes in your KPIs and the target levels for each individual. For example, you can simply increase the revenue targets for individual team members if you find that your sales process has become more efficient – but the team members will still strive for the same green bracket of your achievement percentage system.

Let's look at an example for an AE target (or "quota") in the table below. For this individual AE, "New ARR" is the single key performance indicator. The example shows that the AE will have to generate a minimum of €80,000 ARR per quarter to enjoy any commission payment at all. At the other end of the spectrum, her variable payout is open-ended if she substantially overachieves her target of €100,000 ARR.

New ARR target		On-target commission	
per year	€400,000	per year	€20,000
per quarter	€100,000	per quarter	€5,000

Target achievement	red	amber	green	green
in %	<79%	80-99%	100-119%	>120%
ARR	€0 - €79,999	€80,000 - €99,999	€100,000 - €119,999	€120,000 - unlimited
Commission payment	€0	€4,000 - €4,999	€5,000 - €5,999	€6,000 - unlimited

Managing achievement levels

The overall and the individual achievement levels in your sales organization give you important feedback for managing your sales organization. If your team or individual members continuously overshoot or underachieve their targets, you should definitely investigate the root cause.

Across a sales team, achievements levels should usually be anywhere between 80-120% most of the time.

It's normal for the top performers in your teams to achieve more than 100% for most quarters – but if achievements are above 100% across the entire team all the time, chances are you just set your targets too low.

Inversely, if achievement levels are below 80% across the entire team too often, your sales team members will start to think that the target is unrealistic (and they will probably be right). The effect is the same: if they can't reach the target anyway, why bother? Sales efficiency will go down in this case as well.

Identify consistent individual underperformance fast and act on it.

Under normal circumstances, any team member who performs under 80% receives no commission payout, and has a strong incentive to shape up. If they are still new, it's your job to give them the chance to do so through sales training or mentorship. If the situation continues, however, act fast and let them go within three to 6 months at the latest.

Acting on an individual's underperformance requires, of course, that you are sure this underperformance is due to the team member's capabilities rather than the company or product context. Usually, the team benchmark is a good indicator if that's the case.

Carefully consider the effect of financial incentive mechanisms for individual overperformance beyond 100% or 120%.

Some companies implement "accelerators" to further reward achievements above 100% or 120%. This means that the commission payout increases disproportionately once the overachievement level of 120% is hit. The goal of these mechanisms is to motivate their top performers to keep going even after achieving their OTE.

For our example of the AE with the "New ARR" target, an accelerator for an achievement above 120% could be that you pay €7,000 instead of €6,000 if your AE reaches 120% of her ARR target (€120,000).

We recommend using accelerator mechanisms only in the *Standardize & Optimize* phase of your sales organization, where the overall system and target setting is more established.

Setting targets

Your sales targets are the basis for any decision on commission payments and individual evaluations. That's why the targets you set aren't just at the core of your remuneration system, they are also a cornerstone for managing your sales team in general.

It's crucial that you get your targets right to keep your sales team highly motivated and performing.

Put another way: Nothing is more demotivating than "management" (in a startup, that's you!) handing down unrealistic targets period after period. Unattainable targets are one of the largest triggers for top sales talents to look for new challenges elsewhere.

At its basis, your variable remuneration system should be driven by simplicity.

When you set a target, include only a limited number of target KPIs, and make sure you know the variables that influence them.

If you have no history or data on a particular KPI, and can only make a wild guess on what could be happening, this KPI does not make for a good target to base commission payments on.

For your startup's own financial safety, only use KPIs that trigger payouts when you have a minimum amount of history on them in your system, and you are sure they don't vary wildly over time.

KPIs that are usually well-understood and simple to calculate are:

- **Activities** (e.g. number of calls, emails, meetings, demos, offers sent out)
- **Ratios** (e.g. number of activities per Opportunity or Contract closed)
- **New Revenue signed**
- **New MRR** (vs. New One-off revenue)
- **Average Contract Value**

Especially in the *Explore & Learn* phase, create separate targets for individuals and teams to foster team cohesion, learning and collaboration.

While activities are best measured individually, separating individual and team targets is particularly helpful for revenue-related KPIs. In any case, make sure to put the emphasis on the individual performance. For example, base >70% of the individual team member's commission on the individual achievement level, and the remaining <30% on the achievement of the team goals. Otherwise, you risk your top performers leaving frustrated because they feel too "dragged down" by new or less strongly performing team members.

Apart from KPIs on revenue-generating activities and results, make sure to establish organizational "must-dos" as a prerequisite for your commission payouts.

This has the simple but powerful background that you don't want your salespeople to neglect the basic, but essential activities within your sales process over their hunger to hit their targets.

In particular, make it mandatory for your team members to

- Input all activities and lead communication into your CRM regularly and in sufficient detail, based on a clear guideline
- Be on time for meetings
- Deliver all inputs for the sales reporting on time

Introducing your remuneration system

As you have seen in the previous part of the chapter, your startup's sales remuneration system includes much more than just a salary spreadsheet. Through its effects on the human side of your sales organization, it ties deeply into the functioning of your sales organization.

That's why it's paramount to carefully think about the way you implement your remuneration system – whether you introduce it for the first time or make changes to it after a while.

When we started to redesign our compensation plan, we had five different objectives in mind:

- Achieve better and fairer pay for the sales team (depending only on the MRR they've signed)
- Offer a real acceleration bonus for the best performers
- Encourage teamwork
- Define precise and reachable targets
- Avoid report effects as far as possible

The resulting compensation plan works as follows:

- Each month, we define individual targets. If the sales person reaches the target, we pay a fixed bonus. In addition, the sales person gets a percentage of every euro they sign. This percentage increases if the monthly target is reached.
- If two-thirds of the team reaches their target, everyone gets an extra bonus. This component is a great way to create strong bonds within the team.
- Because our compensation plan is so straightforward, we just give the team access to the report so that they can monitor their performance in real time.

— Firmin Zocchetto, Co-Founder & CEO, PayFit

Whenever you set up or change your sales remuneration system, we recommend testing its effects in a simulation spreadsheet first.

In your simulation spreadsheet, enter both the commissions for the sales team as a whole and for each team member individually, and link this document with your startup's business or financial plan.

Use the sales targets you set in the commissions spreadsheet to fill in the revenue line of your startup's business plan (including a 10-20% buffer just to be safe). Based on the targets, calculate the exact commission payments for each of the team members (start by assuming 100% target achievement for everyone as a baseline). Link these commission payments back to the labor cost line in the business plan, too.

With your spreadsheet, simulate the effects of your sales remuneration system in different future situations. For example, simulate some team member over- or underperforming on the same or different KPIs and examine the impact that will have on this person's respective payouts.

Cross-check the results of your simulation with your goals and priorities for your remuneration system.

For example, team members shouldn't be able to achieve high payouts only by focusing on lower-priority KPIs (e.g. completing activities or generating revenue types with low margins). Your system should force your team members to actually "earn" their commission by generating real revenue (with a good margin).

It's human nature to always look for ways to "game the system," so the least you can do to prevent this is trying to spot loopholes with a dry run.

More importantly, don't just look at your company's outcome. Put yourself into the shoes of different team members (within and outside of sales) and ask yourself: How would I feel in this situation? This goes toward your general sense of "fairness" between your sales team members, and also between the sales team and your startup's other teams.

To set realistic and achievable sales targets, use historical numbers for your KPIs wherever possible.

Of course, you'll always strive for ways to improve the results you have achieved in the past. However, if you have a well-established KPI that you want to increase, just raising the target obviously won't do the trick.

Instead, look for actual changes you can make across the business in order to enable your intended improvement. There are numerous ways of increasing your sales efficiency, a lot of which we have addressed in this book – great segmentation, product upgrades, well positioned marketing material and messaging, pricing changes, a more structured sales process, optimized hiring/firing, or increased training of the sales team are just a few to name.

Before you actually use the new remuneration system to pay out your commissions, start by introducing it to the team and letting the analytics run in parallel to the existing system for a quarter.

This way, your team members can see clearly how their remuneration would change under the new system, and have time to adjust. Using such a transitional period helps you to make sure the system fits your startup's environment and is accepted within the sales team as well.

Finally, if you want to introduce a variable remuneration system to a sales team that hasn't previously had a commission or bonus in their contract, you'll need to consider a few additional aspects.

Assuming that you are already paying market-level basic salaries, just adding a commission element on top would increase their OTEs above the market.

Under these circumstances, it makes most sense to make the resulting OTE larger than the original basic salary, but to do so by reducing the basic salary and adding the commission element. For example, if your basic salary was €50,000 before, reduce it to €40,000 and add €20,000 in commissions to land at OTE of €60,000.

Strong sales team members will feel confident that they are able to reach their targets, and hence be happy to sign up to your "raise." Less talented team members will worry more about the reduction of the basic salary. If they decide to leave as a result, it shouldn't be a big loss to your sales team.

16 - CUSTOMER SUCCESS

How to grow your business with happy customers

You have finally closed the contract with your customer. The sales process is over! *Or is it?*

In fact, some of the most powerful value drivers for your B2B business come into play *after* the contract is closed.

Of course, now is first and foremost the time to deliver on the promises you have made in the heat of the sales battle. A customer who doesn't see your promises come true will not be a customer for long, and all the effort you put into sales was for nothing. And even worse, the loss may harm your reputation and weaken your investment story.

But there is more to the phase after the closing of the contract that merits consideration. It turns out that helping your customer to successfully use your solution is not just a matter of being nice, but a key prerequisite for a number of ways to generate more revenue for your business.

Because all of the strategies to generate more revenue from your customers after they have signed the initial contract depend on your customers success with your solution, your activities in this phase (and your respective organizational unit) are called "customer success."

Founders need to think of customer success in SaaS as a closed loop system: I know who my best customers are. I know how to find them. I know how to acquire them. I know how to convert them. I know how to make them successful. And I know how to turn them into advocates so each customer refers to a new ideal customer. That's ultimately what SaaS is, winning ideal customers, retaining them customers, growing them, and then they refer new customers who are just like them.

**— Stephen Millard, Operating Partner &
Chief Platform Officer, Notion**

Among the many individual activities that are part of customer success, we will focus on the four most impactful value drivers:

1. Avoiding churn
2. Expanding your business through references
3. Expanding contracts and upselling
4. Increasing your price

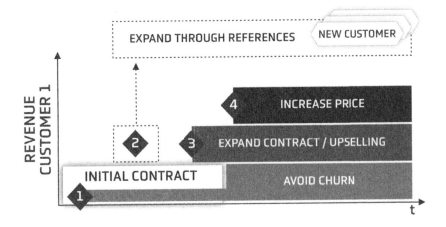

All four measures have a disproportionate impact on your overall profitability. Therefore, they deserve your full attention as founder and leader of a sales team.

Indeed, it often makes sense to separate out the customer success activities from your remaining sales activities. In part, that's because "farming" requires a different mindset from your team members than "hunting." But at the very least, this creates organizational focus:

> When you don't have focus, you're not getting the best of both, you're getting the worst of both. How can you possibly tell a rep: "I want you to go and win 50 new logos. By the way, I also want you to support these other 10 accounts." Naturally customers have questions, they take up time. And what happens is, you are losing on both ends: you're probably not providing world-class customer service to your existing customers, and you're losing ground on the new market, because your competitors have already created focus.
>
> **— Neil Ryland, Chief Revenue Officer, Peakon**

How to avoid churn

Because of its cumulative effects, churn has a significant long-term impact on your startup's profitability, as we've discussed in Chapter 13 on Strategic Sales Analytics.

Churn occurs not only when you lose customers, but also when customers "contract." This means that they reduce their monthly spending, for example through renegotiating your price, or by reducing their usage of your product.

Churn is the arch enemy of every salesperson – because it eliminates any achievements you have won before.

Some churn is inevitable. You'll always have some customers who need to reduce budgets or even go out of business. But avoiding *preventable* churn – that results from your own (in)actions – should be #1 on the priority list for your customer success activities.

Generally, the bigger your accounts are, the lower your churn rates should be, as larger corporate entities move slower in both directions. Balderton Capital gives the following benchmarks for "acceptable" monthly churn levels depending on customer size:

- 2-3% for SMB customers
- 1-2% for midsize companies
- 0.5%-1% for enterprise customers.

Some of the best companies even achieve "negative churn."

This means that their revenue expansion with existing customers more than offsets the churn through losing customers and customer contraction.

In the following, we're going to introduce the six most powerful measures to prevent churn.

1. Ensure successful onboarding

In a narrow sense, successful onboarding means that your product is installed or implemented in your customer's organization and that you have trained the end users in its use.

Depending on the complexity of your product, these steps alone require you to invest ample resources to successfully complete them. Elements that contribute to onboarding success are:

- Easy-to-use product with good, intuitive user interface
- Highly automated and simple set-up and onboarding
- Online and live trainings
- Hands-on support for setup and data import tasks

- Good product documentation and FAQs
- Easy-to-reach customer support
- Proactive check-in calls with your key decision-makers

From the customer's side, however, "successful onboarding" means more than having your product up and running.

Only when your customer starts to experience the value created by your solution, the risk of churn decreases significantly.

In fact, it pays to help your customer measure and quantify their success as part of the onboarding process. Especially with new solutions and business processes, knowing what success looks like can be tricky, as Scoutbee's Gregor Stühler describes:

> Typically, the customer doesn't invest their first million right away. It works rather like a review cascade after we have sold the first couple of licenses. That's why we get the customer to implement reporting committees and KPIs for measuring success as soon as they start using their licenses. We advocate for the committee to be led by our Digital Champion, and then aim to constantly communicate success to the company.
>
> For this to lead to upselling, it's important to use the right KPI. If you pick the wrong one, it can kill your entire upsell process.
>
> **— Gregor Stühler, Co-Founder & CEO, Scoutbee**

2. Provide a high service level

Providing a high service level should be a core element of your customer success strategy throughout the entire customer relationship.

At a minimum, your customers can expect self-service offers, such as manuals and online FAQs (Frequently Asked Questions). Even more comfortable for them is customer support with a live component (phone, chat or even personal visits).

The higher the service level you offer without charging extra for it, the more your customers will appreciate it.

It's up to you to strike a good balance between cost of service and the value the customer support brings you in terms of avoided churn.

In working toward a high service level, make sure to track your operational metrics to identify potential improvements and gaps. Good indicators for the quality of your service are the rate of problems solved, the wait times (for calls and chats) and response times (for emails and tickets), and the percentage of customers raising issues with your customer service.

Personio's COO Jonas Rieke highlights the personnel investment into the entire spectrum of customer activities that the HR company has made in order to achieve low churn rates. This includes roles directly in contact with the customer, but also cross-organizational roles, internally supporting the supporters with technical and product information:

Our Customer team counts about 125 people in the following roles:

- **Implementation (35 people)** - This team sets up customer accounts once they are handed over from Sales. This includes importing data, setting up the right parameters, and training the users.
- **Customer Service and Community (40 people)** - After the active support phase during the implementation, our service becomes reactive, i.e. our team responds to users' tickets and calls. We continuously try to increase the automation rate for these services while keeping service quality at the same high standard that we always strived for. Lately, we are also heavily investing in a Community

team which develops and operates an online community and organizes User Groups Meetups and our Customer Advisory Board (CAB).

- **Customer Success (10 people)** - This team works as strategic partners with the People teams of our larger customers. Customer Success provides additional services to more complex accounts to drive adoption and reduce churn risk of those bigger customers.
- **Customer Growth (20 people)** - They take care of traditional account management and any commercials with customers: renewals, expansion, and dealing with detractors and churn.
- **Payroll Operations and Partnerships (15 people)** - The team is responsible both for training and certifying tax advisors in using Personio in combination with payroll software and winning them as trusted partners and customers.
- **Product Experts** - They are the interface between product and the Customer organization, facilitating beta tests and feature releases as well as reporting feedback back to the Product and Engineering teams.
- **User Education (five people)** - The team owns all channels around self-served and proactive communication with customers: our help center, in-app tours, webinars, monthly product update newsletters. Additionally they organize knowledge management for internal functions.
- **Customer Data and Processes (five people)** - The team aims at improving and automating processes. They closely collaborate with BI, Infrastructure and all customer-facing teams. The further develop our tool landscape and make sure that each function is able to work as data-driven as possible.

— Jonas Rieke, COO, Personio

3. Establish good antennas

If your sales process was successful, it's likely because you have established good personal contacts with key people on the customer's side.

Maintaining personal contact throughout the customer relationship is essential for defending against churn.

By staying in close touch with your contact on the customer side, you'll be able to pick up early warning signs that the customer might churn (see also the "warning signs" in the next section) and act on them.

In an early stage, the initial salesperson will be the one to maintain the customer contact. Once your sales organization matures, you can also transfer over the relationship to a dedicated key account executive who manages the daily operations of the customer account.

Staying in touch also gives your key account executive the chance to seize opportunities for upselling. Through an update or "business review" call, for example, they might learn that the customer is expanding into a new country. Or they might ask the Champion to recommend your solution to a related department. In this regard, the key account executive has both a defensive and an offensive role.

Keeping in close touch with customers also requires a structured process for customer feedback.

Implementing a standardized, structured feedback process allows you to watch for small but critical trends in customer satisfaction over time. We recommend using a standard methodology such as the Net Promoter Score (NPS).

The results of those surveys can also be used to incentivize your teams into the right direction:

> We make sure the New Business rep will not sell a dodgy deal by publicizing our customer NPS scores internally in our Slack feed. Every time we send out the surveys, it goes to the whole company. This is brilliant – because if the survey comes back bad, it says on Slack: Account name, Sold by, Customer success rep. Who wants to have the lowest NPS score of customers? You sold it?"
>
> **— Neil Ryland, Chief Revenue Officer, Peakon**

4. Trigger "Wow!" moments

A proven method to lock in a customer is to exceed their expectations by so much, they can't say anything else but "Wow!"

Ideally, you've already blown away your customer with your product features in the sales process (see Chapter 8 on Process for "Wow!" moments in product demos).

In customer success, make it a principle to go beyond the ordinary when it comes to personal attention, reaction time and effort you put in to fix the customer's issues.

Martin (somewhat inadvertently) created a tangible "Wow!" effect when he was serving in the press office of the World Economic Forum in Singapore for a summit event in the mid-1990s.

All day, the journalists had been asking about the text of the dinner speech by the Singaporean leader Lee Kuan Yew and started to complain that the press office was slow to provide it. When the press office finally got hold of the text, Martin had it quickly printed and delivered it to the room where the journalists were seated. When he handed out the paper copies, he noticed that they were still warm from the printing. And so did all the journalists. When Martin left the room, all tables were still discussing the efficiency of an operation that can deliver warm printouts.

This "Wow!" effect spilled over to creating an excellent working relationship with the journalists for the rest of the summit. The press team had proven an exceptional service level, resulting in exceptionally happy customers.

In contrast to many other customer success measures, "Wow!" moments don't have to come at a high cost.

They are powerful simply because they show that you have recognized the most urgent need of your counterpart and delivered the solution on-point.

5. Get your customers "on your team"

If your customers are satisfied with your product and happy with you as their provider – why not let that happiness work for you?

There are many ways to get happy customers involved in your sales efforts. For example, ask them to co-sponsor a case study that you can use as a reference use case for your marketing and sales materials. Even better, ask your customers to act as a reference for you, or join as a speaker at a conference discussing your product.

Seeing happy customers publicly support and promote your product will not only greatly enhance confidence of future customers, but also psychologically get your customers "on your team."

It's much less likely for a customer to churn if they feel like they are "on your team."

Someone who's truly mastered the game of getting customers on his team is serial founder Avinoam Nowogrodski:

Our most successful format is our "Champions' Meetings": we fly out our customers to a meeting where they present to each other what they did with Clarizen. In the end, they receive a "Champion's Certificate." Our customers love it so much, they even pay to participate!

— **Avinoam Nowogrodski, Co-Founder & former CEO, Clarizen**

6. Work hard to win back churned customers

Despite all your efforts at customer success, you'll see some customers cancel their contracts.

Don't let your customers go without making an effort at winning them back.

Winning customers back who have already made the decision to cancel is rather difficult, but not impossible. Even if you just win back 10% or 20% of your churned customers, it will have a significant impact on your revenue line.

If you want to have a chance at winning back your customer, it's essential to react quickly after receiving the cancellation note. Reach out systematically to all key decision-makers to understand exactly why they made the decision to cancel their contract.

In this process, you might learn that the customer is facing a short-term budget problem during a restructuring, which you can bridge with an extra (temporary) discount instead of a cancellation. Alternatively, if they are having a problem with your product, you can try to fix the problem to rescue the situation.

Whether you manage to win back the customer or not – at a minimum, the results are a great learning opportunity about your product and how it is perceived by your customer.

Even if your efforts to win them back fail in the short term, your customer will value the time and attention you invested to reach out and to understand their issues. This will give you a good starting point to contact them again at a later date, for example with an enhanced product version (ideally showing how you reacted to their feedback), or with a new product adjacent to your former offering.

How to expand your business through references

If your customers are happy, use them as stepping stones to new business.

Similar to upselling, this saves you the effort to identify and warm up a cold lead to your product first. Your customers are an important shortcut in several regards:

- They know their industry well and have a clear idea of who else has a problem similar to theirs.
- They can make introductions to specific persons, giving you warm leads to follow up on.
- Their references and use cases are the most credible to other potential customers in the industry.

You will still need a new sales process to convert your customers' referrals into customers. But these factors make a sale much more likely.

Neil Ryland has institutionalized the idea of using happy existing customers to generate new business in Peakon's customer success organization:

When people say "upsell" they usually associate it with increasing just the customer. No, no, no: the customers drive your new business! Your customers are your best weapon for growth – through referrals, case studies, G2.com, crowds turning up at your events and your webinars... I think sometimes people just miss that trick when they think about upsell.

We ask our customers for referrals as soon as they buy. Because that's when people are at their happiest: "Yes, we're over the line, we've started using Peakon." That's the time when they're gonna go: "Yeah, I know this person, this person!" So that's the time to strike and use their network.

— Neil Ryland, Chief Revenue Officer, Peakon

Avinoam Nowogrodski advocates for using customers as your ambassadors – and demonstrates that it can absolutely be a win-win situation for both sides:

At Clarizen, for example, we've given discounts for customer endorsements, or made a common press release or testimonial video part of our contracts. Because customers love to hear about others' use cases, I also regularly invite a group of them to lunches where they can share what they do with our product – and I bring journalists along who write up an article about this.

— Avinoam Nowogrodski, Co-Founder &
former CEO, Clarizen

How to expand contracts and upsell

The third pillar of customer success is expanding and upselling to your existing customers.

Don't underestimate expanding and upselling as a major value driver for your business – often even more important than the initial sale!

> We could double the business next year if I didn't sell one new deal, based on the new products and the amount of seats that I have available. This is how important upselling is to building sustainable and efficient growth.
>
> **— Neil Ryland, Chief Revenue Officer, Peakon**

Expanding contracts

Expansion in the context of customer success means that you sell more of the same product to your existing customers.

For example, you sell another set of seats for a new department, or you charge more for increased usage of your features.

Expanding the use of your product within your customer base is another major value lever for your business.

The difference to upselling is that expansion happens automatically when your customers use your product more.

The advantage of a strategy based on expansion is that you can start with a small ticket (which is easier to sell) and then grow into your customer base step by step.

We wanted to make sure our new pay-as-you-go pricing was encouraging expansion. With our old pricing, you had to pay at least $50,000 a year to have access to certain features. And expansion was starting to stagnate because our pricing wasn't the right model. Now you can start with $1.5 dollars. When expansions happen automatically, the entire sales process changes. Today, our customers start at a smaller base, but they expand faster.

— Nicolas Dessaigne, Co-Founder &
Board Member, Algolia

Expanding your customer requires that your product and your pricing structure have an inbuilt dynamic element – you earn more if your customers' consumption expands. At Algolia, for example, the product is priced by search queries run by the user. Other examples for dynamic pricing parameters are:

- Number of software seats used
- Number of transactions completed (e.g. payments made, signatures filed)
- Data volume used
- Number of analyses run

If your contract specifies a dynamic element, there is no need to do anything extra to earn the additional revenue. Just make sure you can reliably track the dynamic metric and establish a convenient charging method for claiming your dues.

You can also actively drive expansion within your customers by targeting neighboring departments or parallel organizational units (like other regions or countries).

This is an organic growth path: after all, if one business unit within your customer is already successfully using your product, why shouldn't the others use it, too? Because you've already taken the initial hurdle, the cost of acquisition for expanding in additional business units are relatively low.

Make sure your sales organization fully harvests these low-hanging fruits. Simply implement the question "Who else in your company could benefit from our solution?" as part of each customer check-in from your customer success team.

Upselling

Upselling means that you sell additional products or services to existing customers.

For example, you add an additional product feature or an enhanced customer service package to an existing contract with a customer.

As we've mentioned previously, upselling is a separate sales process on its own. Therefore, it's often done by a separate business unit within customer success.

Successfully using the potential of upselling also requires a product architecture that supports separating out "upsellable" components.

Simply put, if you sell your entire product suite at the initial sale, there's no value left that you can charge for in an upsell.

Providing high value to your customer with the first sale while reserving some potential for later upselling is a delicate balance. It requires a lot of strategic thought, as Peakon's Neil Ryland explains:

Think about all the variables that allow you to drive upsell. Our product has very simple tiers: Essential, Business and Premier. By using range pricing, we ruled out being too expensive or looking too cheap. But not all customers need to upgrade their tiers. That's why we offer other products to drive uplift as well. For example, we now offer more service packages. This year is the first year we've become a multi-product organization.

— Neil Ryland, Chief Revenue Officer, Peakon

The power of upselling lies in the head start you have.

For the customer, you're already established as a trusted supplier and business contact who has passed the approval of the key decision-makers once before.

How to increase your price

Price increases are the second essential lever for increasing your revenue from your existing customers.

In Chapter 6, we already discussed the need to get your pricing right for new customers as well as the need to push for the limit by raising your list prices regularly. In this section, we want to draw your attention to price increases for existing customers.

In our experience, many startup founders are not aggressive enough about increasing prices for their existing customer base.

They are afraid of the extra effort it takes to explain and communicate the price increases to all customers. They are also worried about the added risk of losing customers.

However, we've seen again and again that the benefit of extra revenue significantly outweighs these costs. After the dust of the price increase settles, we often see a revenue (and margin) increase of 10-20% across the board at the cost of losing just 1-2% of customers.

When considering whether the risk is worth it, keep in mind that all extra revenue from increasing your price flows directly into your bottom line.

A sales campaign that adds the same revenue from new customers always entails extra costs for customer acquisition (including failed attempts), sales commission, installations and ongoing support. In comparison, the administrative and communicative cost of a price increase is negligible.

Good and bad situations for a price increase

Price increases are sensitive situations because they wake sleeping dogs: they give your customer a reason to critically reevaluate the value of your product. If your customers have any reason to think that the (new) price isn't appropriate for the value they're getting, they might cancel their contract altogether. Instead of getting 10% more revenue, you end up with 100% less.

Before you increase your price, make sure the status quo gives room for an increase and the timing is right.

Positive indications

If you see many of the following positive indications (and only a few warning signs), it's relatively safe to go ahead with a price increase:

- Your product is performing as promised (or even exceeding your customers' expectations) and you have a great track record of delivering on time and according to specs with a stable product and high uptime.

- Your support is solving problems at a high solution level and is available at minimal wait times.
- Your customers on all levels (End Users, Economic Buyers, Champions) are happy and have experienced the value of your product.
- Your customers regularly and increasingly use your product. You can verify this with usage data.
- At the market level, you gain ground versus the competition. Your product is distinctive and sticky enough that it cannot easily be substituted by a competitor's product.
- Your contract structure allows for a price increase, e.g. at the end date of a predefined contract duration. (If your contract includes automatic renewal, that's not possible without renegotiation.)

Warning signs

The following indicators are warning signs that a price increase probably isn't a great idea at this time:

- There are problems with your rollout. Your product is not running stable and/or contains bugs.
- Your price increase would lift you above budget thresholds that may complicate approval at the customer side.
- Your support is performing poorly in terms of availability and/or solution rate.
- Some customers (End Users or Economic Buyers) are unhappy.
- Your customers use your product, but you are unsure whether the End Users or Economic Buyers have fully experienced the value it creates.
- Product usage is volatile or declining (in terms of licenses, daily users, or transactions).
- Your competitors are ready to fully substitute your solution with limited switching costs.

If you are confident that you can improve on some of the parameters relatively quickly, we highly recommend doing this first before launching the price increase.

Maybe some warning signs are relevant only for a subgroup of your customers, for example those who use a specific feature. In this case, exclude this feature from the increase process for now.

Smart ways to increase your price

A flat-out price hike – "Starting today, our monthly rate is 15% higher" – will raise some eyebrows. Your customers will wonder what justifies this (beyond your wish to earn more).

As so many things in life, pricing increases are a matter of "how you say it."

If you use one of the following four smart ways to implement and communicate your price increase, chances are good that your customers will either accept it as fair, or not even fully notice it at all.

1. Combine the increase with the rollout of new features

Time your price increase to coincide with a rollout of additional product features. But instead of charging directly for usage of the new features, increase the price for your entire product – the basic message being that your entire solution just became more valuable.

Ideally, the customers will actually benefit from the added features. But even if they don't: it should come across that you're offering more value, so it's fair that they're now paying more.

2. Combine the increase with a complete change of the pricing mechanics

Sometimes it makes sense to not only change how much the price is, but also *how* you price your product.

Naturally, this is not an option for every time you do a price increase. Your revenue model is a cornerstone of your business and it requires a significant administrative effort to change it (as we have pointed out in Chapter 6). However, if you are planning a change in your revenue model, it will be a good time to raise your pricing along with it: it makes it harder for customers to compare how much they paid before and after the change.

In Personio's case, a change in their pricing mechanics was overdue because the existing product packages didn't capture the structure and needs of the customers anymore. Because the new product packaging made more sense to the customers, Personio managed to introduce a relevant price increase along with the new packaging. With impressive results:

> By making changes to our product packaging and pricing, we were able to increase MRR, practically without any churn. Plus we gained references by giving discounts for early customers for whom we raised prices less in the process.
>
> It was a huge success, but we also worked hard to accompany the pricing structure change for every single customer with a lot of information and discussion. We wanted customers to understand our thinking and not just increase prices. This is key to a process like this and only works authentically if you mean it.
>
> **— Jonas Rieke, COO, Personio**

3. Build the increase into the contract from the start

Other than the previous two alternatives, automatic price increases in the contract are smart because they do not require any dedicated communication or explanation.

In fact, it is common practice in many B2B contracts to build in a small annual price increase labeled "inflation adjustment" or "cost of living adjustment" into your contract.

An annual increase of 5% or 7% might not seem much, but thanks to compound interest effects, it will add nicely to your customers' profitability in the long run.

4. Put an expiration date on initial discounts

Expiring discounts are another way to implement price increases that have a chance to pass under the radar of your customers when the time comes.

> Our discounts expire after a year. Then the customers can either re-negotiate a new discount or cancel the contract. But the default is that the contract renews automatically for another year at the regular price, without the discount.
>
> — **Veronika Riederle, Co-Founder & CEO, Demodesk**

The advantage of expiring discounts is that the customer has to become active to prevent the price from increasing. You should be ready for that to happen. But if your product provides the value it promises, the customer might just as well continue the contract at the higher price level anyway, without any further action on your side.

17 - CONCLUSION
Looking back, looking forward

We have taken you with us on the long journey from learning and exploring the market to standardizing and optimizing your sales processes and organization.

Hopefully, we showed you a few shortcuts along the way by avoiding the most frequent mistakes in B2B sales we introduced at the beginning of this book. But no doubt, you'll make other ones. And that's okay!

Failures are the best tool to make progress. Successfully going through the process of understanding *why* you were failing is the most important skill of an entrepreneur. So don't avoid failure, don't ignore it, don't deny it – embrace it!

**— Avinoam Nowogrodski, Co-Founder &
former CEO, Clarizen**

The challenge is not how to avoid mistakes, but to learn from them. More than any other lesson, we hope that you have taken away from this book the idea that you don't have to start out perfect. You just need to get started at all and then put everything you've got into observing, learning, and improving.

What took you a couple of hours to read will likely take months, even years to implement. And the road will never truly end – there's always another corner you haven't turned, another bridge you haven't crossed. And that's precisely what we love about sales and entrepreneurship in general: the endless potential to get better, to learn more, and to challenge ourselves.

With our book, we hope that we have given you the tools and ideas you need to get your B2B sales machine up and running.

We hope that it takes you wherever you dream to go next: from zero to one, from one to ten, from ten to €100 million in revenue – and beyond.

ACKNOWLEDGEMENTS

First and foremost, we would like to thank all of our contributing founders and experts for sharing their wisdom, expertise, and personal experiences with us. You have given us what is most valuable: your time and wisdom. Your input has been an invaluable contribution to this book and will be as inspiring to our readers as it was to us.

For her support in writing and editing this book, Matthias and Martin are extremely grateful to Rike Brand, our editor, researcher, and sparring partner who has been with us since the beginning. A two-time startup founder herself, Rike represented the voice of the target customer in our book-related discussions and helped to give the book a clear and consistent structure.

We also want to thank Rebecca Gischel, whose extraordinary ability to create elegant and understandable graphics from our rough sketches and ideas made a huge contribution to our book. She also created our beautiful cover.

Thank you also both Eric Wyman and Jay Polmar for proofreading and layout, respectively. The results speak for themselves.

Furthermore, we would also like to thank you, our friends and colleagues, for the time and effort you invested in giving your detailed feedback on our draft.

Natalia Karbasova
Enno Kuntze

Jens Lapinski
Philipp Nägelein
Michele Oglietti
Shuli Shwartz
Konstantin Stoytchev
Nina Wang
Steven Willmott

Your thoughtful comments helped us sharpen our arguments and highlight new angles that we hadn't thought of. You pushed this book forward – thank you!

APPENDIX

Sales systems in contrast: Deer vs. Elephants

As we have discussed throughout the book, B2B products, business models and the companies built around them vary widely. Your sales strategy and system will reflect these variations in almost every aspect, from your segmentation to process and organization.

This doesn't mean, however, that every sales system is completely unique. Rather, many of the elements in your system are oriented toward one or the other side of a prototypical divide: the difference between what Christoph Janz calls "Deer" and "Elephants."

In the table below, we describe the key differences between these systems to illustrate how your sales system (and ultimately the profitability of your business model) is tied to your type of market and customer.

When reading through these two concepts, please keep in mind that there is no clear-cut divide between the two, but that our descriptions merely try to highlight the respective contrast.

		Deer	Elephants
ARPA/ARR		€10,000	€100,000
When to target		Early/Mature product	Mature product
Market segmentation	Employees	250-1,000	1.000-100,000
	Revenue	€100M - €1B	€1B+
Decision-making unit	Decision-maker	Managing Director/CEO	Management Board level -1 (EVP, SVP)
		MB level -1 (Director, Head of)	MB level -2 (VP, Director)
	Involvement of Purchasing department	Possible	Mandatory
	Involvement of Legal or IT departments	Likely	Mandatory
Standardization	Product	Standard SaaS	Customized SaaS
			Professional Services
		Standard Hardware	Customized Hardware
	Contract and T&Cs	Standardized	Customized

	Signature	Online button	Physical signature or Purchase Order (PO) only
Process	**Lead time**	1-6 months	3-24 months
	PoC	Possible without	PoC mostly mandatory
	# interactions prior to sale	5-10	10-50
	# people in decision-making team	2-3	3-10
Pipeline sizing	**Prospects per month**	1,000+	100+
	Leads per month	100+	10+
	Opportunities per month	10+	5+
Sales automation	**# tools in sales tech stack**	10-20	5
Operational Sales Reporting	**Focus**	Pipeline & team focus	Deal focus
		Conversion rates	Qualitative deal progress
Organization	**Sales team size for €1M ARR**	20	5
	Focus	High velocity hiring/firing	Senior industry expertise
		Sales academy	

Remuneration	Salary level vs. market	Above average	Top quartile
	Commission	Sophisticated commission system	Standard commission system
		Monthly commission payouts	Quarterly commission payouts
Motivation		Varied contests and incentives	
Channels		Direct	Direct
			Indirect & Integrators

List of contributors' companies

Alex Meyer –
Co-Founder &
Partner, **42CAP**

42CAP is a Munich-based VC fund founded
in 2016 by Alex Meyer and Thomas Wilke.
For their investment activities at 42CAP,
Alex and Thomas build on their long-time
experience as entrepreneurs, where they co-
founded a marketing tech SaaS company with
more than 500 employees and $50 million in
revenue before selling it to Teradata for $240
million in 2012.

Nicolas Dessaigne –
Co-Founder & Board
Member, **Algolia**

Algolia was founded in 2012 in Paris by
Nicolas Dessaigne and Julien Lemoine with
the mission to allow developers and business
teams to build and optimize delightful search
and discovery experiences that increase online
engagement, conversion rates, and revenue.
More than 9,500 companies including
Under Armour, Lacoste, Birchbox, Stripe,
Slack, Medium, and Zendesk rely on Algolia
to manage over 95 billion search queries a
month. Algolia has raised more than $184
million in capital.

Bastian Nominacher
– Co-Founder &
Co-CEO, **Celonis**

Celonis was founded in 2011 by Bastian
Nominacher, Alexander Rinke, and Martin
Klenk. Its process mining software helps
companies unlock the capacity to maximize
business performance. Headquartered in
New York and Munich – and with 15 offices
worldwide – Celonis currently has over 1,000
employees and more than $100 million in
revenue. To date, Celonis has raised $370
million and is valued to be in excess of
$2.5 billion.

Arun Srinivasan – Founder & CEO, **Clarisights**	Clarisights was founded in 2018 by Arun Srinivasan and Ankur Gupta in Berlin. As the decision platform for growth, Clarisights provides real-time reporting for high-performance marketing teams at companies such as Delivery Hero, Hello Fresh, or Omio, and employs more than 30 people.
Avinoam Nowogrodski – Co-Founder & former CEO, **Clarizen**	Clarizen was founded in 2005 by serial entrepreneur Avinoam Nowogrodski and Tanya Epstein. As a leading cloud project management platform, Clarizen has more than 2,000 enterprise customers and 100,000 individual users in 79 countries. After raising $90 million, the company was acquired by the private investment firm K1 in 2018.
Charles Delingpole – Founder & CEO, **ComplyAdvantage**	Comply Advantage was founded in 2014 by Charles Delingpole. The company offers AI-driven financial crime risk data and detection technology with the aim to neutralize the risk of money laundering, terrorist financing, corruption, and other financial crime. Today, more than 500 enterprises in 75 countries use ComplyAdvantage. In total, the company has raised $88 million in venture capital.
Tai Alegbe – Co-Founder & CEO, **Contingent**	Contingent was founded in 2019 by Tai Alegbe and Rajpal Wilkhu in London, United Kingdom. Contingent provides an AI-powered platform that helps proactively manage supply-chain and third-party risk both for private and public enterprise customers. The company employs 13 people.

Paul Salazar – Head of Sales Central Europe, **Couchbase**	Couchbase was founded in 2011 in Santa Clara, California, as an open-source platform providing an enterprise-class, multicloud database with the robust capabilities required for business-critical applications. As Head of Sales for Central Europe, Paul Salazar joined Couchbase in 2020, where he contributes 35 years of experience in technology along with his hands-on executive leadership in sales for startups and established firms.
Veronika Riederle – Co-Founder & CEO, **Demodesk**	Demodesk was founded in 2017 by Veronika Riederle and Alex Popp. Demodesk offers the first intelligent meeting platform for remote sales and success teams. Today, more than 150 customers across Europe and the US use Demodesk to close deals and have better customer conversations. In 2020, the Y Combinator alumnus announced its $8 million Series A funding round.
Michael Wax – Co-Founder & CEO, **Forto**	Forto was founded in Berlin in 2016 under the name FreightHub by Michael Wax, Ferry Heilemann, Erik Muttersbach, and Fabian Heilemann. Forto stands for groundbreaking, scalable, digital logistics technology, and services that go beyond transportation from Point A to Point B. With over 2,500 customers and 10 global offices, Forto currently employs more than 400 people and has raised over $126 million of capital to date.

Matt Robinson – Co-Founder & Board Member, **GoCardless**	GoCardless was founded in 2010 by Matt Robinson, Hiroki Takeuchi, and Tom Blomfield. Today, the recurring payments platform processes $13 billion in transactions a year and counts TripAdvisor and the Guardian among its 50,000 business customers around the world. Including a Series F round in late 2020, GoCardless has raised $217 million in venture capital.
Moritz Zimmermann – Co-Founder & former CTO, **Hybris**	Hybris Software was founded in 1997 by Moritz Zimmermann together with two co-founders as a provider of software for omni-channel customer experience and commerce (CEC). The company was acquired by SAP in 2013 for $1.3 billion – the highest-value private acquisition of a technology business at the time. Until recently, Moritz has overseen all product innovation and development as CTO at SAP Customer Experience.
Ben Stephenson – Co-Founder & CEO, **Impala**	Impala was founded in 2016 in London by Ben Stephenson and Charles Cowley with the mission of building one API platform that provides the key to thousands of hotels and billions of data-points. With more than 60 employees, Impala partners with companies such as Philips and TripAdvisor and has raised over $32 million in capital today.

Erez Galonska – Co-Founder & CEO, **Infarm**	Founded in 2013 by Osnat Michaeli and the brothers Erez and Guy Galonska, Infarm combines highly efficient vertical farms with IoT technology and machine learning to offer an alternative food system that is resilient, transparent, and affordable. The company distributes its smart modular farms throughout urban environment to grow fresh produce for the city's inhabitants. Infarm has raised more than $300 million and employs more than 600 people.
Daniel Metzler – Co-Founder & CEO, **Isar Aerospace**	Isar Aerospace was founded in 2018 by Daniel Metzler, Josef Fleischmann, and Markus Brandl. The company offers flexible, sustainable, and cost-efficient access to space for satellite constellations through its self-developed launch vehicle. The Munich-based startup is supported by Bulent Altan, former VP of SpaceX, and has raised more than $100 million in venture capital.
Dr. Oliver Trinchera – Co-Founder & CEO, **Kinexon**	Kinexon was founded in 2013 by Oliver Trinchera and Alexander Hüttenbrink. The company's products and services leverage customary sensors to connect and automate objects, people, and processes in real time in the Internet of Things. Its main target markets are professional sports and media applications as well as industrial processes. In 2020, Kinexon added a digital solution for proximity warning and contact tracing to prevent COVID-19 infections. Clients include the NBA, NFL and MLB and leading industrial clients such as BMW and Continental.

Jörg G. Beyer –
Co-Founder &
former Co-CEO,
LeanIX

LeanIX was founded in 2012 by Jörg G. Beyer
and André Christ in Bonn, Germany. Today,
the company has more than 230 employees
in its German headquarters and its offices in
Boston, USA, and Hyderabad, India. Among
the more than 300 enterprise customers for
LeanIX's enterprise architecture and cloud
governance tools are brands like Volkswagen,
Adidas, DHL, Merck, Vodafone, and
Zalando. In four funding rounds, LeanIX has
raised about $120 million in venture capital.

Philipp Koch-Büttner
– Co-Founder &
COO, **Lengoo**

Lengoo was founded in 2014 by Christopher
Kränzler, Philipp Koch-Büttner, and
Alexander Gigga. The language tech company
provides professional language translation
services using a combination of machine
translation technology and linguists for more
than 3,000 customers worldwide, including
National Instruments, Sunrise, and Sixt. In
2019 and 2020, Lengoo won the Deloitte
Fast 50 Award as one of the fastest-growing
technology companies in Germany. Lengoo
employs over 90 people and raised more than
$34 million in capital.

Bill Aulet – Managing
Director, Martin
Trust Center for MIT
Entrepreneurship,
**MIT Sloan School of
Management**

As Professor of the Practice and Managing
Director of the Martin Trust Center for MIT
Entrepreneurship at MIT Sloan, Bill Aulet
has led the development of entrepreneurial
education across MIT. He builds on over 25
years of business success, first at IBM and then
as a three-time entrepreneur. His 2013 book
"Disciplined Entrepreneurship" is an award-
winning international bestseller.

Dr. Felix Reinshagen – Co-Founder & CEO, **NavVis**	NavVis was founded in 2013 by Felix Reinshagen, Georg Schroth, Robert Huitl, and Sebastian Hilsenbeck. The company's 3D scanning technology enables the accurate mobile mapping of indoor spaces and enterprise-ready digital twin solutions. Between Munich, New York, and Shanghai, NavVis currently employs more than 200 people. The startup has received $68 million in funding to date.
Peter Carlsson – Co-Founder & CEO, **Northvolt**	Northvolt was founded in 2016 in Stockholm, Sweden, by Peter Carlsson and Paolo Cerruti with the mission to build the world's greenest battery to enable Europe's transition to renewable energy. With more than 800 employees, Northvolt partners with industry leaders such as ABB, Siemens, Volkswagen, and BMW, and has raised more than €3 billion in capital to date.
Chris Tottman – Co-Founder & General Partner, **Notion** Stephen Millard – Operating Partner & Chief Platform Officer, Notion	Notion was founded in London in 2009 by SaaS entrepreneurs and operators Ben White, Chris Tottman, Ian Milbourn, Jos White, and Stephen Chandler. The venture capital fund is exclusively focused on European SaaS and enterprise tech. It has made more than 60 investments and has invested $500 million in early-stage SaaS startups.

Kai Leppanen –
former SVP, Global
Accounts, **Opera** &
Chief Global Sales
Officer, **Liana**

Opera Software was founded in 1995 by Jon
Stephenson von Tetzchner and Geir Ivarsoy
out of Telenor, Norway. Opera is one of the
world's leading browser providers for more
than 350 million people and a pioneer in the
field of integrated AI-driven digital content
discovery and recommendation platforms.
Liana Technologies was founded in 2005 in
Finland focusing on the marketing technology
stack. Among the 3,500 customers worldwide
are Hertz, Toyota, Ikea, and Starbucks.

Firmin Zocchetto –
Co-Founder & CEO,
Payfit

Founded in 2015 by Ghislain de Fontenay,
Florian Fournier and Firmin Zocchetto,
PayFit digitizes and simplifies payroll
management and HR processes for over 4,000
companies across France, Spain, Germany,
UK and Italy. Fast, intuitive and automated,
the PayFit solution allows employers to easily
manage payroll on its own, saving valuable
time and money. Payfit has raised more than
$100 million and employs more than 500
people.

Neil Ryland – Chief
Revenue Officer,
Peakon

Peakon was founded in 2014 in London by
Phil Chambers and Dan Rogers. Peakon is
an employee success platform that converts
feedback into insights you can put to work.
With more than 260 employees and $68
million in capital raised, Peakon delivers
solutions to more than 1.000 customers,
including Trustpilot, Easyjet, and Verizon.
On Jan 28, 2021, Workday announced its
intent to acquire Peakon for $700 million.

Jonas Rieke – COO, **Personio**	Personio was founded in 2015 by Hanno Renner, Roman Schumacher, Arseniy Vershinin, and Ignaz Forstmeier shortly before Jonas Rieke joined the company. The scaleup offers a holistic HR software for small to mid-sized companies. In four offices, Personio employs 600 people. Personio has raised more than $250 million in venture capital to date.
Christoph Janz – Co-Founder & Managing Partner, **Point Nine Capital**	Point Nine Capital, founded in 2011 by Christoph Janz and Pawel Chudzinski, is a Berlin-based venture capital firm focused exclusively on early-stage SaaS and marketplaces. Point Nine has backed Delivery Hero, Zendesk, Algolia, and Typeform from their earliest stages. Christoph Janz runs a popular startup blog at christophjanz.blogspot.com and is the author of the "animal hunting" framework for SaaS companies.
Ognyan Vasilev – EMEA B2B Industries Advisory and GoToMarket, **Salesforce**	Ognyan Vasilev has been with Salesforce since September 2018 as the Manufacturing and Automotive Business Development Lead. Before joining the market leader in customer relationship management (CRM) software, Ognyan was part of The Boston Consulting Group and Accenture Digital, advising leading global enterprises on their digital agenda and supporting them end-to-end, from strategy definition to implementation.

Tiffani Bova – Global Growth Evangelist, **Salesforce** and WSJ Bestselling Author, Growth IQ

Salesforce, founded in 1999, is the market leader in customer relationship management (CRM) software with more than 150.000 customers worldwide. Tiffani Bova is Global Growth Evangelist at Salesforce and the author of the Wall Street Journal bestselling book GROWTH IQ: Get Smarter About the Choices that Will Make or Break Your Business. Bova has been named to the latest Thinkers50's list of the world's top management thinkers and is a welcomed guest on Bloomberg, BNN, Cheddar, MSNBC, and Yahoo Finance, among others.

Gregor Stühler – Co-Founder & CEO, **Scoutbee**

Scoutbee was founded in 2015 by Gregor Stühler, Christian Heinrich, Thimo Schraut and Lee Galbraith. The startup maintains a supplier discovery platform powered by artificial intelligence and big data. With currently 130 employees, Scoutbee serves more than 100 customers from its offices in Southern Germany. To date, Scoutbee has received $76 million in venture capital funding.

Miki Yokoyama – Managing Director, **TechFounders**

TechFounders is a B2B tech-startup accelerator by Munich-based entrepreneurship center UnternehmerTUM, led by Managing Director Miki Yokoyama. In addition to a 20-week program with intensive training and coaching on all kinds of business topics, participating startups collaborate with one of TechFounders' leading corporate partners to further develop their product or service with a €25,000 project budget.

Dr. Stephan Rohr –
Co-Founder & CEO,
TWAICE

TWAICE was founded in 2018 in Munich by Stephan Rohr und Michael Baumann. TWAICE provides battery analytics solutions to accelerate the transition to emission free mobility and green energy. Its core technology is the digital twin, a software that combines deep battery knowledge and artificial intelligence to determine the condition and predict battery aging and performance. This makes complex battery systems more transparent, effective, and reliable. With more than 50 employees and customers such as Porsche, Audi, Hero and Munich Re, TWAICE has raised over €14 million in capital today.

List of abbreviations

ACV   Average Customer Value

AE   Account Executive

ARPA Average Revenue per Customer

ARR   Average Recurring Revenue

B2B   Business to Business

B2C   Business to Consumer

CAC   Customer Acquisition Cost

CEO   Chief Executive Officer

CIO   Chief Information Officer

CLV   Customer Lifetime Value

CRM   Customer Relationship Management

CRO   Chief Revenue Officer

CSM   Customer Success Manager

CSO   Chief Sales Officer

CTO   Chief Technology Officer

CxO   C-Level Executive

DMU   Decision-making unit

ESOP Employee Stock Option Plan

EVP   Executive Vice President

ICP   Ideal Customer Profile

KPI   Key Performance Indicator

LTV   Lifetime Value

MB   Management Board

MOU   Memorandum of Understanding

MQL   Marketing Qualified Lead

MRR   Monthly Recurring Revenue

NPS   Net Promoter Score

OTE   On-Target Earnings

PoC   Proof of Concept

RFP   Request for Proposal

ROI   Return on Investment

SaaS   Software as a Service

SDR   Sales Development Representative

SE   Sales Engineer

SMB/
SME   Small and Medium-sized Business/Enterprise

SOM   Sales Operations Manager

SQL   Sales Qualified Lead

SVP   Senior Vice President

UI/UX   User Interface/User Experience

VP   Vice President

VSOP   Virtual Stock Option Plan

FURTHER RESOURCES

Books

Amos Schwartzfarb	**Sell More Faster** Amos is Managing Director at Techstars and has written a great sales book for founders.
Bill Aulet	**Disciplined Entrepreneurship** Bill is a serial entrepreneur and Senior Lecturer at MIT. His book and the accompanying workbook offer a highly structured approach to building successful startups.
Geoffrey Moore	**Crossing the Chasm** This is a useful framework on how to adjust your product and sales approach as you move deeper into any given market.
Pete Kazanjy	**Founding Sales** Pete is Co-Founder of Atrium as well as the Modern Sales Pro community. His book on startup sales is a great complement to Fast Forward.

Philip D. Broughton	**Life's a Pitch**
	An entertaining and insightful guide to the art of selling from rug-peddlers to life-insurance salespeople. Especially relevant if you sell directly to end customers (B2C).
Rob Fitzpatrick	**The Mom Test: How to Talk to Customers**
	Lots of advice on how to get meaningful and actionable information from customer interviews and avoid misleading feedback.
Robert B. Cialdini	**Influence: The Psychology of Persuasion**
	A leading psychologist, Robert B. Cialdini, wrote this classic and intriguing guide on how to persuade a client.
Robert B. Miller and Stephen E. Heiman	**The New Strategic Selling**
	This is the modern edition of a classic B2B sales book. It is one of the origins of key concepts, like decision-makers.
Roger Fisher and William Ury	**Getting to YES**
	This classic textbook establishes many of the fundamental principles of WIN-WIN negotiations.

Presentations & Videos

Balderton Capital   **B2B Sales Playbook**

A good overview presentation from one of the top tier VCs.

Becc Holland   **Flip the Script**

Probably the best videos and material available on how to optimize outbound sales in detail.

Dirik Iskender   **The Sales Operations Playbook**

A 100-page overview on how to approach sales as a B2B startup by a Microsoft ScaleUp Managing Director.

Steli Efti   **Sales for Startup Founders**

160 pages on SaaS sales from the founder of CRM Software Close.io.

Tiffani Bova   **The Future of Sales 2020**

How the sales team structure will fundamentally change in the next few years, how human sellers can work in sync with technology to provide personalized, real-time value to buyers, and how to future-proof your sales organization through incremental improvements.

Blogs

Jason Lemkin   **SaaStr**

Founder of EchoSign, writing probably the most widely read blog on SaaS and sales.

Mark Suster   **Both Sides of the Table**

Perspectives of a two-time entrepreneur turned VC with strong sales credentials.

Lincoln Murphy   **Customer Centric Growth**

Author and extensive writer on customer success and growth.

David Skok   **For Entrepreneurs**

Five time serial entrepreneur turned VC with a focus on SaaS and sales.

Christoph Janz   **The Angel VC**

The European institution on SaaS (and the author of the "animal" framework).

Tomasz Tunguz   **Blog**

Prolific VC writer about everything startup, including sales.

Bill Aulet   **Disciplined Entrepreneurship Blog**

Lessons on entrepreneurship from Bill Aulet and the Disciplined Entrepreneurship community.

Pipedrive, Close, Hubspot, Salesforce   **Corporate blogs**

Useful (if sometimes also a little biased) articles from some of the top CRM tool providers.

Printed in Great Britain
by Amazon